ISLAND DREAMS

Life on a Wild Island in the Georgia Strait

CHARLIE WALTERS

iUniverse, Inc.
Bloomington

Island Dreams
Life on a Wild Island in the Georgia Strait

Reproduction of information from Canadian Hydrographic Service charts in this publication are for illustrative purposes only, they do not meet the requirements of the Charts and Publication Regulations and are not to be used for navigation. The appropriate charts, corrected up-to-date, and the relevant complementary publications required under the Charts and Publications Regulations of the Canada Shipping Act must be used for navigation.

iUniverse books may be ordered through booksellers or by contacting:

iUniverse
1663 Liberty Drive
Bloomington, IN 47403
www.iuniverse.com
1-800-Authors (1-800-288-4677)

Because of the dynamic nature of the Internet, any Web addresses or links contained in this book may have changed since publication and may no longer be valid. The views expressed in this work are solely those of the author and do not necessarily reflect the views of the publisher, and the publisher hereby disclaims any responsibility for them.

ISBN: 978-1-4502-3326-2 (sc)
ISBN: 978-1-4502-3327-9 (ebook)
ISBN: 978-1-4502-3328-6 (dj)

Printed in the United States of America

iUniverse rev. date: 12/01/2010

Photo Credits: Cover - Dag Goering, (hiddenplaces.net), Charlie and Carlos Kayaking – Theresa Girard-Walters, Charlie and Theresa in aluminum boat – Peter Stanley, and *China Cloud* - Sue Schoonover

This book is dedicated to my wife Theresa, the love of my life and enthusiastic companion in adventure. And to my sons, Chris, Ryan and Chas, who still keep me on my toes.

"I am tormented with an everlasting itch for things remote."

—Herman Melville, *Moby Dick*

CONTENTS

PREFACE

As the 1970s were ebbing, my wife Theresa and I joined our good friends, Ken and Claire Pickard, on a sailing vacation through British Columbia's Gulf Islands. Pushed by the wind and living off of the fish we caught, we lost ourselves in those rugged isles, some small enough to embrace with a glance.

Like gulls circling a herring ball, we were drawn to a shimmering island name Lasqueti. Lasqueti is a seldom-visited wonderland in the middle of the Strait of Georgia, floating among a clutch of small islands that attend it as ducklings nuzzle their mother. One of these islands had a hand-hewn floathouse anchored in its intimate lagoon, and we were captivated by its dreamy beauty. We didn't learn its name, but could not forget its charm.

A few years later, Ken and Claire bought a cove on Lasqueti and pestered Theresa and me to get some waterfront nearby. Though we cherished our memories of that enchanted coast, diapering our newborn children won out over island dreams. We were content with our life on Puget Sound, snuggled among rhododendrons overlooking a small bay.

Determined to give me no peace, Ken tempted me with each Lasqueti property that came on the market. Though I resisted valiantly, he eventually aroused my interest with news of a small island that was for sale. Olsen was its name, and it sat just across False Bay from Ken's Lasqueti cabin. I was firmly hooked when Ken told me Olsen was the floathouse island that had entranced me years before.

Like Alice tumbling down the rabbit hole, I fell into a fantasy world. For months I put myself to sleep each night formulating plans of how to settle this uninhabited gem. Theresa finally tired of my trance-like scheming about a place we didn't even own, and suggested that we go ahead and buy the place. I appreciated her spunk, as we had never landed on Olsen and had cruised by it only briefly. My fantasies were far more detailed than any memories, for I was at a loss to give even a vague description of the place.

Attempting to bridge the gap between dream and reality, I finally called the owner. To my dismay he told me that the island had just been sold.

After a year of sulking, I began a search for property on Lasqueti, but everything I heard of failed to measure up to my Olsen Island fantasies.

Months of frustration had passed when our Canadian real estate agent mentioned offhandedly that Olsen Island had come back on the market. Though Theresa, I and our boys were busy with last minute preparations to float the Colorado River, we were determined to not let the island slip through our fingers again.

In a week we were going to step into a raft heading through the Grand Canyon and out of any contact with the outside world. After a short discussion with Theresa, I called our real estate agent and got negotiations rolling. When the owner and his agent heard our intent, which was to buy the island without even visiting it, they struggled to take us seriously. They couldn't believe we wanted to purchase a place we had never set foot on and hadn't even seen for fifteen years. Accordingly, they dragged their feet, unsure of whether they were dealing with legitimate buyers.

To complicate matters, time was short and I was in Gig Harbor dealing across the border with a part-time Vancouver Island real estate agent. She, in turn, was trying to coordinate with a Saltspring Island agent representing an owner from the mainland.

My challenge was to negotiate an international real estate transaction in five business days with a seller who questioned my sanity. Through dogged persistence, however, I was able to close the deal from our Nevada hotel room the night before we set out to raft the Colorado.

***

What follows is our tale of settling and living on Olsen Island.

Time is not linear on the islands of the Strait. Life on these islands flows like the waters that surround them, with dangerous rapids and languorous calms. Currents of intrigue capture everyone who lives there, carrying them to uncharted destinations.

My island dreaming took me to distant times and places as I attempted to understand this island world. Just as I kayaked to the many islands that surround ours, so did I travel through the stories of their formation and settlement and to the home of the wind and the depths of the sea.

Such trips of fantasy and discovery are an essential part of living on a small island.

***

Island Dreams is a work of non-fiction. The people, places and events are all real, though I've taken a few liberties with dates.

The science and natural history of the islands, though written to make it readable, is as accurate as I can render it. Where I've projected myself into the bodies of sea creatures, I've done my best to keep their biology correct.

When I've reported on events that I didn't witness firsthand, as with the capsizing of Verner's kayak and the sinking of the *Kella Lee*, I've followed Coast Guard reports and other official documentation as closely as possible.

For, as I've found on my journey of exploration, the wonders of life on a wild island need no exaggeration.

ACKNOWLEDGMENTS

My thanks to these folks, whose inspiration and help made this book what it is:

My parents, Mary Ann and Gene Walters, introduced me to life on the beach, and gave me the unmatchable childhood I spent on the shores of Vashon Island. Shortly after I was born, I was swaddled home to our house on Magnolia Beach on Vashon in Washington's Puget Sound. Though a few years later we moved to Tacoma, we returned to Vashon each summer. The day after school ended, we'd pack up the family station wagon and head for the island ferry, not to return to town until the day before school started up again. Our new island home was a small cedar cabin on Burton Beach. My daily chores were spent among the beach logs, collecting bark for our wood cookstove. Then I'd run off in search of my friends, pulling bark slivers from my fingers with my teeth. This island childhood was a period of living dreams.

My wife Theresa has a spirit of adventure that helped make our island dream come true. She ceded me the hours to write this book in a time when our lives were overwhelmed with careers and children. She also gave me the big, red, overstuffed chair in our living room where much of this book was written and rewritten, and a stream of abuse whenever I sank too deeply in that chair, neglecting her and our boys.

My sons Chas, Chris, and Ryan helped me pursue my dreams through their enthusiasm for our life on Olsen. Whenever their schedules permitted, they were anxious to get up to the island. They turned island life into a family affair, and enriched the times we spent there.

Ken Pickard introduced me to Olsen Island and pushed me to join him exploring the world around Lasqueti. In our friendship, he has helped me focus on the important things in life. He takes time to live, always lives beyond the boundaries of what most folks find comfortable, and is a discoverer of new places. Ken is my fishing partner, soulmate, and best friend. Island life is a way of life for Ken, and in drawing me into it, he's pulled me into happiness that most people can only fantasize about.

Phil Kallsen, my lifelong friend with whom I've prowled beaches, depths, and peaks, helped me develop my passion for water and wild places. He also keeps me from taking myself too seriously, finds humor in everything, and inspires me in his dedication to spending time in the wilds. Besides designing our home, he's kept it full of laughter through his summer visits.

Ray Lipovsky, from his own experiences settling a small island, helped me deal with many of the unique challenges we faced on Olsen.

Eve Llyndorah brought flowers on stormy days, and a smile that calmed the roughest seas.

Dick Grinnell helped us build a home on Olsen that captured the spirit of the islands and waters of the Straits of Georgia. His sensitivity to my unvoiced enthusiasms and concerns was extraordinary. Terry Theiss managed the books and allowed Dick to live his life of irreverent enthusiasm. As editor of *Our Isle and Times*, she has kept us up to date on island happenings through our months of absence.

Ruth Bottel of Port Hardy sent me the articles from local papers that chronicled rescue efforts for the *Kella Lee*.

A number of people from the Canadian Coast Guard and Vancouver Island Rescue Centers, and pilots from their associated air wings, helped me gain access to the official records chronicling their attempts to search for and rescue Verner and the crew of the *Kella Lee*. Their personal insights into these tragedies, and those related to me by Jan's and Verner's friends and families, were touching in their grief, detail, and understanding. One Canadian official in particular, who patiently tolerated my pestering through the years it took to produce the official report on the *Kella Lee's* sinking, must remain unnamed. He potentially risked his career by sharing facts with me that were scrubbed from this report as the government progressively sanitized it in response to competing legal interests.

Greg Jensen and Miles Logdon, both oceanography professors at the University of Washington, reviewed some of my sea-scribble and helped get it closer to correct.

Dana Lepofsky, Associate Professor of Archaeology at Simon Fraser University, challenged my research on First Nations history. Any errors there are due to my stubbornness and not her thoughts or advice.

My Aunt, Frances Bentley, is a retired high school English teacher, and she attacked my manuscript mercilessly with her red pen. I'm humbled by the hours she spent brutally exposing its flaws. Any grammatical errors which remain are the fault of my rewriting. Aunt Frances taught me lessons in my mid-fifties that I should have learned much earlier. She deserves many thanks for her diligent help.

Maria Coffey critiqued my first manuscript, and gave me good advice on how to take an axe to it and shape the remains into a book.

Thanks to Dag Goering for the photograph that graces the cover of *Island Dreams*.

Laure and John Nichols and Jack Thomas had the patience to review one of my numerous "final" drafts and point out its shortcomings. They know me well enough to catalogue my many personal deficiencies, so highlighting problems in the book came easy. Thanks for your honesty.

Melody Stalk helped me get my manuscript ready for publication, and her diligent husband, Bruce, ferreted out errors in format and grammar that even my professional editors missed.

Pam Swanes was kind enough to proof the entire book just before it went to print. Any flaws that remain are the result of gnomes that trashed the pages after Pam combed through them.

Shirley Molenda, my secretary of over twenty years (now retired), deciphered my illegible scrawl and tolerated my penchant for rewriting and reorganizing. The first drafts of this book were written longhand, and Shirley translated that mess into something readable. Her patience was truly a gift, for as she told Theresa, she was sure that the book would never be finished. Thankfully it is.

CHAPTER 1
ARRIVAL

Since time immemorial, man has suffered from island fever. It is a highly contagious malady, and once contracted, there is no hope of recovery. Everyone has felt its symptoms … the longing to live simply, fully, on a dab of land surrounded by sea, sky, and trees where even the air you breathe is all your own.
—David Conover, *Once Upon an Island*

August 7, 1996

Fifteen years had passed since my wife Theresa and I sailed by Olsen Island, and a year since we'd bought it sight-unseen. Crossing the Strait of Georgia in our small boat, we leaned forward in anticipation as we watched our dream materialize out of the haze joining water and sky. As I slowed just offshore, I spotted our good friends Ken and Claire Pickard fishing nearby, a special welcome by the adventurers with whom we'd discovered this enchanting place.

Standing in our boat just off Olsen, I let my eyes roam over its cliffs, in and out of the woods above, and into the clear depths that surrounded it. Theresa just sat there smiling. The sun was hot, and our boat rocked gently.

We looked at each other and laughed at our luck and audaciousness.

Motoring slowly, we cruised around Olsen as if to confirm that it really was an island. Once we satisfied ourselves, we looked back and forth between the island and each other.

"Shall we?" beamed Theresa.

"Might as well, it's ours!" I laughed.

With that, we swung our bow into the narrow cove where the floathouse was moored. In more ways than I could comprehend, I was home. And at the same time, just starting a journey.

After dumping our gear on the floathouse porch, Theresa and I clambered up the rocks between forest and sea. We felt the blood of ancient species course through us as we stood where two wildernesses met. Something deep in our brain stems recognized the wildness of this place and twitched with pleasure at our homecoming.

As water and trees cleared my thinking in a manner that only wild things can do, our small island took hold of me. I had lived on the waters of Puget Sound for most of my life, but now saw how tame the south sound was. I had spent my time with friends who skied and windsurfed and climbed mountains, whose daring now seemed strangely civilized. I wondered what type of folks we'd find living in this remote place.

We came from a world that used money and possessions to measure success. It didn't take long for me to realize that the people living on these islands employed different yardsticks.

Along with this thrill of the wild came a sense of deepening peace. Olsen was perfect and self-contained. While we had little in the way of comforts, we lacked nothing and were far richer for it. Our island was human-sized, bringing the world down to dimensions that were pleasingly comfortable.

We also live on the water in our home at Minter Creek. It's a pristine spot bordering a small bay with an abundance of salmon and oysters, where eagles perch in old growth firs that tower over the woods behind us. But the difference between Minter and the island is like the difference between a dog and a wolf. One is tame, mine to train and command. The other is wild and unpredictable, beautiful and mysterious, but potentially dangerous. It will not be possessed.

Though I'd spent much of my life on the water and in the woods, when I looked into the mirror of the Strait I found that what I didn't know was broad and comprehensive. It pretty well covered the whole gamut of how to prosper, and even survive, on a remote island.

***

Below where we stood on the island, rock walls plunged into the depths. The Strait is a massive body of water that sets its own rules, an accelerator of bad weather and dangerous seas. It fills an immense valley between mountain ranges, and to the north and south fades into its own horizon.

Huge tides flow in and out, raising and lowering the surface like the chest of some slow-breathing beast. Rivers of current wave back and forth—at times boiling upwards in seething slicks.

Like some great serpent, the Strait's underbelly coils around islands and shoals, crushing the depths and scattering the bones of the drowned. Its deep is a place of millions of tons of brine, a disphotic zone where the water is cold and silent and dense, and the airy bodies of surface creatures collapse under giant pressures.

But on days of calm, the Strait reveals itself as a nursery of swimming marvels. Kingdoms of diatoms drift like miniature galaxies in a limitless universe. Salinae twitch and gibber, desperate to move mere inches and escape the roving mouths that devour them. Schools of fins shimmer, suckered pads flex over nearby rocks, and giant flukes create their own whirlpools.

On its fringes, the Strait curls around boulders and flows into intimate spaces between pebbles and sand, burnishing driftwood and polishing agates. At night it is a fantasy kingdom where phosphorescent creatures dance. Its shallows host underwater blossoms of brilliant color—purples and oranges and greens and golds.

Where its flanks descend gradually, thickets of seaweed give way to forests of kelp. In other places, underwater cliffs drop into darkness, hosting only abalone and rock scallops.

The depths of the Strait have plains and ravines and hills and mountains. This deep is a place of geologic instability, the birthplace of mountains and islands, a duct between realms.

Vessels are relative newcomers to the ancient Strait. Their shadows never reach its abyssal plain, where generations of sailors have fed innumerable scuttling things. Hidden under barnacles and slime, sunken ships have been mourned and then forgotten. The living bottom of the Strait has decorated them with glass-like corals, transforming them into caves for wolfeels and ratfish. At times more savage creatures glide through their rigging, vague presences that haunt the dark.

CHAPTER 2
LANTERNS AND ICE CHESTS

Lulled into ... unconscious reverie is this absent-minded youth by the blending cadence of waves with thoughts. In this enchanted mood, thy spirit ebbs away to whence it came.

—Herman Melville, *Moby Dick*

Day One, Continued

As we continued our first walk around Olsen, we discovered that at high tide our island becomes two islands, separated by the small cove where the floathouse sits. On the larger of the two, the highest point is a meadow of moss and lichen that offers magnificent views of the surrounding waters and isles.

The north side of the island twists and turns, with steep rock cliffs that flank the back pass. Though this pass is navigable only at high tide, there is always water in its western end where tiny Dragon Island sits. At low tide most of the back pass gives way to eel-grass flats of oysters and sand dollars.

Forests of arbutus and fir cover most of Olsen's main island. Near the water, these woods thin into stands of juniper, the only trees that tolerate the spray thrown up from the waves. Stunted and twisted by the wind and salt, the junipers endure as silver bonsais long after they die.

Our junipers are Rocky Mountain Junipers, which can live as long as 1,500 years. After death, they can stand for a century, protected from rot by the natural preservatives in their wood. These magnificent trees are adorned with dusky blue berries, whose seeds are prepared for germination by passing through the digestive tracts of island birds.

Various First Nations' clans, regarded the juniper as sacred, and believed that juniper smoke could prevent sickness and ward off evil spirits (First Nations' is the term used to refer to the aboriginal people of Canada). Some burned it to purify their homes or for good luck prior to hunting. Others drank juniper berry tea to stimulate urination, cure kidney problems, or encourage digestion.

In medieval Europe, juniper was used to induce abortion, and herbal literature suggests that while juniper is effective for treating a variety of problems of the bladder and urinary tract, it does stimulate contractions and can be hazardous for expectant mothers.

Through unspoken assent, islanders are loath to cut down a juniper. But our reluctance pales to that of the residents of Wales, where it was traditionally believed that felling a juniper would result in the woodcutter's death.

***

After grabbing a quick lunch of bread and cheese, Theresa and I boated out to the nearby Finnerty Islands with Ken and Claire. We tried a bit of fishing and had what we wanted to believe were bites from a monster salmon that fought for a minute before stripping off our hooks.

Though most fishermen know that only dogfish bite hooks off like that, no fisherman worth their salt will ever admit it. These huge lunges come from salmon swimming in our fantasies, fish that flash and leap in our imaginations. These are the ravenous fish that school in the *Reader's Digest* tales of fishermen who masterfully condense a lifetime of bad weather and boredom into a series of battles and conquests.

Fishermen fish for dreams, and no-one dreams of catching dogfish.

That evening, Theresa and I ran our boat over to Ken and Claire's for a barbecue of salmon that Ken had caught the day before. Cruising home slowly in the dark, we were followed by faeries of phosphorus playing in our wake. Sitting on the floathouse deck with the lanterns extinguished, we were awed to find so much phosphorus blinking in the lagoon that it out-twinkled the stars.

August 8, 1996, Day Two on the Island

Reading on the deck after breakfast, Theresa and I saw an eight-point buck swim to Olsen from nearby Lasqueti. Distracted by a racket overhead, we looked up and spied an eagle chasing an osprey.

We were delighted by the charm of Olsen's floathouse, a small cabin resting on a raft of large float logs. It was built by Larry Aites, who handcrafted it throughout the thirteen years he lived there with his wife Millie.

Locally our floatie is referred to as the "Hobbit House." Misshapen doors are fitted with handles made of gnarled juniper branches. Small tree limbs serve as rafters, and four-foot-long shakes cover the outside walls, meticulously hand split from cedar beach logs. All the wood was scavenged from Olsen's forest and nearby beaches.

The top of the floathouse roof curves like a derby hat, and its skylights bathe the inside with natural light. Small overhangs arch gently skyward like those of a Japanese temple. A menagerie of odd-shaped windows provides views of the surrounding islands and waters.

Anchored in its cozy lagoon, the floathouse rocks gently in the waves at high tide as its walls and float logs creak. Such tides also float the beach logs around it, turning homecoming into an acrobatic adventure. We climb onto bobbing logs from our kayaks, walk nimbly along their rolling lengths, then scurry up the plank that bridges the logs and the floathouse porch. This plank bounces perilously as we ascend it, alternately bending down far past its suspected breaking point and shooting us skyward as it rebounds.

In search of excitement after hours of reading, Theresa and I went fishing again at the Finnerties. On the first pass, I caught a seven-kilo (fifteen-pound) Chinook. Having forgotten to bring a net along, I had to land the fish with my trusty halibut gaff, and in the process sprayed blood all over our boat. After thirty minutes of celebration and a bit humbler clean up, we tried our luck again. Her first time down Theresa nailed an even bigger salmon. I admired her sense of humor as I tried to beat it off her hooks with my gaff, finally sticking the fish on the third try.

We decided to stop fishing as there was no way we could eat or store all the salmon we'd caught. Stopping by Ken and Claire's, we left the big fish and a fillet of the smaller one in their refrigerator as a surprise. The rest went into our ice chest.

After harvesting a small load of prawns from the trap we'd set out the day before, we finally made it home after dark. Dodging mosquitoes, we smoke-barbecued salmon and prawns over a beach fire.

I was very careful with the fire, isolating it from anything burnable and dousing the coals with water when I finished cooking. The charred trunks of the island's older trees made it clear that Olsen had completely burned at sometime in its past.

Washing our feet in our water bucket before retreating to the floathouse for the night, we were delighted by its own population of glowing phosphorus. Climbing into the sleeping loft, we read by lantern light before drifting off to sleep.

August 9, 1996

There aren't even game trails on some of the neighboring islands, whose only visitors are the sun and wind and waves.

The delicacy of island flora is such that it disappears when more than a few people tread inattentively. While the staples of the northwest coast are present—arbutus, fir, salal, and huckleberry—so are a variety of foreshore plants that are never seen in more settled areas. Seldom visited islands such as Olsen provide a tantalizing glimpse of how the coast probably looked centuries in the past.

Just above high tide, gray and yellow lichens cover the rocks. These give way to a carpet of dark green moss, interspersed with pillows of brilliant white-green reindeer moss. Tiny thick-lobed succulents nest in crevices on vertical rock faces, and in special places, small patches of cactus grow.

Cactus. On a coastal island in British Columbia.

Olsen has no island water supply, and we get by with what we bring in large plastic jugs. Like nearby Lasqueti Island, Olsen also has no electricity. We read by propane lanterns, navigate the dark with headlamps, and mark forest paths with oyster shells so we can follow them by starlight.

We cook on a small propane hot plate and our refrigerator is an ice chest. After our ice melts, we simply do without. Though the Lasqueti store occasionally stocks frozen lake-water in used milk jugs, the availability of this sickly brown offering is unreliable at best.

Gas for our boat is sold only sporadically at the Lasqueti dock, and the store nearby carries just a limited supply of basic items. Therefore, we live off what we bring with us or can harvest from the sea, happily cut off from the rest of the world.

While our supplies were limited, on this particular morning they allowed us a delicious breakfast of french toast slathered with maple syrup.

My chore for the day was to set up our hammock between two old junipers overlooking False Bay. Afterwards, I walked the rocks above the back pass and mapped its underwater outcroppings, which were covered with starfish and oysters.

After a morning of leisure, Ken and I motored out to the Finnerties. Though we were met by schools of dogfish and swarms of mosquitoes, we managed to battle off these pests long enough to catch a couple of salmon. Ken boated a six-kilo king and I reeled in one just a bit larger—a short, fat fish that fought like crazy, taking line time after time.

Inspired by the salmon that were swimming around us, I later dove into reference books I'd brought with me to the island. I wanted to get to know these salmon more intimately.

CHAPTER 3
SALMON'S WORLD

*The salmon people dwell in huge houses far under the sea,
where they go about in human form. When the time comes for
the annual runs they put on their salmon skins and convert
themselves into fish, voluntarily sacrificing themselves for the
benefit of mankind.*

—First Nations Legend

Far inland from where I fished on the Strait, ancient lakebeds rest quietly under untold feet of sedimentary rock. As erosion wears away the lid of this primeval sarcophagus, dawn salmon emerges from the darkness. Fifty million years of patience are finally rewarded with a glimpse of the sky. Nearby fossils are the remains of other freshwater fish, perhaps prey that dawn salmon was chasing.

Swimming upward through the overlying strata, countless generations of offspring eventually evolved into sabertooth salmon, a fifteen-foot predator weighing 227 kilos (500 pounds). Cruising lakes and rivers some six million years ago, its mouth held an enormous pair of curved teeth.

Finning forward through four million years, sabertooth evolved into hooknose salmon. Surviving determinedly when ice ages drove them from lakes to the sea, hooknose retained its taste for the waters of its ancestors. In homage to its freshwater biology, it continued to return to rivers to spawn.

In the bays and rivers of the Pacific Northwest, salmon recolonized postglacial barrens in the same millennia that humans first arrived.

As glaciers retreated, strays from refuge salmon populations probed meltwater rivers draining the glacial wakes.

In these years, large conifers migrated north and south from unglaciated botanical preserves. The trees provided the stream structure, shade, and detritus-based aquatic food chain that nurtured the salmon's spawn.

Hooknose salmon has evolved into five unique species: king (tyee, spring, chinook, smiley), coho (silver, blueback), sockeye (red), chum (dog), and pink (humpey). Kings and cohos are what we catch most often near Olsen.

Kings are the monarchs of the salmon world, weighing up to fifty-seven kilos (126 pounds). This incredible fish was caught commercially off Alaska, where tales of a sixty-six kilo (145 pound) king still echo around the docks.

Kings spawn in fast, high-volume rivers, sometimes 1,610 kilometers (1,000 miles) from the sea. They typically return after four or five years in the ocean, though large fish may remain in the saltchuck for up to seven years.

Cohos are the kings' closest relatives. They typically spawn in smaller streams and tributaries, spend eighteen months to two years at sea, and have a maximum age of four years. The record coho, weighing fourteen kilos (thirty-one pounds), was caught in Cowichan Bay, British Columbia.

Each salmon is a member not only of a broad taxonomic species like king or coho, but also of a subgroup from its own particular river. These subgroups are marked by distinct scale and flesh color, size, and their own unique schedule for fresh and saltwater migration.

Most young Pacific salmon migrate north to the Gulf of Alaska. They typically stay in the coastal current in this journey, carried at speeds up to ten times what they could achieve on their own.

Some kings and coho stay in the coastal waters over the continental shelf off of British Columbia and Alaska year around. Others join the sockeye, pink, and chum as they journey thousands of miles offshore to swim out their lives in the North Pacific, returning to the coast only to spawn. They are travelers that range up to 16,000 kilometers (10,000 miles).

In their years of wandering the ocean, salmon gorge themselves on its riches. Swimming open-mouthed through shoals of plankton and herring and squid, they store the bounty of millions of square miles of marine life in their flesh. And as urgent signals from ripening sperm and eggs overcome their compulsion to feed, the salmon carry their storehouses of nutrients back to the coast.

Extremely sensitive to their place on the earth's electromagnetic grid, salmon find their way back to the river of their birth.

With a sense of smell a thousand times more acute than a dog's, the homebound fish can detect the equivalent of one drop of perfume in 500,000 barrels of water. Following clues as subtle as the bouquet of particular stones or the smell of water washing over unique fir roots on a stream bank, the salmon return to the exact patch of stream from where they emerged as fry.

Finally, a female slows her pace, intrigued by scents from her past. Circling lazily in growing recognition of her birthplace, she gathers energy for her final duty. Throwing herself onto the rocky stream bottom, she furiously fans the gravel. Sacrificing fins and flesh, she excavates a nest from the stream-packed stones. Squeezing her flanks with what energy she has left, she spills a brilliant treasure of rosy pearls into the newly formed redd.

Orbiting the nest is a rush of hooked jaws and butting heads, finally reduced to a lone male. In a life-ending surge, he clouds the nest-water with his milt.

Exhausted and aimless, male and female drift listlessly in the currents. Soon they join their dead brethren on the riverbanks. Eagles cluster in nearby trees, and wolves slink out of the surrounding forest. Pulling spent carcasses from the river, they bring ashore such a quantity of sea-grown nutrients that the size of the year's salmon run is recorded in the growth rings of nearby trees.

Nestled in the gravel, the abandoned salmon jewels slowly transform. Tiny slashes of life eventually emerge next to the nourishing yolks.

Struggling against the membrane that enfolds it, a growing alevin finally escapes its confines. Straightening its spinal cord for the first time, it twitches the tiny fins and tail that make it a salmon. Defenseless and transparent, it hides in the gravel to live off the remaining yolk.

Absorbing the yolk sac that gives a pregnant curve to its belly, the diminutive fish eventually finds the gravel barren and constricting. Wriggling its way into the stream flow, it begins feeding on its own. And depending on the species to which it belongs, at some time it acquires a taste for salt and heads downstream for the sea. Driven by a genetic code that insists it face into the current, the fry navigates its way to the sea tail-first, carried backward by the stream flow.

CHAPTER 4
SALMON SONG

I.
In a time long ago,
when the land was flat
and there were no rivers
and nothing lived on the earth,
a large salmon swam alone
through the Pacific.
Though he loved the blue sky
and clear water,
he became bored and lonely
and decided to change the world.
Gripping the shore between his jaws,
he thrashed and shook it until the first mountains formed.
Then he splashed water onto the land with his tail
to form a spray of lakes,
and time and again swam onto the beach
to create a series of rivers.
After resting on their banks,
he flicked some of his scales onto the barren earth.
The large blue scales from his back
grew into cedar trees,
and his small white belly scales
sprouted into various grasses and bushes.
Some of these bushes fruited,
and when their berries
fell on the ground

they changed into the animals of the forest.

But still the salmon was alone in the sea.
One day he came upon a sharp rock,
and swimming headlong into it
he split himself in two.
Healing instantly,
he turned to see a woman salmon of such beauty
that tears came to his eyes.
When the young girl-salmon kissed these away
she became with child.
Together the happy couple
journeyed up one of the new rivers
so that their children would have sweet water to drink
when they were born.

Their offspring sang often
in those forgotten times.
The stars were much closer then,
their spirits drawn near
by the enchantment of the salmon's voices.

II.

I am sitting among the rocks
of a secret cove
on our island.
A ghost salmon hovers
in the clear water just beyond my feet,
his large spotted tail swinging slowly
back and forth in the current.
He meanders languidly along the shoreline,
working his mouth and gills
with such elegance
that my own breathing seems clumsy by compare.

Watching him makes me feel

as old and heavy as the rocks themselves.

I have seen him here before,
and the many hook scars on his jaw
are proof of the tales he tells.
He has starred in the stories told by generations of fishermen,
though he has never seen the inside of a boat,
never known the warmth
of a charcoal fire upon his back.

I have fished with fishermen who themselves have salmon powers
and can call these fish onto their lines.
The ghost-salmon told me that such men and women
are the offspring of salmon.
They got lost as youngsters
when their curiosity got the better of them
and they swam out of the water
to explore the beach and forest.
Finding themselves gasping for breath,
they transformed
into young boys and girls.

The people who found these young salmon-people
believed them to be orphans
and took the them into their families
and raised them as their own.
These salmon in human form remember
the language of their youth,
and use it to call fish from their reveries in the sea.
The sea-salmon
come to help their lost children
when they call,
and are happy
to give themselves up
as food.

While I have no such salmon powers

I can smell salmon
when they swim close by,
just as I can smell approaching rain.
The smell is much the same,
clean and fresh,
youthful and quick,
shiny and silver.
Even if you have never seen a salmon,
you can imagine it perfectly
from its undersea smell.
It is this smell that draws me to sit
by my secret cove
when I am walking the island,
knowing that my friend
the ghost salmon
is near.

At times during my talks with the ghost-salmon,
when I hug my knees
and let the tide creep over my toes,
I see scales begin to shimmer on my legs
and the outline of a fish tail
flicker around my feet.
As we speak
I feel cool water on my sides
where fins begin to grow.
With slight popping sounds
I hear gills opening for the first time
on my neck.
I know that this is my friend's way
of inviting me to swim with him
and marvel at the wonders of his world.
One thing he has told me of,
which has tempted me to join him,
is the song of the salmon.

Salmon are usually silent when they meet each other.

But solitary salmon,
alone with the moon,
will often sing a love song to it.
They tempt the moon
to come down
to the end of its silvery path across the water,
so that the salmon might leap through it
and swim into the heavens beyond.

Schools of salmon,
sending scouts to make sure
that no killer whales can hear,
will sometimes sing as a choir,
joining together in songs of such purity
that even old lingcod
weep as they listen.
Nearby herring swim in tightly
around the salmon when they sing like this,
forming a blanket of tiny fish
to help keep the forgetful salmon warm
as they lose themselves in the ecstasy of their song.

These choirs of salmon
sing to the stars,
believing them to be the eyes of lost lovers
who journey nightly across the sky.
They sing to bring the heavens nearer,
and leap with joy
when a shooting star
breaks free from the distant school,
streaking homeward
to embrace
some undersea love.

CHAPTER 5
A QUALICUM STEALS OUR BOAT

*Often, in mild, pleasant weather … [the whalers] were engaged
in the boats … paddling after whales … calmly awaiting
their uprising … At such … times of dreamy quietude, when
beholding the tranquil beauty and brilliancy of the ocean's skin,
one forgets the tiger heart that pants beneath it and would not
willingly remember that this velvet paw but conceals a remorseless
fang.*

—Herman Melville, *Moby Dick*

August 10, 1996

I spent much of today reading and dozing in our hammock. The sea
was calm and the day hot, luring me deep into languor.

Theresa finally pried me from my cocoon in late afternoon so we
could kayak to Ken and Claire's for a salmon barbeque. Over dinner
we got to know Eve Llyndorah and Ray Lipovsky, who we discovered
were our neighbors. Ray and Eve are talented artists who live on Higgins
Island, which lies in the outer reaches of False Bay just east of Olsen.

From our first glances, all four of us knew we were kindred spirits.
Ray and Eve didn't leave Higgins Island often, but the Lasqueti grapevine
had been buzzing about the new owners of Olsen Island, so they came
over to get to know us. Excited over our shared love for small islands, we
made plans for breakfast together the next morning at Ray and Eve's.

August 11, 1996

I awoke this morning to strong westerly winds pushing monstrous swells through the narrow pass behind Olsen. Looking anxiously to where I'd anchored our boat, I found that it had disappeared! Hurriedly pulling on my pants, I ran outside in a panic.

My mind raced through fears of finding our boat on Olsen's rocks, battered by the night's storm. Even more upsetting was my dread that it had been blown out of the back pass entirely and thrown up on distant shores, mauled to pieces by breaking waves and leaving us marooned.

Theresa and I had been on Olsen Island all of three days. Helpless in my ignorance of its rocks and beaches, I scratched my shins and banged my elbows as I clambered distractedly over foreign terrain. I quickly discovered seaweed-slicked rocks and errant blackberry vines. Sweat trickled off my forehead and blood ran down my legs.

After a frantic search, I found our boat in a small cleft in the rocks near our island's northeast end, its anchor tangled in its chain.

Luckily the hull suffered only minor damage. All could have been much worse. But we *were* stranded. The tide was going out, our boat was high and dry, and we were due for breakfast on Higgins Island with Ray and Eve.

The falling tide, however, presented a solution to our problem. Near low-ebb we were able to wade to the nearby shore of Lasqueti, hike through the forest, then wade to Wolf Island and finally out to Higgins. Luckily these islands were connected by shallows that we could walk across at low tide.

When we sheepishly presented ourselves at Ray and Eve's door, we were wet up to our waists. Playing the perfect hosts, they initially ignored our sodden pants dripping on their porch. After we abashedly admitted what had happened, they offered us towels and dry clothes and invited us inside. While toweling off, we were instructed on the perils of "Qualicums," the unpredictably savage winds that had torn our boat from its anchorage. As Ray pointed out, our escape with only minor damage was our "freebie."

After breaking the ice with our foolishness, we fell into an easy rapport with our new friends. Over an extended breakfast we learned how they too had come to purchase their own small island. They had considered buying Olsen seriously enough to have picked out sites there for their house and wind generator. Lucky for us they chose Higgins instead.

Ray and Eve had faced the same challenges we were facing. They had arrived to live on a forested piece of rock, surrounded by a moat of water, periodically lashed by storms, without water or power. Animal paths were all that cut through the woods, where nighttime travel had to be done by flashlight.

Through four years of living on Higgins, they had found answers where we were just discovering questions.

After several hours of fine conversation, Ray ran us home in his skiff. The tide had come in and floated our boat, allowing me to extract it from its place in the rocks. Moving it into the lee of Olsen, I set out two bow anchors and tied the stern to a deadweight of rusty iron I found buried in the sand. My goal was to keep the boat from swinging in the wind and re-wrapping its chain around the anchor. Later I moved it farther into floathouse cove so I could sleep in peace.

***

Delving into local lore about Qualicum winds, I learned that while Olsen's back pass is an enticing anchorage in prevailing north and south winds, freak westerlies spring up that make a lie of its apparent shelter. On sunny days when the Strait is a sheet of glass, a glance toward Vancouver Island might reveal a line of white caps rushing toward Lasqueti, pushed by forty-knot winds. These Qualicums come with little or no warning and send large swells through the narrow passage between Olsen and Dragon Islands.

Locals know to keep their heads up while on the water and not take any western anchorage for granted. Qualicums bring big winds and seas from a direction that newcomers wouldn't expect.

Larry and Millie Aites, Olsen's last year-round residents, had made the island their home for thirteen years. Living in the floathouse and depending on sail and oar power, they were very attentive to the dangers of Qualicum winds. As these blew up suddenly in day or night, summer or winter, Larry always kept an eye to the sky. He was on guard whenever the barometer changed abruptly, or when the prevailing winds shifted from one point of the compass to another. He knew that danger was at hand when clouds obscured Vancouver Island's mountains and the pass above Qualicum Beach suddenly cleared, or when the sky was clear and clouds began to appear in the pass. When he saw a black line on the water to the west, he always headed for shore.

Allen Farrell, a local sailor of considerable renown, tells of a particularly nasty Qualicum in the summer of 1993 that drove three-meter swells into False Bay. Ken remembers this Qualicum throwing huge logs into his front yard, where they landed with such force that they shook his house.

Several deaths have been attributed to Qualicums, and all local mariners have come to respect them. Lasquetian lore asserts that False Bay was named by early settlers after their encounters with Qualicum winds. Although the bay itself is real enough, it provides only false protection from the fury of a Qualicum's wind and waves.

The zone of a Qualicum's strongest winds is only about three kilometers wide, and Olsen Island sits smack in its middle. Since these winds are very localized, nearby Sisters Island is the only weather station that reports them. And as they blow down from the mountain pass above the Qualicum River and shoot across Qualicum Bay, they've been dubbed "Qualicums."

A look at Vancouver Island's terrain helped me understand how these Qualicums are born.

On the west coast of Vancouver Island, Barkley Sound and Alberni Inlet form a long, narrow funnel from the Pacific Ocean that plunges three-quarters of the way through the island. Qualicums are a classic example of what meteorologists refer to as "gap winds." Blowing up Alberni Inlet, winds from the Pacific double in speed through its confined passage, increasing down channel and becoming their strongest near its terminus. The effect this narrowing channel has on the wind is the same that a nozzle has on water flowing from a hose.

When the accelerated onshore flow from the Pacific encounters Vancouver Island's Coast Range, "barrier damming" produces a lake of high pressure against the mountains' western flanks. But the mountains' barricade does not entirely stop the flow. A pass above the end of Alberni

Inlet allows the wind to pour through the mountains above Qualicum Bay.

In the pass, this wind is subject to additional gap and nozzling effects, squirting out in a concentrated stream at much accelerated speeds.

All this explains the speed of Qualicums, but not their sudden onset. These surprises come from the interplay of another unique set of mechanics.

Meteorologists have noted that there is often wind flowing through this pass that remains aloft. The western slope of the mountains acts like a ramp, shooting the wind skyward as it crests the summit.

When this wind streams out of the pass, it forms waves in the lee airflow, causing significant turbulence where the wind rushes over the underlying air. As my neighbor Ray said to me in a letter, "The clouds seem to spill over the tops and down the east side. The spillover creates an interesting turbulence that looks to me like a rotating horizontal tube."

These wind waves can "break" just like waves in water. Such breaking waves add to the growing instability of the boundary between the upper and lower air parcels.

As gravity exerts its pull on the relatively cold and dense air flowing aloft, it finally pulls the upper winds through the less dense air below it. Breaking onto the surface, the wind rushes over the smooth Strait with little friction to slow its speed. There, it becomes a Qualicum.

CHAPTER 6
FIRST WATER, FIRST LAND

At first there was only water. There was no land at all. The duck swam over the water. When the time came for her to give birth she saw her eggs would sink if she laid them on the water. She pulled out her own fluff and made a nest. Her babies grew up strong and healthy. In their own time they made more nests for their own babies. Gradually there got to be so many nests that they joined together and formed an island. This is how the earth began.
—Vadimir M. Sangi, in *First Fish, First People* (Roche and McHutchinson 1998)

August 12, 1996

I started off the day with a bracing outdoor shower. Standing on the beach near the floathouse, I lathered up under the small shower-bag we'd tied to an overhanging limb. I tried to warm it by adding a tea-kettle of water heated on the stove, but the temperature remained stubbornly cool. I responded by dancing a jig as I washed myself off.

While toweling dry, I noticed some yellow jackets working a seep at the bottom of the bank beside me, a sure sign of fresh water. Exploring above, I found a small dry well. As I learned later, this had been dug and redug by past island residents without offering any water.

In the morning quiet, I heard a deer nearby in the forest. When these island deer see us they never run away, but rather freeze or lie down in the brush in a usually successful attempt to disappear. After I returned to the floathouse, a buck came down to browse on greens near the seep and left only when Theresa went over to shower.

Though Theresa had thoughtfully planned out an evening of social obligations for me on Lasqueti, just before we were scheduled to leave Ken called and hatched a plan for a fishing expedition.

Ken and I were *supposed* to accompany Theresa and Claire to John Cantrell's for dinner. John is one of the original group of long-hairs that settled on Lasqueti in the 70s. We'd become friends when we first sailed around the island years ago, seen him periodically since then, and were looking forward to renewing our friendship. My first catch of the evening was thus a ration of abuse from Theresa about my poor manners in abandoning John's dinner invitation.

In Ken's boat, we followed the west side of Lasqueti down to Jenkins Island. No luck until sunset when I nailed a hard-fighting eight-kilo (seventeen pound) king. When we rendezvoused with the women after their dinner at John's, the fish and our enthusiasm were enough to thaw their frosty hearts.

Theresa and I cruised home slowly in the moonless dark, watching for shooting stars. As I lost myself in the stars and sky, I shared Melville's musing that "beyond the visible horizon our seas inter-flow with the heavens and so form the white breakers of the Milky Way."

Lying in bed gazing at the stars through our skylight and reading about the history of our solar system, I drifted off to sleep sailing through celestial seas filled with wonder at how our world came to be.

***

In a time known to only the oldest stars, there existed an immense cloud of dust and gas. Perhaps twenty-four billion kilometers (fifteen billion miles) across, it floated quietly in interstellar space.

As the cloud rotated slowly, it began to contract. With gravitational forces that were infinitely small, larger dust particles pulled smaller ones toward them. This allowed the cloud to spin faster, which in turn eventually caused the spinning mass to flatten into a disk. As the particles in the center gradually fused into a single mass, the dark predecessor of our sun was born.

Increasingly intense compression drove the temperature of the mass to over a million degrees Celsius (two million degrees Fahrenheit), which set off nuclear fusion that radiated its energy as sunshine. Out of our black cloud finally came light.

The earth and other planets were born of the gasses, dust and rock held in orbit by the gravity of the nascent sun. In a coalescing process similar to the one that formed our star, the orbiting material drew together to create the planets.

The earth grew violently, in a chaos of impacts and annealing. Since meteorites and comets were larger and more frequent in earth's early years, and as there was no atmosphere then to burn them up, their landfalls played a large part in building our planet.

As these extraterrestrial pilgrims smashed into the growing earth, their energies melted its rock. In a feverish rain from space, a spinning mass was built and cauterized, and by about 4.5 billion years ago the ball of our planet had formed.

Our moon is thought to be the result of a collision of a super-meteor with early earth. Spared the destructive erosion of an atmosphere and surface water, the moon and its craters are fossils of that period of frequent collisions. Waves up to 6,000 meters (20,000 feet) high in the moon's crust are evidence of meteors that crashed into it with explosive energy in the billions of megatons—equivalent to a 240-meter (800-foot) layer of TNT covering the entire United States.

Earth's water came along with the rock from outer space. Even today, water molecules are abundant in molecular clouds in space. Though they exist as minute amounts of ice on the surface of frozen dust grains, their aggregate bulk is enormous. In our galactic cloud alone, the volume of water is roughly the mass of a million suns.

In our frigid outer solar system, the bodies that coalesced were particularly icy. Much ice-laden material was left over from the debris that formed Jupiter, Saturn, and Uranus, and some of this collided with the post-moon earth. This icy debris from our outer solar system could have delivered enough water to eventually fill our oceans.

At least some of our planet's water was delivered by comets. Formed before the earth or even the sun itself, their water molecules were relics of the mother-cloud from which our solar system condensed, frozen into ice in the cold depths of ancient space.

During these times, decaying radioactive elements, the compression of accumulating ice and rock, and the energy from colliding meteors heated up the earth's guts. This heating wrought great changes in the body of our planet.

As different minerals approached their melting points, heavier elements sank to the earth's center. A solid core of nickel-iron developed, surrounded by a molten outer core of the same material. Lighter elements rose to the surface, gases pumped out of volcanoes and ice boiled into steam. The strength of our world's gravity held these gases on the surface and built our atmosphere.

As the tremendous heat vaporized our planet's water and ice, a blanket of steam came to shroud it. Our present-day rivers and oceans all flooded the sky, weighing down with an atmospheric pressure over one hundred times what it is today.

Eventually rain began to fall. But this deluge was unlike any downpour we've ever known. It was a collapse of the heavens, a hellish event that went on for millennia. With its one-hundred atmospheres of pressure, our ancient cloud cover of steam condensed out scalding rain. This rain created a boiling ocean that was revaporized where asteroids or comets of sufficient size collided with the young earth.

In time, our planet lost its heat and its present water fell out of the atmosphere. Over eons this water grew to form an endless ocean without continents, interrupted only by volcanoes pushing above its surface. By about 3.5 billion years ago, the crustal plates grew thick enough to rise out of the ocean, creating the building blocks that would later fuse into our first continents.

CHAPTER 7
SECOND SUMMER

Far away in the mists of time, the king of the eagles flew over an Indian village on the coast. Spying the monarch circling above their homes, some small boys could not resist the temptation of shooting arrows at him. Instead of flying away in fright, the giant eagle continued to soar above the village. His boldness attracted some older warriors and they joined in the shooting.

Possessing supernatural powers, the eagle kept circling defiantly as the arrows glanced off his feathers. In a short time all of the tribe's warriors and chieftains were stringing their bows and whistling arrows skyward.

Finally tiring of the tribe's impertinence, the eagle swooped down and grasped one of the braves by the hair. As the warrior rose off the ground, another member of the tribe grabbed hold of the ankles of the first. With magical strength the eagle continued upward, as though bearing a feather.

In panic to save their loved ones, all the men and boys of the village sought to restrain the rising bird. One after another they clutched the legs of a neighbor, until finally they were all pulled into the sky.

Though some sought to release their holds, they found they could not do so.

Flying straight toward the sun, the eagle rose with the human chain dangling below. When he could finally see the whole coastline beneath him, the eagle began swinging the Indians in ever-widening circles.

When the eagle released his hold at last, the men and boys fell into the sea. Where each entered the water, an island rose above the surface.

The size of each island was determined by the rank of the person who had fallen.

— First Nations Legend

August 2, 1997

Our first stay on Olsen left us smiling through the following winter. The charms of the island and its floathouse were even richer than our fantasies had been. We couldn't wait to get back, and spent the intervening months thinking of what we should take with us. Included were our three sons: sixteen-year-old Chas and fourteen-year-old twins, Chris and Ryan.

Locking the door on our Gig Harbor home, our family miraculously accomplished an 8 AM departure for our distant island.

By this hour, I had wound myself up into a frenzy that no one in our brood could understand. To me it was already late. To Theresa and the boys, it was a Saturday morning usually spent in sleep. They were blissfully ignorant of the planning mania I had escalated into over the last several weeks.

In my opinion, our packing and departure had all the organizational challenges of a military campaign. I approached it with only slightly less seriousness than an admiral might apply to an invasion. We had borders to cross, a weaving boat-trailer to tow, a ferry to catch, and fishing licenses to buy.

I believed we were laying siege to exotic foes.

My family thought we were just going on vacation.

We had been out of our driveway for only twenty minutes when the whining lot of them insisted that we stop at Starbucks for lattes and hot chocolates.

I fumed about the importance of a forced march to our objective.

They threatened mutiny and pointed out flaws in my personality.

We made our stop, and I sat pouting in the car as they ran with glee to collect their morning delights.

Our car and trailered nineteen-foot boat were loaded with two kayaks, a propane refrigerator, four fifty-gallon water barrels, three prawn traps, one huge ice chest, three big water jugs, a barbecue, a pump for the water system we hoped to build, several large buckets, two buoys, hundreds of meters of rope, a tent, five sleeping bags, and piles of duffle bags filled with clothing and food for two weeks for five people.

Any hope of a peaceful journey was drowned out by the river of testosterone pouring out of our three teenaged sons. Before long, I resorted to threats of work detail and streams of profanity to keep the peace.

Successfully weaving our way through the day's maze of obstacles, we finally reached French Creek and launched our boat. Leaving the activity of the harbor behind, we cruised to where we were kilometers from any land or vessel. Dusk was settling in and I started to relax as I spied our island in the distance.

Just then, in the middle of the Strait of Georgia, our motor's high-heat alarm sounded—perhaps to test my sense of humor. Fearing the worst, I immediately shut the engine off. Glancing at my family, I found them staring at me in uncharacteristic silence, waiting for answers. We were dead in the water, overloaded, kilometers from shore, and night was falling.

And all aboard were grimly aware of the limits of my mechanical skills.

I was luckily able to restart the motor without incident, however, and we arrived at Olsen in the growing dark. I fancied myself some type of conquering hero. No doubt Theresa and the boys had private speculations over what failure of mine had caused the alarm to sound. But they kept their thoughts to themselves, wary of the dragon that had been at the helm all day.

Qualicum paranoia demanded two shore lines and two stern anchors to secure our boat. Chris and I swam in from it in the dark, delighted by the phosphorus rolling over our eyes as we opened them underwater.

Even though Theresa and I had banned video games and other electronic distractions, our boys were excited about our isolated isle. It warmed me that our family could share this dream and revel in its wonders.

All five of us slept in the floathouse, snuggling contentedly among our bags of clothing and food.

Reading before I drifted off to sleep, I learned how the surrounding mountains and gulf had been formed, and how our rocky enclave came to push above the waters.

***

Geophysicists have calculated that the amount of heat generated by the decay of early earth's heavy metals was three to four times what our planet produces today. In those eons of high heat, unknown mechanics shaped the earth, mysterious predecessors of the tectonic plates that now sheath it.

But in time the plates did form, perhaps many more than exist today. In the oceans above them, countless volcanic islands vented the roiling heat trapped beneath. These islands gradually amalgamated into small protocontinents, though only speculation remains of them. While the present continents are essentially unsinkable due to their relatively light and buoyant rock, they are modern creations. The world's first continents were formed when global heat and tectonics were much different, and all may have submerged into the mantle and been completely recycled.

By about 3 billion years ago, the history of our planet comes into better focus. Many granitic microcontinents spread over the globe and had begun to coalesce. At 2.7 billion years ago, the building blocks of the core of North America were themselves being formed and began to approach one another through the oceans.

Two billion years ago, the drifting Wyoming craton was surrounded by abyssal ocean. Through the next 200 million years, a number of microcontinents collided with it, sometimes sandwiching the remains of oceanic islands in between. By 1.8 billion years ago, these had coalesced to form the Canadian shield, the heart of North America that contains its oldest rock.

This foundation covered no more than a quarter of the area our continent covers now, a roughly triangular shaped minicontinent that extended north from a tip near present-day Colorado. In its center, in the Canadian Northwest Territories, is what's been generally agreed to be the planet's oldest known rock. It is 3.96 billion years old, a highly deformed gneiss which itself was formed by the partial melting of even older material. Though researchers have recently suggested that there is yet older rock in Northern Quebec, with an age of 4.28 billion years, there is controversy over the reliability of the method used to date it.

The rest of present-day North America grew on the margins of this continental core via the docking of countless island arcs.

About 1.1 billion years ago, something began to tear this North American massif apart. Perhaps it was a gigantic thermal plume rising from deep within the mantle. Whatever its origin, it resulted in a mid-continent rift that was pushing the two sides of the continent away from each other. Basalts flooded into the rift valley from below and, at night, lava fountains lit the sky. Finally, the junction broke open under what is now Lake Superior.

If the rifting had continued for some 200 million years, like the mid-Atlantic rift did, North America would have been divided in two just as the Atlantic divided Europe from North America's east coast. But remarkably, it stopped after only twenty-two million years.

The compressional forces that stopped this rifting were massive. They resulted from no less than a collision of continents, wherein the West Africa Craton and Amazonia Craton pushed up against the eastern and southern edges of North America, creating supercontinent Rodina.

For countless millions of years, as lethal winds of ammonia and cyanide scoured the planet, this immense landmass brooded. It was a lonely, treeless massif that hunkered through eons of terrible rains and storms, existing in a time of rock, water, and wind.

In the blue waters off its black shores, single-celled organisms had finally evolved.

With a measure of patience that only the universe knows, subterranean currents of molten rock slowly flexed and stretched the tectonic plates that were home to this ancient continent. In a parting that itself covered millions of years, the tides of middle-earth again had their way with the rock above them. They separated the Amazonia and Africa Cratons from Rodina and annealed them to other masses, and in the following millennia of millennia, inexorably moved these continents to their present positions.

For all their size, these continental islands were dwarfed by the limitless seas. One ocean in particular was vaster than all others combined. It would later be named the Pacific.

The history of our plant is one of rising and falling sea levels, of oceanic basins opening and closing, and of continents building and splitting apart. When huge oceanic ridges pushed up, they displaced so much volume that the oceans were forced over much of the continents, at times nearly submerging North America. When the ridges collapsed, the oceans receded.

At one time in the past few hundred million years, we could have stood in central Nevada on what was then the continent's western margin. Continental shallows were just offshore, teaming with pelagic squid and accumulating sediments that would form the rock atop the Sierras. Roughly in eastern California, the deep ocean began, studded with immense volcanoes. To the west, the ocean floor stretched all the way to the China Sea.

Deep under the western Pacific, colliding gyres in middle-earth rose and pushed apart the techtonic plates above them. Where the plates separated, an immense rift valley formed on the ocean floor. As the underlying gyres continued to push the sea-bottom plates east and westward, rising magma fused new rock to the plates' trailing margins.

Through the same millions of years, wind and rain lashed the continents. Rocks eroded mote by mote, and then rode to sea in rivers that drained the land. Explosive volcanic eruptions pumped tremendous amounts of ash into the atmosphere, which in time also settled into the oceans.

All this rock drifted slowly downward and settled the tectonic plates of the ocean's floor.

Yet bits of rock were not the only things that settled there.

In the waters above, more advanced forms of life had developed. Plants absorbed minerals from the water, and plant-eating animals transformed these minerals into a variety of shells and skeletons.

Diminutive mollusks and brachiopods burrowed. Trilobites and plankton swam. Glass-like diatoms drifted. And in the end, after their trillions of brief lives were over, their hard remains all joined the dust from the continents in a rising accumulation on the ocean floor.

While the annual fall of such dust and shells was infinitesimal, the result over millennia was impressive. Compressed by its own weight and the pressure of the water, this debris was forged into immense plains of sedimentary rock.

At times, this seabed ruptured. Molten rock seeped slowly out of fissures as undersea volcanoes built their way upward and finally pushed forth as islands.

The ancient Pacific knew a number of such archipelagos, similar to today's Hawaiian Islands. They and the sedimentary seafloor rode the gyre-powered oceanic plates eastward as they crawled inexorably toward North America.

Such migrating island chains and distinctive limestone seafloors are called terranes. Though the terranes crept forward at only five to thirteen centimeters (two to five inches) a year, their crawl moved them up to 120,000 kilometers (75,000 miles) in a billion years. Since the Pacific Coast is mere thousands of kilometers away from the mid-ocean rift where these plates originated, the accumulating sediments and volcanic islands rode a virtual conveyor belt under the ocean to collide with our coast.

When the leading edges of the oceanic plates hit the continental margin, they dove deep to where intense heat and pressure bonded the descending slab to the over-riding mass. For a time, the subduction process stopped, presenting an immovable collision zone to the incoming oceanic plates. Pressing relentlessly forward, the plates and their terranes fused with the continental mass.

But the tremendous momentum of the trailing plates could not be halted for long. As they sheared off behind their welded termini in massive subduction earthquakes, they proceeded again below the continent. As their dives continued, huge pieces scraped off their backs to join the continental margin.

Riding the crustal plates east under the Pacific, these terranes and island arcs built our continent westward when they smashed against the immoveable coast. Some parts of the plates thrust inland over the continental margin by as much as eighty kilometers, some annealed to the edge, and still others dove beneath it. Some, like Vancouver Island and southeast Alaska, were forced northward thousands of miles along transform faults. These two masses formed near eastern Australia, rode tectonic plates thousands of miles to Peru, and then were pushed north to their present locations.

Each of the terranes that pressed onto the coast had its own unique birthplace. Some were formed of high-latitude sedimentary rock created deep under cool waters. Others were composed of tropical island chains fringed by coral reefs. Still others were volcanic archipelagoes that rose off our coast. The origin of these exotic terranes can be deciphered by examining their unique fossil records and the magnetic fields in their volcanic rocks.

Some one hundred identifiable masses annexed to the Pacific shore in this manner. Each grew the coast westward by tens of kilometers from where it meandered through eastern British Columbia 300 million years ago, when the Old Cascades were offshore volcanic islands.

Our Pacific Coast was built through this complex joining of exotic fragments. These rocks are their own history books, each with a story to tell.

The pressure of these incoming plates on our coast folded the continental crust in front of them. Upward folds produced the mountain ranges of Vancouver Island and coastal British Columbia, and the downward fold between them formed the Georgia Basin, an immense trough beneath the Strait of Georgia.

As the integrity of the rock failed during this folding, the mountains and basins fractured into a spider web of faults. And when the subducting slab melted far below the surface, liquefied rock found its way up through these cracks to form the area's volcanoes and igneous rocks.

Through millions of years of erosion of the adjacent mountains and the sinking of countless dead marine organisms, the Georgia Basin accumulated upwards of 10,000 feet of sediment. Under the pressure of that sediment, the original bottom of the basin bowed downward as it accommodated the increasing load.

When the compression of colliding terrains relaxed, the crust thinned in a rebound of decompression. At the same time the underlying plates changed directions, tearing the attenuated crust. Fissures opened in the rock under the Strait of Georgia and molten basalts oozed slowly forth.

Lasqueti and its nearby islands began as a silent explosion. Thousand-degree rock spewed into the depths, flashing water to steam. In moments, the Strait heaved skyward as if blown by massive depth-charges.

In a rise to the surface that may have taken decades or centuries, an underwater peak grew. On its flanks were a number of smaller peaks, pillows of basalt that pushed out of the central massif. Amid bubbles and steam, these nascent islands pushed toward the light.

To ancient seabirds, the first hint of new land was a change in water color. Eventually the presence gave way to persistent foam, a new place where waves broke. At first the birds avoided the area, fearful of some monstrosity lurking below.

One day when the waters calmed, a low hump protruded above the blue. Again the gulls screeched and wheeled, mistaking rock for leviathan. But as the massive thing persisted in its breach, in time it became a place to perch above the waves. Soon other shadows surfaced and eventually a pod of islands hovered in the center of the Strait. Far in the future, the largest would be named Lasquetti.

Lasquetti and its clutch of islands perch atop layers of ancient rock. Down deep is the rock of the Wrangallia super-terrane, itself of offshore origin. On top of this is the sedimentary rock that formed in the Georgia trough. The islands were created by basaltic flows of partially melted remnants of exotic terranes flowing sluggishly out of fissures that opened when the Georgia basin was deformed by tectonic plates smashing against our coast.

In its earliest years, Olsen was a peninsula of ancient Lasqueti. Over time the glaciers of succeeding ice ages ground off Olsen's top and gouged out a trough that separated it from its much larger neighbor. In the most recent ice age, the weight of kilometer-thick ice depressed Olsen and Lasqueti as much as 230 meters (750 feet). But when the ice melted and the land was freed from its overburden, the islands rebounded to their present levels.

Only the Strait knows how Olsen and Lasqueti looked before the glaciers had their way with them.

Chapter 8
Settling In

*As soon as Billy found an affordable floathouse, he bought it,
and ... towed it from Richmond Bay in Drury Inlet to Insect
Island ... Southeast winds of 70 knots began to blow as they set
out. It would have been easier to wait out the blow, but half
the fun was not knowing for sure if they'd make it. The little
house was wet and salty clear to the roof peak ... It was probably
a good thing that neither Yvonne nor Billy owned a stick of
furniture, because there was no place to put it ... the house was
so small, with a built in bed and breakfast nook, and a stove,
that there wasn't even room for a chair ... There was no indoor
plumbing ... despite it all, Billy and Yvonne loved their new
home. It was warm and had the cozy breakfast nook where they
lingered over Yvonne's good cooking.*
— Alexandra Morton and Billy Proctor, *Heart of the Raincoast*

August 3, 1997

I woke early and sat on the floathouse porch, enjoying the morning's
peace. An eagle feathered the air and landed in a tree above me, then
screamed at its mate across the lagoon.

After breakfast, the boys and I ran over to French Creek to pick up
the rest of our gear. With two overflowing boatfuls, we felt sufficiently
prepared to remain out of touch with the outside world for the duration
of our stay.

As I was enjoying the day's heat, a neighbor dropped by to tell us a cow had fallen into the Lasqueti well that used to serve the floathouse. Unfortunately, the cow had died and decomposed before it was discovered. Though we'd never used this well, images of the decaying cow prompted me to set up the water system I'd planned through the winter.

Step one was to haul one of the empty blue barrels we'd brought up to a flat spot on the rocks above the floathouse.

Step two involved a boat trip to the Lasqueti dock at high tide, where I filled the remaining three barrels with water. Piped to the dock from Pete's Lake and of questionable potability, it would do fine for showers. Never mind its beautiful brown color.

Step three came after I ran back to Olsen and maneuvered our boat deep into floathouse lagoon. After partially tearing apart the boat, I hooked up my homemade pump system to the boat's battery. Then I placed the pump's feed line into a barrel in the boat and pulled its discharge hose up the rocks to the awaiting cistern.

With a flip of a switch I was in business. The only thing I hadn't planned on was the cloud of blue smoke spewing from my 200 horsepower motor, which I had to keep running to keep my battery sufficiently charged to power the pump.

In step four, I flipped the switch off, grabbed a beer, and yelled to the boys to haul the now empty barrel from the boat to the ledge above.

After repeating this latter sequence two more times, I had three full barrels up on the island and one empty in the boat. I was also buzzed from beer and exhaust, so I left the rest of the hookup for the following day.

Following my swim in from the boat, the two small panfuls of fresh water I poured over my head brought dreams of future showers.

***

Basic Island Courtesies

   1. Pee in the woods, not in the outhouse.

2. Pour a scoop of dirt down the outhouse hole after using it, and do so with the toilet seat raised. Who wants to sit down on a film of dust?

3. Take off your shoes before coming inside the house.

4. Take your garbage with you.

5. Be careful with fire.

6. Be careful about breaking anything, because there's no way to replace it.

7. Don't step on the lichen.

8. Conserve water.

9. Share with neighbors.

10. If you're going somewhere after dark, bring your own flashlight.

11. Be considerate about using up someone else's stash of supplies that can't be replenished locally. Which is everything.

Frequently Asked Island Questions

1. Where should I pee so it won't stink?

2. While walking to and from the floathouse at high tide, will I break this bowing gang-plank or roll off this floating log?

3. Am I going to hit an unseen rock with my motor?

4. Why am I losing track of things in a three by five meter floathouse?

5. Where can I put my foot so I don't step on the lichen?

6. How much water is left in the barrel?

7. How many more things should I do now that my hands are dirty before I wash them and use up precious water?

8. How much shampoo should I use so I can get clean in one rinse, and not need extra water to wash off?

9. Why doesn't the outhouse stink?

10. Where shall I put the boat so it won't go dry, get blown by the wind, or bang against the rocks?

11. What day is it?

12. How deep do I dare put the prawn traps?

13. How much propane do we have left?

14. Now that the outhouse stinks after ten days of five people using it, how do I get it to stop?

August 4, 1997

The most prized item we lugged to Olsen this year was a propane refrigerator salvaged from a derelict motor home. We hoped this would allow us to move our perishables out of our ice chest and stem their inevitable rot.

Moving a new refrigerator in its protective box on a hand truck into a suburban house is one thing. As we quickly discovered, lifting a sharp-cornered old appliance in and out of a boat, carrying it up a wet beach and over uneven beach logs, and then moving it carefully along the narrow walkways of an antique floathouse, was entirely another.

The boys and I spent a good part of the morning getting this beast set up in the shed on the side of the floathouse. When I finally touched a match to its burner, however, I ignited a pressure-leak in the propane line. Chris rushed to fetch our fire extinguisher, though by reaching past the flame thrower I was luckily able to turn off the gas before the tinder-dry floathouse went up in flames. After scavenging repair materials, I used a piece of an old plastic bag to seal the loose fitting, and then wrapped it with some used electrical tape.

When we first explored the floathouse's beautifully handcrafted drawers, we'd shaken our heads at what a packrat Larry Aites had been. Each drawer was full of meticulously sorted junk: rusty screws, short pieces of twine, plastic bags, dead batteries, mysterious parts from dismantled appliances, specially modified hand tools, broken gears— the variety was staggering. We had the very real sense that through his thirteen years in the floatie Larry had thrown nothing away.

Larry hadn't been sure what the twist ties off loaves of bread would be good for. He just knew that in some unpredictable moment of crisis they'd be exactly what he needed. Like his island neighbors, Larry was an oasis of self-reliance in a world addicted to buying easy fixes.

When it came time to fix our leaking propane line, Larry's junk collection began to sparkle like precious jewels. As the fog of our naiveté cleared, we realized that we were gazing at our local hardware store. On a remote island, improvisation and self-sufficiency were keys to survival. There was no repairman to call, no store to visit. The original uses of our junk were irrelevant; all had limitless potential restricted only by our imagination and the depth of our need. This accumulation of rusted paraphernalia, utilized with proper ingenuity, would keep us warm, dry, watered, and fed.

A prior promise to the kids to go fishing saved me from more work, as the falling tide necessitated an immediate departure from the lagoon. We caught a few nice dogfish near the Finnerties, and then motored to a little cove where we swam and dove off the rocks.

The kids played chess by lantern light after dinner, and then we sat on the deck in the dark looking for shooting stars. The Milky Way was out in all its glory, rewarding our patience with an incredible meteor shower. When it's dark here, it's really dark, with no city-glow to compete with the stars.

***

In the deep quiet of the island, there are two clocks that set the rhythm of our lives.

One is the sea, whose cadence is deep and underlying. This slow-beating heart pumps to the cycle of the moon, powering a monstrous chest that rises and falls twice a day.

On low tides when the back pass goes dry, we gather shellfish and walk to nearby Lasqueti. But such low water also deprives us of our sheltered landing area in floathouse cove. Boats tethered to the floathouse become stranded for hours, and we must disembark on the steep rocks bordering False Bay. If these low tides are at night, and the water is rough, we choose to be island-bound.

On incoming tides, waters advance over the sand flats of the back pass and absorb their stored heat, inviting swims and saltwater rinses before outdoor showers.

When the tide is high, we fish off the rocks facing False Bay. Friends motor into floathouse lagoon in their runabouts, landing on the bobbing logs next to our home.

Equally as powerful as the timepiece of the tides is the clock of the winds. Though this is a clock without rhythm, it determines our schedules nonetheless. Calm days put the world at the water's edge and journeys to everywhere are contemplated.

On windy days our travel is restricted and fraught with anxiety. In storms we raise the drawbridge to all things off our rock. It's then that we truly become an island.

August 5, 1997

As usual I was the first one up, enjoying a calm and sunny morning. After Theresa arose, she and I kayaked over to Higgins Island to visit Ray and Eve. We stayed for three hours, chatting and enjoying a leisurely breakfast.

Upon our return, the boys and I bent to the task of relocating our propane refrigerator. Extracting it from the floathouse's cramped shed was an awkward four-person wrestling match. After lowering the fridge off the floathouse raft, we humped it over the beach to a small rock platform I'd built on the island, determined to keep all possibility of fire away from the floathouse.

After more patchwork with more used materials I finally got the refrigerator going without igniting another flame thrower. Then I hooked up a hose to a water barrel on the rocks above and put a nozzle on its end. Theresa and I stood admiring our day's work, smiling at the unspeakable luxury of having refrigeration and a shower on our island!

Finally we put some oyster shells around the fridge's base and a juniper branch on top to make it presentable for the dinner guests we were expecting.

As we were starting a beach fire to cook our dinner, another neighbor from Lasqueti stopped by to welcome us to the island. His name was Dick Grinnell, and his canoe was full of tools. The carpentry job he had near tiny Dragon Island was typical for him. Someone on the water needed something done. So Dick packed his tools in his canoe, paddled to the job, and then paddled home at night. Dick lives on the water, commutes on the water, and works on homes on the water—living a life that completely captivated me.

Shortly after Dick departed we were visited by a representative of the Lasqueti Fire Department. The volunteer fireman said that, out of the ever present worry about home and forest fires, someone on False Bay had phoned when they saw the smoke from our campfire. Initially I felt intruded upon, but then appreciated the concern. Ray and Eve told us they experienced a similar courtesy call when they first settled Higgins Island.

As the sun settled toward the horizon, our island's arbutus and junipers let out their shadows to roam across the rocks. The trees held these shadows gently by the wrist and let them crawl further away as the sun dipped lower in the sky. Then called them quickly back at sunset to sleep together through the night.

Looking at each other in the floathouse, I see that we've all turned brown, our hands and feet cut from life on the rocks and beach. Chess and card games by lantern light graced the waning hours before bed.

August 6, 1997

It's obvious that the more conveniences we bring to the island—such as our fridge and water system—the more time I spend setting up and getting and keeping things working.

This goes for people as well, as evidenced in my full-time job refereeing kids. After I broke up the first fight of the day, the boys fled to the beach with masks and snorkels to go crabbing. No doubt they swore among themselves at the big shore crab they were escaping.

With most of the major settling-in chores completed, I gave myself over to the pleasures of island life. As I swung slowly in our hammock under the shade of bay-side juniper trees, the book I was reading sank slowly to my chest. I heard the wind sighing, a raven croaking, and seals blowing as they surfaced in the bay. Ospreys cried, eagle wings whistled, and waves whispered to the shore.

Chapter 9
Hammock Time

Languor is sunny and hot. It is at home near the sea and is best appreciated in environments of beauty.
  —Kevin Patterson, *The Water In Between*

From the time I was an infant in the house in Aracalca I had learned to sleep in a hammock, but only in Sucre did I make it part of my nature. There is nothing better for taking a siesta, for experiencing the hour of stars, for thinking without haste, for making love without prejudices.
  —Gabriel Garcia Marquez, *Living to Tell the Tale*

August 6, 1997, Continued

How long have I been dozing in the hammock, two hours or two days? I do not know and it does not matter. I only know the bay is calm and the sun hot. My hammock has changed the shape of time, stretching it to embrace the day's heat.

The hammock has allowed me to become something less than human. As the sun warms me, I slide back millions of years to when distant ancestors emerged from the sea, where my only dream is to float and swim and warm myself on the rocks. The heat touches the reptilian part of my brain, causing me to spread my arms in the most basic form of ecstasy. I move only for pleasure or hunger or flight.

Indian gods visit me as I drift through shallow dreams, totems that explain the universe.

44

Though I move in and out of consciousness I feel no weariness. The world around me is alive with the magic that lives at the boundary of sleeping and waking.

As I succumb to the enchantments of the island, the membrane separating the real and dream worlds becomes increasingly porous. Each begins leaking into the other, and as the day grows warmer it becomes impossible to differentiate between the two.

While my body is in the hammock, I am swimming through the bay like a salmon. I revel in cool water rushing over my skin, taking in great droughts of oxygen through hungry gills. I leap into sky and spread fins that miraculously become feathers as I wing my way above the trees. My eagle eyes take in the Strait and its islands and surrounding mountains. Within me grows something spawned by the grandeur of such places, an awareness that requires the immensity of the sea and beauty of the islands to be born.

Ironically this languorous fruit of island life carries some poisonous seeds. For as an old mariner once told me, the slide toward disaster usually starts when you relax and take things for granted.

So it is on the island. Days of sunny hammock-time allow me to withdraw into the fantasy worlds of the books I read. Gazing out across the bay, I find it incomprehensible that its gentle waters could be capable of any violence. Our seas get progressively warmer, inviting me to dive in and swim slowly along the shore.

Lulled by day after day of heat, I leave my float coat hanging on its hook when I go fishing. Pushing my kayak onto the rocks just above high tide, I neglect to tie it up. I moor our boat carelessly, closer to shore than I know is safe.

The lack of wind encourages me to glance at frayed ropes and forget them. I stop listening to the weather radio, take my eyes off the sky, and ignore swells that start rising beneath my feet.

Such lassitude allows me to smile benignly at things that break. I defer necessary repairs and maintenance, and draw our gas tanks down to reserve levels.

My spirit expands as I wax philosophically about my communion with the wild. Laziness takes root as I'm hypnotized by the siren's song of days that seem to have no beginning or end.

And in all this I forget Ishmael's warning of the sea's tiger heart. My state of enchantment leaves me woefully unprepared for the fangs of the Strait, fangs that sink in with paralyzing suddenness.

On a dead calm day when the wind blows up to forty knots in thirty minutes, the sea metamorphoses from friend to foe. Waves build from benign to breaking, from placid to prowling.

Yet the biggest threat comes not from the weather itself, but from my lack of preparation for it. And more ominously, from my seeming inability to respond to the storm-dragon's attacks. In such attacks I have difficulty believing my senses.

After days of dreamy quietude, when my brain is out of its normal habit of problem solving, I stand ape-like looking into the wind and waves as I fail to grasp that the sea is stalking me. I'm stunned by a world turned upside down, shaking my head as if groggily awaking from Gulliver's sleep.

But Komogwa, the aborigines' malevolent undersea God, rides in on the storm to collect his due. He considers each act of forgetfulness a stinging insult and wants his revenge.

Komogwa comes calling when the wind and waves besiege us, and he reveals himself through their nasty handiwork. Frayed lines break. Kayaks wash off the rocks, then are hurled back against the shore and smashed. My hydraulic lift fails as I attempt an emergency landing in a wind-swept cove. As my mind races to recall the details of a weather forecast I neglected, all I can hear is Komogwa whispering in my ear.

In this I've learned an important lesson: If I fail to read the danger signs, I lose. Perhaps my boat or a loved one.

Komogwa is a greedy bastard, and he holds grudges.

The worst fear thus has a painful twist to it, for it doesn't come from confronting the threats of a storm. It grabs me when I finally realize I've been perilously tardy in doing so. I'm past due, and the debt collector is staring me in the face. He is uncomfortably close, baring fangs awash with spittle.

CHAPTER 10
THE DEEP

When you look long into an abyss, the abyss looks into you.
—Friedrich Nietzsche

The water is clear and deep beyond our island's rocks. These depths draw me into them … to dive, fish, or gaze as if into fire.

Similar depths have made me recoil in fear. Snorkeling off Panama's San Blas Islands, I panicked as I finned over the abrupt edge of an atoll. Suspended over the void, I backpaddled furiously to where I could see the bottom beneath me. I could venture out again only by reminding myself that I was only meters from shore.

Years later I was diving for lobsters off Mexico's Revilla Gigedo Islands, young volcanic cones whose flanks plunged into the abyss. As I hovered next to the underwater cliff, beneath me the depths receded into the deepest of blues, where the seamount lost itself in darkness.

Grabbing a lobster from the wall, I surfaced to show it to my friends. Two were snorkeling close by, but my buddy Dave Treat was out of the water clinging to the cliff like a crab. Sensing something wrong, I swam back in alarm. Try as I might, I couldn't convince him to get down, and ended up swimming back to get our boat. Dave was paralyzed with fear. "It's the blue … so deep … can't swim … my chest knots up … can't do it!" He was shaking as I picked him off the rocks and helped him into the boat.

Thinking back on these experiences, I've realized this response is sparked by the sudden falling away of land's edge, not the depths themselves.

Cruising back from the Revilla Gigedos, our captain glided to a stop in waters 4,000 meters deep (12,000 feet). Donning masks and snorkels, we jumped in for a swim above unimaginable depths. Hundreds of miles from any clouding sediments, the sea was crystal clear. Shafts of sunlight danced around us, shifting columns of brilliance that disappeared into the abyss.

Dave was swimming with us then, and felt not the least discomfort.

***

In the waters just off our shore, a rockfish hovers above the descending seafloor. Peering upward at Olsen, it sees no island at all—just a curving wall with a seam of water at its top. Strange shapes and warbling sounds suggest things living beyond the wall, but they are too alien for the fish to comprehend.

Hiding cautiously behind some kelp, the rockfish eyes the opaque world above the water's edge. Suddenly a shadow looms and something explodes through the water just off the rocks. Flaring its spines defensively, the fish stares at a clumsy pink animal that emerges from a rush of bubbles, padding gracelessly with skinny appendages that must dream of webs and fins.

Turning from the dangers beyond the waves, the rockfish glides deeper into its world. It wanders through limitless plankton and diatoms and krill, tiny plants and animals that wash over the fish's eyes as it swims. Though some of these minute organisms migrate vertically in the water-column in search of food, others are capable of only the smallest twitching movements. Still others are drifters, sedately riding the currents through the entirety of their lives. To creatures their size, seawater has the consistency of honey.

The swim of the rockfish reveals that the undersea Strait is not one place but many. Our island has many counterparts below the surface, submarine environments with their own miracles of plant and animal life. Pinnacles sport rock scallops and abalone and capes of waving seaweed, all of which disappear at an inverse "tree-line" where the walls descend into gloom. Schools of herring hover in the lee of rocks, feeding on smaller creatures caught in their eddies. These herring attract salmon, which in turn draw rigid boat-shadows to the surface, shadows that send down filaments that slice through the currents, creating seams where none should exist.

This is a world of brilliant anemones, wondrous animals whose trunk-like bodies are anchored to rocks and mouths are surrounded by hydras of wandering tentacles.

Above the anemones float diaphanous creatures without backbones, medusas made entirely of jelly. Trailing long, sticky tentacles, they fish patiently for anything careless enough to swim into their blood-red nets.

Finning lazily over the edge of a cliff, the rockfish swims into limitless blue. There is no surface or bottom to see, nothing in any direction but water. But for a glow in one direction and darkness in another, there is no up or down. To the fish with its neutral buoyancy, gravity does not exist. The up-current zone from which all odors come is the only hint of direction.

Other fish glide noiselessly by in a world cloaked in silence. Colors dim and disappear as the rockfish descends to the bottom of the Strait, where only one percent of daylight penetrates. This is the realm of mud-eaters, of worms and sea-cucumbers that continuously consume and excrete the sediment.

These depths crush with incredible pressures, which increase by one atmosphere for every ten meters the rockfish descends. Yet rockfish, jellyfish, and even fragile, brittle stars move from surface to abyss with impunity, displaying abilities far beyond those of the pink animal swimming above.

The depths are a place of scavengers and predators. Nothing grows here, and food is either taken by force or found at random as it drifts down from above. Some feeders are constantly searching, beating up-current at the least scent of prey or death. Others hover motionless in the gloom. Extremely sensitive to movement, they wait patiently for prey to blunder near.

Here dwell creatures seldom seen on the surface, vaguely known from occasional body parts that wash ashore. These are monstrous things that have risen from the abyss to swim through aboriginal myths. In the open ocean they battle sperm whales, leaving rows of sucker-scars on the leviathans' giant heads. Their beaks, found by the thousands in stomachs of slaughtered whales, attest to their incredible numbers. They hang quietly in the dark, draping huge tentacles to catch the unwary. Collecting dim light in eyes the size of dinner plates, they see where others only feel.

***

Hundreds of feet below the waves, a hunter prowls the depths. Amid the particles that eddy around it are a few with favored tastes: traces of specialized gills and bits of shell that encase delicate meats. Although the currents are vague, their subtle scent trails are enough for the hunter to follow.

Pursuing these odors, the hunter slides its tentacles over slime-covered rocks, silently pulling itself forward. Its suckered arms reach inquisitively through fluids that are only slightly more or less opaque at midnight or noon.

Halting momentarily, the predator savors the strengthening scent-trail. Excited into tense stillness, it gathers its waving arms in readiness, its sphincter-jet dilating and contracting with its slow breathing. Its sensitive skin picks up the nearby beating of a small heart guarded by a brittle carapace, slow and cold-blooded.

In a rush of movement, the hunter attacks. Eyes on stalks glimpse suckered terrors looming suddenly overhead. Feathered mouth parts taste danger in the strangely distorted waters. Odd sensory receptors flash alarms to a brain incapable of foreboding.

Overcome by the pure fright of discovered prey, the shelled-one drives a clutch of segmented legs into frantic movement. But it is not enough. The prehensile predator lashes out and puts a quiet end to the shelled-one's frenzy. In an instant, it is pulled apart.

The dark waters shudder intensely and then quiet. Wrapping shadow around itself, the sinuous hunter disappears. There is a slight movement of sand grains as if something brushed them and was gone. The silence is as perfect as a porcelain vase.

When the disturbed silt settles, a collection of cracked chitin remains. Its pieces rest on the bottom like pottery shards for some future interloper to discover and interpret.

As the tentacled thing glides forward, it comes upon a cave of deeper darkness. Resting in it is an immense danger that appears to be sleeping. Meaty lips part slowly, drawing water over inward-curving teeth. Gill covers work with the same somnambulistic rhythm. Notwithstanding these signs of sleep, something in the shallowness of the head's breathing betrays its wakefulness.

Turning on its camouflage too quickly, the tentacled thing reveals its intent to flee. But before it can jet away, its Martian-like brain sac is yanked forward as the giant maw opens and swallows.

Tentacled arms are swaddled by the muscular gut that lies behind the huge head. Stinging digestive juices gag the cephalopod as it tries to breathe. Frantically jetting and changing color, it finds escape only in the approaching quiet of death. As awareness dims, its last sensation is the intense burning of its highly sensitive skin.

Resting quietly in the cave, the large predator goes back to the task of fanning a large egg cluster with its tail. Sinking into a sated torpor, it slowly digests its favorite prey. Relaxing within confines of protective rock, its hunting instincts are allowed to sleep. It will not feed again for days.

But something hard and alien bounces off the rock around the mouth of the cave where the giant head rests. Up from this bouncing thing stretches a filament that slices through the depths, unlike anything the giant head has known. The head knows instinctively that these things are neither food nor prey, nor any part it's world. But they are certainly a threat to the eggs.

In a crush of razored teeth, the head attacks the alien thing, which responds by sinking barbs of pain into the head's huge lips. With a power beyond its diminutive body, the alien thing jerks the head upward.

The head has ruled the depths near its cave for a hundred years and it fights the alien with incredible fury. Its immense tail is worked by great bands of enraged muscle, straining to regain the bottom. But in time, the monstrous fish begins to tire and the blinding light of the surface looms. Finning exhaustedly just below the boundary between realms, the giant head suddenly finds itself lifted skyward in a hammock of knots. In moments it is slammed upon something impossibly hard and flat as a wash of air begins to desiccate its gills.

Gazing downward at the fish, a two-legged creature displays an upturned flash of teeth. Ignoring the building seas and threatening sky, it unhooks the claws from the giant head and throws the alien thing back into the water. And with a certainty that only the head and suckered thing know, it moves unwittingly toward becoming one of the eaten in the food chain beneath the waves.

CHAPTER 11
EXPLORING A MIDDEN

*The broad white clam-shell beach speaks of a thousand years
of clam feasts. Rising up from this beach is a high, flattened
midden, the soil black from pre-historic fires. The extent of it
announces that grand Kwakiutl longhouses once stood there.*
— Alexandra Morton and Billy Proctor , *Heart of the Raincoast*

August 12, 1997

I awoke slowly today, still tangled in dreams. My body was heavy and relaxed as I listened to the sounds of the morning: a light wind blowing through the trees, cedar shakes creaking overhead, and an occasional bird call.

My son Chas and I clambered aboard our boat and went to pull our prawn traps. We found that if we kept tension on the line we could let the swells do the lifting for us. Shortly, we filled a five-gallon bucket half-full with beautiful jumbo prawns.

Chas and I then beach-combed the south end of the Finnerties for some cedar logs we needed to rebuild the steps leading from floathouse beach onto the island. After tying them to a rope trailing behind our boat, we let out our fishing lines and trolled for salmon as we towed our bounty home.

As we maneuvered the boat, logs, and tow line while attempting to pick one last log from Olsen, we caught the tow line in our prop. Although this stopped our motor cold, no damage was done.

Later our family cruised over to Ray and Eve's for dinner with a group of friends from False Bay. We feasted on our load of prawns, a salad from Eve's garden, and homemade lemon-lime ice cream. Afterwards, Ken played his accordion and Ray his stand-up bass, and everybody joined in playing spoons, clapping hands, and stomping feet.

After our evening of fun was over, I ferried our Lasqueti friends home in the dark.

August 13, 1997

I've developed a system of rotating work duty among the boys: washing dishes, separating garbage, and filling up the dirt bucket for the outhouse. If I keep good written notes on "whose turn it is," I can hold their arguing down to a manageable level and preserve a semblance of family peace.

When there is hard work to do, however, I make sure everybody joins in. Today the boys and I cleared some rocks out of the lagoon entrance and then grunted logs into place for our new set of stairs. This was hard work, made frustrating by horseplay, bickering, and swearing. Angry and disgusted at our antics, Theresa kayaked off for some peace.

When we spied Theresa returning, all of us hastily agreed that an escape in the boat was in order.

Attempting to climb along the rocks and board our boat in the deep water next to them, Chas slipped and dove for our bow. He smashed down hard, almost slid into the water, and was laughingly miffed that I was more concerned about the fate of the fishing pole he carried than whether he'd hurt himself.

In this critique of my character, Chas finds a kindred spirit in Theresa, who never misses a chance to tell the story of when we were "wading" across the Skykomish River while steelhead fishing. It was a bit deeper than we expected, with water up to Theresa's chin. She grabbed onto me as strong currents swept her feet off the bottom and her flip-flops away. My concern, of course, was that she not drop the fishing rod I had entrusted to her care. She was not amused by my priorities.

While the boys and I were fishing, Theresa returned home and salvaged her afternoon by making a gin and tonic with real homemade ice. What a luxury, especially while pouting.

Arriving back at Olsen and needing to cool off after a hot afternoon in the boat, I swam in from the boat's mooring pulling my kayak behind me.

We barbecued half a salmon over a bark fire for dinner and roasted foil-wrapped potatoes in the coals. Theresa unveiled a blackberry pie for dessert, which was an unexpected surprise for the family males considering our earlier conduct. Our clan ate the pie off one community plate, devouring it with scrupulous respect for each other's portions. I found this remarkable, having expected a feeding frenzy to ensue. Perhaps residual guilt from our morning rudeness kept us all under control.

In the waning light, we threw our salmon scraps into the lagoon and watched the crabs enjoy a feast of their own.

August 14, 1997

Our water usage in eleven days: twenty-eight gallons of "clear" water, equaling 2.5 gallons per day, and used mostly for drinking, cooking, and brushing teeth; 150 gallons of "brown" water, equaling 13.6 gallons per day, and used mostly for showering. This wasn't bad for a family of five. Our consumption would have been a lot higher if the kids had showered daily, but the cold water feeding our shower served as an effective deterrent to frequent use.

***

The immense shell piles left by the First Nations Peoples who lived in this area are known as middens, and I'd spied one on a small Lasqueti beach facing the floathouse. Today I waded over at low tide to check it out. This collection of old shells was two meters (six feet) deep and covered nearly thirty meters (one hundred feet) of shoreline. Large arbutus and fir grew on top in the soil that covered the last shell layer. No doubt this midden had been used for thousands of years.

All types of shells were mixed in—cockles, blue mussels, butter clams, and steamers—along with many sea urchin spines. The shells in the top meter were unbroken, often appearing in distinct layers of one type of clam.

Throughout the midden were many fire-scorched cooking rocks. To heat water inside their wooden cooking vessels and woven cooking baskets, Indians heated up these rocks in their fires and then dropped them into the cooking water.

Staring at the midden from the beach below it, I realized I beheld a signpost of past millennia that pointed to countless generations shelling clams on this spot. Aboriginal families passed such sites down to their descendants, and the ancestors of the last clan who came here may have clammed the same beach for hundreds of generations.

Prowling the forest above the midden, I knew that I was in an abandoned Indian camp where untold numbers of shamen had supplicated their gods, burying offerings of their finest blades in forest and sea. But so far, the beach and the trees had kept silent about where these treasures were hidden.

Sitting on the beach below the midden, I contemplated the journeys that brought these natives here.

CHAPTER 12
ABORIGINAL EXPLORERS

Raven was alone and lonely in an empty world, and one day wandered down to the beach. From the wet sand at his feet came a faint sound. He saw a partially buried clam shell, cocked his head to listen, and heard a sigh as the two halves of the shell began to open. A small face peered out, then shyly withdrew. Raven called to the face in a whisper. It slowly reappeared, stretching its neck as it looked up at him, and then quickly retreated again. Once more the Raven whispered to those in the shell to come out. Another sigh came from the shell, and another face peered from between its two halves. Soon there were more small faces, until a whole row of them appeared along the edge of the shell. Little arms came out, pushing the clam shell open wider. Unfolding and stretching, hordes of little people emerged from the open shell and went off to populate the land. These were the first people. Born of the shore, they stayed by the shore to live.
—Haida Legend

Since the days of early earth, our planet has wandered in and out of a succession of ice ages. Its eccentric orbit and wobbly axis, along with changing levels of atmospheric carbon dioxide and continental drift, combined to produce an ongoing series of freezes, some so deep that glaciers met at the equator. Some of the intervening warm climes brought temperatures to the Yukon similar to those of present-day Florida, allowing alligators to live above the Arctic Circle and forests to grow where now there is only tundra.

During the deep freezes, so much of earth's water accumulated in the ice sheets that there were millennia-long droughts and land bridges between the continents. These droughts were likely responsible for the very evolution of our human ancestors, who migrated over the land bridges as they spread around the globe.

About seven million years ago, extended glaciation desiccated much of Africa. Before then, primates had been forest creatures that swung from tree to tree, knuckle-walking on all fours in their short jaunts across the ground. Their feet, like their hands, were structured to grip branches, with four long toes and an inner fifth toe that grasped like a thumb.

These tree-dwellers were the smartest animals on the planet. Communicating with hoots and grunts, and perhaps some chest-banging or fang-bearing, they epitomized animal intelligence. But they made no tools and lacked the brain size and vocal structures necessary for speech. They carried no torches and sat around no fires, and the only light at night came from the moon and stars.

In search of food in what had once been a lush forest, a family of these simians clambered from limb to limb in one of their favorite fruit trees. But the drought had not been kind to the tree, and in too short a time the hungry animals had picked it clean. Previously they'd have swung to the branches of adjoining trees, but in the succession of dry years many of these had died and fallen to the forest floor. So the primates descended and scrambled on all fours to the closest trunk they could find.

As the years of drought continued, the forest fragmented and grasslands crept into the spaces between the trees, making islands of the patches of woods that remained.

The primates feared these grasslands, as dun-colored cats lurked hungrily within their cover. So when the chimps were finally forced by hunger to cross the grass to other stands of trees, they reared up on their hind legs and ran.

The African grasses were tall, and the chimps that ran upright were better able to spot cats lurking in wait. As the trees fruited less and less, the families that learned to dash upright began to breed with one another and drift genetically from their brethren that remained on all fours.

In a world where large teeth grabbed those who were slow a-foot, tree climbing offered less and less refuge and limb-grasping feet no longer necessarily assisted survival. As natural selection favored speed and an upright posture, a succession of supporting adaptations found their way into what were to become our ancestors.

These adaptations started with the mutation of our big toes, which straightened and strengthened and allowed these simians to balance on two legs. In time their other eight toes straightened, their heels thinned and lengthened, and a complex system of small bones and tendons came to surround muscled arches in their feet. Bowed legs straightened, the pelvic girdle morphed to support the upper body's weight, and spines evolved from straight to S-shaped. Together these allowed our distant ancestors to run, and run progressively faster than other savannah primates.

This running generated a lot of heat, and to cool themselves these simians shed their body hair and developed an enhanced circulatory system in their heads. This flow of blood also allowed their brains to expand in size and complexity.

As these early ancestors began preying on creatures of the grasslands, natural selection favored the planning, cooperation, and tool-making skills necessary to bring down game animals. As far back as 1.8 million years ago, some ancient human species developed the hand axe, believed to have been thrown to injure game. These tools have been found by the thousands around ancient watering holes where prey congregated.

Meat eaters would not have needed as large a digestive tract or as much energy to digest food, which may have precipitated shifts in how our ancestors' bodies functioned. Energy previously used in digestion may have shifted to the brain, and the concentrated protein from meat could have allowed more cerebral growth.

Standing upright with a head that was repositioned on their curved spines, our ancestors' throats straightened and lengthened, their voice boxes dropped, and pharynxes changed shape. But though they had evolved to be the smartest creatures around, with the physical apparatus for speech, the most they could do was to grunt and hoot.

To talk, they'd need to further develop their thumbs.

In this our ancestors' upright posture cooperated, as it freed their front feet to become hands. Eventually these developed specialized opposed thumbs that could twist and turn grasped objects and purposefully strike them together, which enabled our ancestor to make tools.

Toolmaking's need for planning ahead and manipulating objects favored the evolution of a brain with the neural structures for arranging ideas in an orderly manner. And as our ancestors' brains evolved to support increasingly complex toolmaking, they were configured so that they understood the world in the same organized fashion that their hands manipulated it. The unique function of these brain structures and the way hands organized toolmaking are thought to be the foundations of the proclivity for logic and syntax that allowed the development of speech and language.

The evolution of our thumbs and dexterous hands was thus central to our evolution as humans. Handling and manipulating things around us helped select neural formations unique to the human mind.

Though our first meat-eating ancestors were most likely scavengers, when their successors developed tools they could feast more easily on the carcasses they found. They became hunters when they learned how to work together and employ these tools against large game. Increasing protein in the diet allowed them to grow yet larger brains, and the need for better communication while hunting caused natural selection to favor further increases in brain size and complexity. Larger craniums were required to house these growing brains, which meant that we had to be born increasingly premature to pass through the birth canal. Earlier birth favored learning over instinct, as the young were born so helpless that instinct couldn't guarantee survival. This in turn led to higher survival rates of those with more developed brains, which over time became three times larger than scientists would predict for primates of similar body size.

Homo erectus of 300,000 years ago would have looked much like we do, but would have had a brain only two-thirds the size of ours. While they were accomplished hunters, grimaces and grunts and gestures and screams would have defined the outer limits of their communication. It would be the arrival of *homo sapiens* about 195,000 years ago, with the cerebral cortex that their predecessors lacked, that brought our direct ancestors into being. *Homo sapiens* were the first primates to have the capacity for complex thought, language, and speech.

In the preceding million years, a number of primate species had migrated out of Africa, only to vanish in the mists of time. But when the world slid into our most recent ice age some 100,000 years ago, at least some of our fully human ancestors did something that their ancestors had never done. When they migrated out of Africa to spread across Eurasia, they survived.

Dramatic climate swings punctuated this last ice age. Game died out in some geographies and humans either followed the game into oblivion or moved on to where animals were more plentiful. The wild climate swings never allowed the small clans of people to remain in one place for very long, and traditions of migration were developed in order to stay alive.

Sometimes there were abrupt and dramatic population collapses, as when the supervolcano Toba violently erupted in Indonesia some seventy-four thousand years ago. Ejecting 3,000 cubic kilometers (1,700 cubic miles) of material into the sky and leaving a sixty by one hundred kilometer (thirty-seven by sixty-two mile) caldera, it shrouded much of the earth from the sun and caused a precipitous drop in worldwide temperatures. The resulting die-offs of plant and animal life may have caused the global human population to drop to less than fifteen thousand people.

Survival always depended on finding a hospitable place to live, and Eastern Siberia eventually became such a place. Encouraged to stay by its abundant game and benign climate, modern humans began living there some thirty-five thousand years ago.

The rigors of life and challenges to survival were still daunting, however, and skeletons from this period show that less than half the people lived past twenty-one. Those who reached forty were definitely into "old age." Men lived thirty-five years on average and women to only thirty. Though worldwide population had bounced back from the cataclysm of Mount Toba, it still consisted of only a few hundred thousand people.

The depths of the last ice age put additional challenges to Northern peoples, and as the climate deteriorated the residents of eastern Siberia increasingly struggled to feed themselves. So in the tradition of their forbearers, in search of more favorable living conditions, some of these Asians moved on. Genetic studies indicate that these people separated from their Siberian kin between thirty-four and seventeen thousand years ago, eventually journeying to the coast of an area known as Beringia.

Beringia was created when the lower sea levels of the last ice age exposed a 1,500-kilometer-long coastal plain connecting Siberia and Alaska. During the height of this freeze, sea levels dropped by 130 meters (430 feet), and exposed over twenty-five million square kilometers (sixteen million square miles) of the world's continental shelves. The minicontinent Beringia, often referred to as a "land bridge," was part of this.

As the changing climate made eastern Asia even less hospitable, more people continued to make their way into Beringia. Genetic studies indicate that there were possibly a number of waves of migration, perhaps as many as six, and possibly from diverse places: Mongolia, Siberia, Tibet, North China, and Japan, or perhaps a single extended migration from one area that split into genetically isolated groups. Finally, when Beringia became fully passable by foot or by boat, these Asians crossed it.

Through thousands of years of coastal living, some of these people had developed maritime cultures of fishing and sea travel. These mariners boated eastward along the Beringian shore, and without fanfare or knowledge of where in the world they were, they eventually camped on the virgin beaches of North America.

***

Paddling into a sheltered bay one evening, fur-clad Asians headed for the outfall of a small stream. After carrying their skin boat high up the beach, the tired paddlers laughed among themselves as they slaked their thirsts from a pool of fresh water just above the shore.

Then, as one, the paddlers suddenly fell quiet. Something large was splashing its way downstream, hidden for the moment around a brushy bend. An unfamiliar grunting reached their ears, unlike anything their ancestors had mimicked around the fire. When they caught the approaching animal's scent, it too was totally new. Quietly hefting their spears, they tensed as the unknown thing approached.

Snorting its way into view, as it rooted through the stream-side brush, the massive creature reared when it saw the hunters. Hairy and some two meters at the shoulder, it flared its nostrils as it tried to catch the explorers' scent. With no reason to fear them, it went back to its feast. Though the hunters had no name for the creature, they knew it was meat. In moments, a dozen spears bristled from the creature's back and its blood flowed freely into the stream.

In succeeding days and months and years, the travelers encountered still more new creatures.

There were short-faced bears nearly twice as big as grizzlies and lions significantly larger than current African species; dire wolves with great fangs and beavers as big as black bears; cheetahs and saber-toothed tigers; multiple genera of horses and sloths as big as elephants; mastodons, camels, and stag moose bigger than any antlered animal living today. Though tales of this fantastic menagerie passed down through to succeeding generations of travelers, by 12,000 years ago all of these magnificent North American creatures had disappeared into the mists of extinction.

***

During these times, the Cordillera Glacier covered the coast between Alaska and Washington's Puget Sound, and extended inland to blanket most of British Columbia. The Georgia Strait lay under 1,600 meters (one mile) of ice, which smothered all but the highest peaks on Vancouver Island.

But glaciers didn't prevent the migrating Asians from continuing south. Equipped with well-developed sea-going traditions, they traveled south by boat and lived off of fish and seals and clams.

On their way, they were beset by cataclysms that shot ice through their bowels. Warming temperatures created immense lakes around the melting ice sheets, and in what is now Montana, massive Lake Missoula repeatedly formed and burst its ice-dam through the years of glacial melting. The onslaughts it released stampeded for the coast with a power that altered the very geography of the land.

These outbursts were dwarfed by those originating in the center of North America, where Lake Agassiz and Ojibway merged into a melt-water behemoth containing seven times the total volume of the modern Great Lakes. When their glacial dams collapsed, catastrophic floods raged seaward, devastating everything in their path. These were so massive that they altered oceanic circulation and changed the world's climate for years.

As the earliest explorers paddled south along the icebound coast, they made landfall at ice-free enclaves like the Queen Charlotte Islands. Other potential landing sites had been created by lower sea levels exposing previously submerged offshore volcanic peaks, and by the kilometer-thick ice pressing new offshore islands up, as if on a seesaw.

It's possible that some early inhabitants witnessed these offshore peaks rising above the water, as the oral traditions of the Haida speak of a time when "islands rose out of the sea, and people walked on the open ocean" (Glavin 2000). But when the glaciers melted and their tremendous pressure on coastal lands came to an end, these temporary offshore islands sank down again, taking their aboriginal remains with them.

Oceanographers have located some of the beaches established during these times of lower water levels. Diving on underwater seamounts off British Columbia's Pacific coast, they discovered relict beach terraces covered with rounded pebbles and mussel shells characteristic of coastal shores, at depths corresponding to the sea levels of the last ice age.

During these years, the continent's shroud of ice deterred non-maritime Asians from following the south-leading coast. The ice-covered land was impassable for those traveling on foot and, in most places, lacked the animals that big-game hunters depended on. These mammoth-seekers may have continued eastward into Canada, and then thousands of years later made their way south through an ice-free corridor between the Cordilleran and Laurentide ice sheets.

Some descendants of the first migrating Asians pressed on far to the south, and remains from Monte Verde in Southern Chile show they'd reached there by fourteen thousand years ago. Since the inland ice-free corridor through North America's massive ice sheets did not open until about the same time, and in its early centuries would have been barren of both vegetation and animals to hunt, the most likely route that the first Asian travelers followed south from Beringia was down the coast by boat. In their migration, they simply continued the nomadic seagoing traditions their ancestors had followed for thousands of years.

Scientists have carbon dated remains from British Columbia's coastal archaeological sites to 12,000 years ago, but changing sea and land elevations make locating older coastal settlements extremely difficult. The earlier migrations down the coast were likely made by very small groups of paddlers who left little evidence of their passing, and their campsites may have been erased by glaciation or located near relict beaches that are now hundreds of feet under water.

Finding *any* early sites is made even more difficult by what the land itself was doing during these millennia.

Billions of tons of glacial ice had pushed the underlying land down, sometimes by hundreds of meters. Stubborn in its depressed elevation, this land stayed down as sea levels rose. As the glaciers melted, rising seas flooded inland valleys and plains that had been compressed by the glaciers, which later rose up *above* sea level when the crust rebounded to its "normal" elevation. Shorelines during some of these millennia would thus presently be located 100-140 meters above current shorelines.

The consequence of these changes in sea and land elevation is that the coastal campsites of early Asian explorers would now be on the bottom of the sea (if they paddled here before the glaciers melted), or far inland (if the paddlers camped there after the glaciers ebbed, when the land began to flood before the underlying crust began to rise).

Archaeologists have been attempting to retrieve evidence from the depths to confirm aboriginal settlement on ancient shorelines, and have had some success. In the Pacific Northwest, a stone tool was pulled up from fifty meters (175 feet). And in the North Sea, a trawler dredged up a clod of peat from thirty meters (one hundred feet) containing an exquisite deer-antler spearhead. "This artifact was dramatic evidence of how early humans exploited the broad expanses of land that had been created during the last ice age, and were only reclaimed by the sea some seven thousand years ago" (Burroughs 2005).

***

The migration down our coast was not a quick dash south by a single clan, but rather a series of nomadic passages that may have spanned fifteen thousand years. Though well-suited for the chilly temperatures of the north, skin-boats eventually rotted in warmer climates. Skin gave way to wood over years of trial and error boat construction, no doubt involving some tragic failures. Along their way south, the travelers were forced to develop entirely new boat-building technologies.

The speed of the boats did not set the southward pace, however. More determinative were the myriad issues facing a people on the move.

Young children were along, as were leathery-skinned grandparents. Tools and cooking utensils crowded the boats, as did shelters of hide and stores of food. Dolls and amulets had to be tucked into bedrolls, medicinal herbs stored, and favored idols protected.

So laden, the crafts progressed slowly. Young children needed time to play, their grandparents time to rest. Hunters and gatherers required time to hunt and collect food, and still more time to preserve it.

When the salmon were smoked and berries preserved, and the camp made ready to launch again upon the waters, there were battles to fight with the weather gods. In some seasons, travel became so perilous that progress was halted for months. These months stretched into years if the camp site was an especially hospitable one, and eventually into permanent settlements when the coast became more habitable.

And so the journeys south were extended ones, moving forward in fits and jerks.

Generations were born and died en route. Groups of families splintered off to found the Tlingit, Haida, and other First Nations populations that settled the coast. Occupying enclaves with limited contact with the outside world, they developed their own languages and traditions.

The scarcity of archaic coastal sites indicates that perhaps only a few hundred people lived on the shores of the Strait of Georgia during these early millennia. They stayed close to the water, living a nomadic life that depended on hunting, fishing, and gathering.

CHAPTER 13
GONE FISHIN'

Shall I go to heaven or a-fishing?

—Henry David Thoreau

August 9, 1997

In the middle of the night, Theresa lit our lantern with a determined huff. She'd finally had enough of mosquitoes dive-bombing us while we tried to sleep. Our scent had concentrated in the floathouse loft and apparently acted like a magnet on all the local pests.

We had tried to create a sanctuary in the loft by cordoning it off with mosquito netting. Our bed was fully surrounded by this gauze barrier, which was tacked securely to the ceiling and tucked carefully under our mattress. We sought refuge in this enclave through a zippered entrance, which we fastidiously closed behind us. But tonight, the persistent mosquitoes had managed to get in through minute cracks in the floor and tears in the netting. Perhaps two dozen were inside, using Theresa and me as their private feeding grounds.

T attacked with her book, intent on dispatching every one of them.

Some of the pests were wary opponents, escaping at the last minute from her descending club and then zigzagging through the air to land in some unseen spot.

Others flew slow and lazily. Theresa's book slapped them out of the air and pancaked them on the low ceiling, decorating it with their small payloads of our blood.

Theresa's jaw clenched and her eyes blazed. With grim determination she hunted her prey.

When the ranks of our torturers thinned, we closed our eyes and lay back as human bait. When the vampires whined in our ears as they settled for a drink, Theresa lashed out again. And again.

I was smacked several times, each time with a different smile on Theresa's face. Some were smiles of victory over a wary flying adversary. Others were smiles of satisfaction from extracting payment for some prior offense of mine. Still others were simple smiles of pleasure from tormenting the log-like entity that refused to participate in her mad hunt.

Finally, our small space was cleared of its blood-sucking vermin. Theresa drifted off to a contented slumber, dreaming the dreams of a successful hunter. Battered and trod upon, I was fully awake and had to read for a while before sleep could reclaim me.

August 10, 1997

After breakfast, the boys and I headed over to Lasqueti and hiked the dirt road to John Cantrell's cabin. Heated up from our walk in the sun, we joined John and another Lasquetian (who shall remain anonymous) for a swim in John's pond.

Here I should interject that this other gentleman was a long-time Lasqueti resident who apparently had spent a similar length of time without the benefit of supporting underwear. Nude is the way many folks swim here, and when Mr. No-Name doffed his pants, the effects of gravity on his scrotum were clear to see.

When the boys caught sight of this pendulous snood, their laughter threatened to drown them. I had to shush them to keep them from gulping water as they tried to swim, breathe, laugh, and whisper to one another at the same time. They were driven to further paroxysms of laughter when one of them took inspiration from our family visits to the animal barns at the Puyallup Fair and dubbed this gravity-enhanced gentleman "lamb-nuts."

Returning to Olsen in the late afternoon, we grabbed our gear and went out to fish and pull our prawn traps. Delighted with a haul of jumbo prawns, we started fishing with high hopes. Our optimism was rewarded when I hooked into an aggressive seven-kilo (fifteen-pound) king. Theresa paddled up in her kayak a short while later and was very pleased with our catch.

One of the new friends we'd met on Lasqueti was Morgan Armstrong, and we'd invited her out to dinner tonight. She had arrived by kayak during our absence, and was very impressed with how well we'd settled into the floathouse. We enjoyed her company feasting on salmon and prawns barbecued over a driftwood fire.

When dessert and conversation were finished, Theresa left to kayak Morgan home through the dark. Phosphorus dripped from their paddles as they stroked out of the cove. After the boys went to bed, I sat on the porch, enjoying the night sky and waiting for Theresa's return. When she glided back in toward the floathouse I could see the ghost of her kayak outlined in phosphorus, which spread out in waves from her bow and paddle strokes.

August 11, 1997

Fishing this evening with Ken, I caught a strong-fighting lingcod. It was a nice big fish, but I threw it back as our larder was full.

The determined attack and brutal fight of a lingcod springs from something more urgent than mere self-preservation. For when a ling charges an intruder to its realm, it's defending generations of lingcod yet unborn.

From late fall to early spring, female lings leave their deepwater habitat and begin an annual migration into the shallower territories of the males, where they deposit their eggs in clusters weighing up to twenty six pounds. The males fan these nests with their tails to keep water moving over them, and ferociously protect them from predators. Any interloper is simply eaten—whether it is a rockfish or even another lingcod.

This nest-guarding behavior and territoriality make lingcod particularly aggressive, urging them to strike more readily than most other fish. Lingcod physiology is well-suited to this temperament, dominated by a huge head and canine-like teeth. Their Latin name, *Ophiocon*, literally means "snake-tooth."

Yet, for all this voraciousness, lingcod grow slowly. A meter-long lingcod could be forty years old. The biggest lings—weighing upwards of twenty kilos (forty four pounds) are all females. Mature males rarely exceed nine kilos in weight.

As we motored back to the floathouse, the sky glowed pink, and Ken and I fantasized about what the fishing would have been like when the first native explorers dropped their lines into these waters.

CHAPTER 14
WONDERS OF THE ANCIENT SEAS

There are still places in the world ... where it is possible to find something of the miraculous in nature. In Alaskan estuaries, salmon still gather in impenetrable throngs ... They attract packs of toothy salmon sharks, seals, otters and killer whales ... Great shoals of hammerhead sharks still circle Galapagos seamounts. Mighty boils of tuna still erupt from the Humboldt Current, thrashing their way into dense boils of anchovies ... Such scenes are remnants of the seas of long ago. They offer us windows to past worlds, letting us see the oceans as they must have looked to travelers and fishers of centuries past.
    —Callum Roberts, *The Unnatural History of the Sea*

When Beringians skiffed down our coast, they beheld the signature of glaciers in full retreat. Pregnant rivers birthed huge plumes of silt into coastal waters, dying them greenish white.

During the reign of the glaciers, forests extended no further north than central Oregon. Between these trees and the ice fields of British Columbia, there was only tundra and grasslands.

But trees are persistent colonizers, and as the temperatures warmed they spread northward. By 12,000 years ago, forests of fir and hemlock were spreading over much of our coast.

As the evergreens re-established their magnificent canopies in the glacial wakes, rain reached the forest floor only in drips and trickles. Falling onto a carpet of needles that defied erosion, it was filtered of impurities before reaching rivers and streams. These arteries delivered the sky's tears to the saltchuck in a flow of liquid jewels. As glacial fines settled beyond memory, crystal-clear waters began to embrace the coast.

Initially there were few salmon, as the ice had scoured away almost all spawning streams. But as the growing forests stabilized river-flows and filled streams' gravels with nutrients, local salmon runs were founded by inquisitive strays from refuge populations.

The glaciers had similarly plowed away the coast's mollusks, and changing beach elevations kept clam populations low. But when sea and land levels stopped fluctuating around seven thousand years ago, clam beds were able to proliferate. Though sea levels rose and fell by several meters through the following three thousand years, they did so slowly enough for the mollusks to adapt. As Indian populations expanded along with the ready availability of clams and salmon, extensive shell middens began to appear.

In times of rest, when First Nations People stilled their paddles and drifted in the currents, they gazed down at endless meadows of eel grass and magnificent forests of kelp.

Sea otters interrupted their urchin feasts to stare at the intrepid paddlers. By keeping the populations of grazing urchins in check, the otters allowed the kelp forests to cover the coast. Millennia later, when George Vancouver sailed through California waters, he sighted kelp forests extending as far as three kilometers offshore. Near present-day San Diego, Vancouver wrote of kelp growing in waters up to fifty-five meters (180 feet) deep, where individual plants reached over ninety meters (295 feet) long.

These undersea forests provided food and shelter for staggering populations of herring and other small fish. When frightened, they flashed and veered as one, looking from above as if some huge creature prowled the kelp.

Oliver Goldsmith, a European herring fisherman from the 1700s, spoke of the size of the herring schools that visited his coast to spawn. "When the main body is arrived, its breadth and depth is such as to alter the very appearance of the ocean. It is ... five or six miles in length, and three or four broad, while the water before them curls up as if forced out of its bed" (Roberts 2007).

No doubt similar schools of herring glittered their way along our coast when the First Nations Peoples established their settlements here.

On moonless nights these masses of fish put on incredible shows for folk living near water's edge. Igniting phosphorescent glow over large patches of sea, they were streaked with the lightning tracks of predators diving through.

These herring fed populations of fish and mammals that stunned our coast's early European explorers. "Columbus, Cabot, Drake, Bering, Cook and others ... returned with tales of strange seas teeming with wildlife" (Roberts 2007).

Krasheninnikov, a naturalist on Bering's voyage to Alaska, observed in 1741 that salmon "come from the sea in such great numbers that they stop the course of the rivers, and cause them to overflow the banks. They swim up the rivers with such force that the water seems to rise like a wall before them"(Roberts 2007).

When George Vancouver was exploring Desolation Sound, he observed that "Numberless whales enjoying the season were playing about the ship in every direction." According to Callum Roberts in his book *The Unnatural History of the Sea* (2007), "Genetic estimates by Roman and Palumbi put worldwide pre-whaling population sizes at 360 million for the fin whale and 240 million animals for the humpback," which compare with estimated current populations of 56,000 fin whales and 9,000–12,000 humpbacks. Whales were found in such profusion close to the coast that "early whaling was conducted from shore with boats sent in pursuit once an animal was spotted."

Giant sturgeon were found breeding in estuaries and lower river courses, some longer than five and a half meters and weighing over eight hundred kilograms. Bluefin tuna ranged north through the Gulf of Alaska, where the four-meter-long, seven-hundred-kilo monsters slashed through schools of feed.

The Pacific Coast's ninety-six species of rockfish grew to their full potential in both age and size, and meter-long demons fought fishermen to exhaustion. Off California, black sea bass fed among the kelp, where century old monsters swelled to over two hundred and seventy kilograms.

This profusion of sea life also fed immense populations of the sea's top predators. Sailing the Pacific in 1795, George Vancouver wrote in his log that "bold and voracious" sharks "assembled in the bay in very large schools, constantly attending our boats ... The general warfare that exists between seagoing persons and these voracious animals afforded at first a species of amusement to our people, by hooking ... one for the others to feast upon, but as this was attended with the ill-consequence of drawing immense numbers around the ship, and as the boatswain and one of the gentlemen had nearly fallen a sacrifice to this diversion, by narrowly escaping being drawn out of the boat by an immensely large shark, into the midst of at least a score of these voracious animals, I thought proper to prohibit all further indulgence in this species of entertainment."

Killer whales, actually members of the dolphin family, were also present in great numbers. And with the profusion of real whales, mammal-eating killer whales were not forced to subsist on lesser prey like seals. They instead attacked the great whales, as witnessed repeatedly by European explorers.

This incredible wealth of sea life made for equally incredible fishing. "The first people going to sea in boats found abundant fish for the taking. Dipping their hooks and nets into these virgin seas rewarded them with giants" (Roberts 2007).

Remarked one visitor to the Chesapeake in the 1700s, "I have sat in the shade at the heads of the rivers angling and spent as much time taking the fish off the hook as in waiting for their taking it" (Roberts 2007).

Early New World fishermen were accordingly able to employ even the most unlikely gear to land their catches.

Reporting on an attempt to sail to the Americas, the Milanese Ambassador to England noted, "They assert that the sea there is swarming with fish, which can be taken not only with the net, but in baskets let down with a stone—"

As great herring schools were concentrated by whales and dogfish, "a shovel or any hollow vessel put into the water takes them up without further trouble" (Roberts 2007).

When Walter Russell and Anas Todkill explored the Chesapeake in 1608, they found the "abundance of fish lying so thicke ... for want of nets we attempted to capture them with a frying pan." Though this device failed, "our captain sporting himself to catch them by nailing them to the ground with his sword, set us all a fishing in that manner, by this devise we took more in an houre then we all could eat" (Roberts 2007).

And in 1620, in Newfoundland, John Mason found "Salmond and Cods so thicke by the shore that we heardlie have been able to row a Boate through them, I have killed of them with a Pike" (Roberts 2007). In these years of profusion, bent nails were used in place of fishing hooks, with equally good results.

Incredibly, these reports were from times when coastal Indian fishing had already reduced local fish populations. When early aboriginal explorers paddled down our coast, the profusion of sea life would have been daunting. Speaking in *The World Without Us* of what the seas would be like if they could be given a rest from humanity (Weisman 2007), Enric Sala states that, "In 500 years, if a human came back, he'd be completely terrified to jump in the ocean, because there would be so many mouths waiting for him."

Just east of our Olsen Island home, there are ruins of an aboriginal fish trap used to harvest the tremendous numbers of fish that swam here centuries ago. Curving lines of piled rocks join a Higgins Island point with the nearby Lasqueti shore. As schools of herring or salmon swam between our neighboring islands, they were forced through the small opening of this rudimentary weir. Standing nearby with nets or spears, local Indians were able to harvest their fill from water that was only knee deep.

CHAPTER 15
SALMON PEOPLE

The Northwest Coast culture was unique: No where else on earth was fishing so crucial ...
                    —Terry Glavin, *The Last Great Sea*

When the first people stroked their crafts into the Strait of Georgia, they found a desolate place that scarcely encouraged them to stay. Glaciers still hugged the coast, salmon had yet to start spawning again in the ice-scoured rivers, and rising sea levels prevented clam beds from proliferating. These seafarers were ephemeral visitors, no doubt proceeding south in search of more hospitable territory.

While paddlers in succeeding millennia were also wandering nomads, the warming climate and increasing bounty of the sea enticed them to tarry on the Strait. When the sea levels of the North Pacific stabilized around eight thousand years ago, and the surrounding coastal lands finished rebounding, our coast evolved into a place of incredible resources. Vast schools of salmon swam up coastal rivers and clam beds proliferated in every suitable bay. With such abundant wild foods, coastal tribes were able to settle in permanent villages, expand their populations, trade, and eventually go to war.

Digging through as much as five meters of stratified prehistoric deposits, archaeologists have explored many sites along the Strait of Georgia. Their findings suggest that the salmon and its capture, preservation, and consumption were the center of aboriginal life here. So much salmon and fish oil were deposited in village sites that archaeologists excavating them found themselves covered by an oily black sheen.

The North Coast Salish occupied the lands bordering the Strait of Georgia east and west of Lasqueti. Excavations of Salish sites have yielded spear and arrow points, knives, labrets, sinkers, grinding slabs, wedges, shell beads, harpoon heads, fishhooks, twine, netting, basketry, hand mauls, awls, hairpins, combs, canoe bailers, and other household items. These were made of stone, wood, antler, bark, and shell.

Deformed skulls indicate that the Salish practiced cranial deformation. This was accomplished by binding a child's head shortly after birth, and leaving flattening boards in place for as long as five years. The result was a wedge-shaped cranium with a flat, broad forehead.

By the time of first contact with white explorers and fur traders in the 1770s, the North Coast Salish had evolved into several distinct bands. The Sechelt band appears to have settled on Lasqueti and its surrounding islands.

Coastal natives spent much of their time navigating and fishing the waters of the Strait. They knew the currents, the tides, and the winds that could turn this sometimes gentle ally into a cruel enemy. They developed fishing methods that were marveled at by the first Europeans who visited the area, well-suited to harvesting the abundant salmon in different seasons.

In the seasons before the salmon began their up-river migrations, salmon were successfully caught with hook and line. Lines were made of whale sinew, nettle fiber, and the inner bark of the cedar tree. Leaders were fashioned out of braided human hair, doe skin, cedar bark, or quills. Hooks were carved out of bone, slate, or wood, with a barb attached at the correct angle.

As John Jewitt described in his diary of 1803, speaking of Indian fishing practices he observed while held captive by the Nootka, "One person seats himself in a small canoe, and baiting his hook with a sprat, which they are always careful to procure as fresh as possible, fastens his line to the handle of his paddle; this, as he plies it in the water, keeps the fish in constant motion, so as to give it the appearance of life, which the salmon seeing, leaps at it and is instantly hooked, and by a sudden dexterous motion of the paddle, drawn on board. I have known some natives to take 10 salmon a morning in this manner."

In open waters, the Sechelt also caught salmon in gill nets. Other species were taken at spawning streams by basket traps, fish weirs, fence traps, gaffs, and harpoons.

As natives mastered the art of fish preservation, they settled in permanent villages near preferred fishing sites. Individual families owned specific places on these fishing grounds, which were passed down through families for succeeding generations. These were known and respected by all, and never bought or sold.

The number of salmon the Indians harvested from coastal rivers was enormous. When the Lewis and Clark expedition passed down the Columbia River in the fall of 1805, the Indian catches "were incredible; one man could kill a hundred salmon on a good day, a full ton or more of fish" (Ambrose 1996). "Northwest Coast societies ... produced volumes of fish at a scale comparable to those of the commercial fishery of the Industrial Age ... The tribal fisheries of the pre-smallpox period accounted for a staggering 57 million kilograms (127 million pounds) of salmon annually. To put that figure in context, it amounts to slightly more fish than the annual commercial catch of sockeye on the British Columbia coast during the 20th century" (Glavin 2000).

Researchers estimate that Indian fishery reduced salmon populations nine-fold from what are thought to have existed prior to extensive native settlement. The "walk-across" salmon runs reported by early European settlers were likely a salmon population rebound that resulted from the decimation of tribal populations by smallpox, guns, and whiskey.

Coastal people typically air-dried their catch on outdoor racks, then finished preserving it in cedar smokehouses. Fish were also dried in the lodges close to the fire, or hanging from poles under the roof, and then stored in baskets and bentwood boxes. Fully smoked and dried fish were completely dehydrated and hard, though some people pounded the fish during smoking to keep it soft. Pieces of dried fish were toasted until hot and crisp, or soaked overnight and then boiled.

Chum salmon were the favorites for drying, as their lean flesh dried hard and was well-suited for long storage. Pinks were also smoke-dried, but chinook, sockeye, and silvers were normally eaten fresh. Although the latter were occasionally smoked, this was done mostly for flavor rather than to preserve their oil-rich flesh.

Salmon eggs were stuffed into deer stomachs and dried in the smokehouse to a cheese-like consistency. Chum roe was put in meter-deep earthen pits lined with maple leaves, with holes punched in the bottom to allow the oil to drain off. After two months, the dirt covering this treasure was scraped off, revealing a cheese-like mass that was often eaten raw. Other salmon roe was placed into boxes which were buried in the sand below the high-water mark, and left there to decompose before being eaten.

Putting away a good supply of fish for the winter was a community effort. During salmon runs the sudden influx of huge quantities of fish meant long hours of work for everyone in the community.

***

The mythology of these First Nations Peoples developed out of their intimate relationship with salmon, rivers, and the sea.

It was generally believed that salmon were really people who lived at the edge of the horizon in magical underwater villages. Different submarine settlements housed the five tribes of the Salmon People, each with its own habits and breeding places. At specific times of the year, these people transformed themselves into the five species of salmon and swam up the rivers.

Some Indians believed these fish were led by their chief, who would then offer himself to be the first one caught, and therefore should be accorded such honor as befitted a chief. Others thought the salmon people sent scouts out ahead, and if the scouts were treated with courtesy and respect when caught, other salmon would follow and ascend the river. Out of such beliefs developed the first-fish ceremonies practiced by virtually all coastal tribes. In these ceremonies, the year's first salmon was welcomed with ritualized handling, butchering, and cooking.

It was widely held that twins had great rapport with salmon, that salmon were responsible for the birth of twins, and that twins of the same sex were salmon before birth.

These beliefs led to many customs involving twins. Twin children were sent down to the river bank to call the salmon, singing special songs and shaking rattles to entice the fish into the traps. The father of twins held special powers in the salmon world. During fishing season, he spent a great deal of his time and energy singing and performing secret rituals to ensure a maximum catch.

It was believed that when dog salmon returned to their village in the sea, they brought back songs learned from their journey up-river, and spent most of their time singing these songs. Salmon hanging on the drying racks were thought to play among themselves when no one was watching.

Salmon were considered to enjoy eating the sweet inner bark of the hemlock, just as the Indians themselves did. Balls of hemlock bark were thus rolled up, stuck with feathers, and floated down rivers in the spring as gifts to the fish.

The local Sechelt shared the belief that salmon were supernatural beings, "salmon people" who lived beneath the water and became fish in order to sacrifice themselves to human beings. All salmon bones were returned to the water so the salmon people could resurrect themselves and return in future years.

These aboriginal traditions of salmon worship were built on a simple truth: while a person could trust in luck, a society couldn't take such a risk. If the salmon failed to return, starvation and death would arrive in their stead.

CHAPTER 16
ABORIGINAL LIFE

Often as I walk slowly along a quiet clamshell beach, I think about the people who lived there long ago. Finding an object made by someone thousands of years ago gives me a strong sense of the people who lived here ... Canoes were being built on the beaches from lengths of cedar tree trunks and ... tall totem poles and burial posts were being carved and erected and stone and bone tools ... were being chipped and carved ...
—Proctor and Maximchuk, *Full Moon Flood Tide*

The Sechelt traveled to and from their fishing grounds in dugout canoes made of red cedar. While their one- and two-person hunting canoes were locally made, their prized, large canoes were acquired through trade from the Haida. These magnificent craft were capable of carrying forty people and tons of cargo. As observed by Ivan Doig in *The Sea Runners*, "If the standing cedar tree had decided to transform into the swiftest of sea creatures, this craft of alert grace would have been the result."

Sechelt houses were sometimes massive. Frameworks were made of old-growth cedar logs covered with removable cedar planks. As the Sechelt relocated seasonally from one fishing site to another, they removed the outer planking and took it with them. An entire extended family of twenty to fifty people typically lived in each house.

As a defense against raiding and slave-taking, some houses were surrounded by log stockades with large rocks piled on top to hurl down on raiding parties. Others were protected by deep trenches dug around the perimeter. Ten to twenty such lodges were often grouped together in villages, most often located on sheltered bays. Some of these village sites show evidence of occupation for over seven thousand years.

Temporary shelters were sometimes used on clamming expeditions during the warm summer months. These consisted of simple bough-covered lean-tos and crude pole frameworks covered with mats.

Polygamy was common, with co-wives residing in different compartments of the same lodge. In some bands, women were used for whatever purpose suited the husband or father. Speaking of the Chinookan Indians, who lived near the mouth of the Columbia River, Meriwether Lewis observed that the men "will even prostitute their wives and daughters for a fishing hook or a stran of beads" (Ambrose 1996).

In March 1778, Captain James Cook's ship *Discovery* became the first English vessel to reach British Columbia. Chronicled in the following journal entries, his crew's experiences with the Nootka people on Vancouver Island's west coast would have been much the same had they been with the Sechelt who lived on the Georgia Strait.

> *A considerable number of the Natives visited us daily ...*
> *On their first coming they generally went through a singular*
> *ceremony. They would paddle with all their strength quite round*
> *both ships, a chief or other principal person standing up with a*
> *spear, or some other weapon in his hand and speaking, or rather*
> *hallooing all the time, sometimes this person would have his*
> *face covered with a mask, either that of the human face or some*
> *animal and sometimes instead of a weapon would hold in his*
> *hand a rattle. After making the circuit of ships, they would come*
> *along side and begin to trade without further ceremony. Very*
> *often indeed they would first give us a song in which all joined*
> *with a very agreeable harmony.*
>
> —Journal of James Cook, 1778

> *In the evening, several of the larger Canoes saluted us, by*
> *making a Circuit around the ships and giving 3 Halloos at their*
> *departure. They paddle in most excellent time, the foremost man*
> *every 3'd or 4rh Stroke making flourishes with his paddle. The*

halloo is a single note in which they all join, swelling it out in the middle and letting the sound die away.
—Journal of James Bumey, March 30, 1778

The greatest number of the canoes remained in a cluster around us till ten o'clock ... and appeared very friendly, a man repeated a few words in tune, and regulated the meaning by beating against the canoe sides, after which they all joined in a song, ... A young man with a remarkable soft effeminate voice afterward sung by himself, ... and he finding that we were not ill pleased repeated his song several times. ... A few boats kept paddling around us all that night which was a very cold one.
—Journal of Lieutenant James King, 1778

William Sturgis' journal tells of a night he spent ashore in the Haida village of Tatance, while an Indian hostage was held aboard ship to guarantee his safe return.

Altatsee now took me by the hand and led me towards the house. On entering it you may well imagine my astonishment when, instead of six or eight people as I expected, I beheld about forty people, men, women and children seated round an enormous fire which was made in the middle of the house.
Some were employed in making fish-hooks for halibut, some wooden bowls. The women were busy broiling and boiling halibut. The children waiting upon the old folks and several of the females who were not slaves making wooden pipes. At my entrance labor stood suspended, and they looked at me with about as much astonishment as Hamlet when he first saw his father's Ghost ...
Altatsee then showed me his riches which were contained in the trunk we sat upon. There were some several garments made of the wool of the Mountain Sheep and marked in spots with sea otter's fur which were very handsome. An ornament for the waist made of leather, with several hundred of the small hooves on it that

*belong to the Deer's feet; this is used in dancing and makes a loud
rattling when shook.*
*He had likewise a number of beautiful Ermine skins which it
seems they consider as a kind of money on the Coast.*
                    —Journal of William Sturgis, March 20, 1799

While the local First Nations economies were initially bolstered by fur trade with the Europeans, diseases brought by early traders dealt a crippling blow to the native populations. Within years they were decimated by microbes to which they had no resistance.

Epidemics of smallpox came in devastating waves, and venereal diseases worked a slow course of destruction. Indian populations declined precipitously during the decades after the first European contact.

"As Vancouver's ship, the *Discovery*, made its way through the portal of Juan de Fuca Strait, its officers and crew came upon an eerie landscape of deserted villages, sometimes littered with skeletons ... there were the remains of towns, overgrown with nettles and brambles, scattered with the bones of the dead" (Glavin 2000). Vancouver had obviously been preceded by other Europeans who left a legacy of death in their wakes.

In the well-traveled areas surrounding the Strait of Georgia, most native peoples were essentially wiped out, and government-supported missionaries coerced the remaining tribes to abandon what was left of their arts and ceremonies. Only the groups more remote from contact, such as Makah, Kwakiutl, and Tlingit, retained much of their original culture. The grim reality in these villages, however, was that only skeleton populations survived to breathe life into their ancient ways.

Chapter 17
Finding a Spearhead

We lifted the long bar from the great door of a community house ... stepped inside and shivered ... the only light came from the open door behind us and from the smoke holes in the roof. Searching ... poking ... digging ... It was so easy to let the imagination run riot in these surroundings. All around me, grey and dim, surged and wavered the ones-of-the-past. I picked up a spearhead; smooth brown stone, ground chisel sharp at the edges – and the men of the tribe crowded close. Naked, blackhaired, their faces daubed with red warpaint, their harsh voices rising in excitement. They were pointing at the beach with their spears – the canoes were ready, they were going on a raid, and they raised their spears and shouted.

—M. Wylie Blanchet, *The Curve of Time*

August 14, 1997, Continued

The wind started rising about noon today, and by evening our weather radio reported it was blowing twenty-five knots at nearby Sisters Light Station. From the moans of the trees, however, we could tell it was gusting quite a bit higher.

The boys and I boated out to pull the prawn traps when the wind dragon was in the midst of its attack. The dragon threw one wave into our boat, but we avoided further mauling and retrieved a reasonable load of prawns for our efforts.

Back ashore in search of fun, the twins and I slid into our kayaks. Waves broke over our bows and the wind drenched us in spray when we paddled out past Dragon Island into the teeth of the blow. Rounding the end of Olsen to where we could harness the weather, we put our fishing lines out and let the wind push us along. About halfway down island, we glided into its lee and stopped to jig for rockfish. Our luck was good and we caught quite a few.

After dinner, we spent hours around the table reading and playing cards. It's a testimony to the pace of island life that, for the first time ever, I've witnessed our children fighting over a book! I actually had to make out a book-sharing schedule for Ryan and Chas to stop their bickering.

I eventually had to chase the kids out of the floathouse, as they were reluctant to sleep in their tent in tonight's wind. The gale-whipped woods were alive with alien sounds in the large trees swaying above the boys' flimsy nylon shelter.

August 15, 1997

It's fascinating to behold Lasqueti's middens, laid down through thousands of years before whites came to the area. What lovers touched and children laughed while people cooked those clams for dinner? Only the shells remember, and they're not talking.

After enjoying a salmon omelet for breakfast, I walked over to explore the middens. I hadn't seen any oyster shells in them, and found out why when I talked to a fellow who was harvesting oysters from the back pass. Apparently oysters weren't native on this beach. They were introduced here from Japan, as were the manila clams whose spat rode here on the oyster shells.

Though I'd searched the beaches below the middens on several occasions, I'd never found anything but shells that the Indians left behind. Today, however, my luck changed.

In the rocks below I found two stone tools: a spear head and a sanding stone.

Lasqueti's extensive middens attest to prolonged First Nations occupation. And not surprisingly, modern-day residents have found a variety of native artifacts, including arrow heads, adz heads, fish net weights, and skinning tools.

I was under the impression Lasqueti had been only a First nations summer camp, occupied seasonally when people came to fish, gather shellfish and harvest cedar bark.

Lasquetian Dana Lepofsky has come to a very different conclusion, however. As a long time resident of Lasqueti, Dana has had the opportunity to closely examine the islands' archaeological sites and artifact collections (containing some projectile points 7-8,000 years old). In her position as Professor of Archaeology at Simon Fraser University, she has been able to compare these Lasqueti sites and collections to those as she's seen elsewhere on British Columbia's coast.

Today Theresa and I were in for a special treat. Dana was going to lead our friends Dick and Terry on a guided tour of Lasqueti's archeological sites, and we'd been invited to tag along.

After boating across False Bay and walking part way up the hill above the dock, we clambered into an open area in the blackberry thicket behind the Blue Roof. There Dana started to debunk my misunderstanding of First Nations life on the island.

At a spot fifteen meters above the beach, perhaps fifty meters inland, we were at the base of a three-meter-high midden made of shells, animal bones and charcoal. Though the midden seemed large to me, Dana opined that what we saw was only "a small remnant of what was there before," and that it had been "heavily disturbed by recent construction."

According to Dana what remained was only "the very back of the midden." Originally the midden's flat top had probably extended more than a hundred meters side to side, and perhaps twenty to thirty meters further inland. We were facing the remains of no mere shell pile on the beach, a garbage dump where discarded shells had been tossed after the removal of their meats. It had been a massive plateau built of shells, which had been laboriously hauled, packed down and leveled. A finely crushed cap of burned shells had been applied to the top to create hard living surface. Pointing at its exposed face, Dana showed us brown stalactites that penetrated the white shells—remains of buried posts.

Before she explained her conclusions, Dana walked us past the post office, then down a side road to an older home in the trees overlooking

False Bay. It had been built on a broad, flat area high above the water, which could be reached from the beach only by climbing a steep switch-back trail. Examining a few places around the house where the topsoil had been disturbed, we found that the house had been built on a flat-topped midden similar to the one that had existed where the Blue Roof now stood.

Pointing at several of the other homes overlooking the bay, Dana shared her observation that they too had been build atop middens. Many of the island's first homes had been sited opportunistically among its plumes of rock, on the already-level midden-tops where there was no need for excavation. As we marveled at the view, we shook our heads at the number of back-breaking loads of shells that had been hauled so far above the shore. And gradually came to see that Lasqueti's middens were no mere trash heaps left by summer clam harvesters.

After driving down island, we hiked to the shores of Conn Bay. A meters-thick layer of shells around the cove indicated that millennia of clam harvests had been cleaned here, and level areas spoke of an ancient community of long-houses.

But that wasn't what Dana had brought us here to see. Climbing up a twisting trail to a spot forty meters above the water, she challenged us to look around. We were slightly back in a forest on a steep mountainside, with magnificent views of the Sabine Channel. Around us were the typical humps and hollows of Lasqueti's billowing rock, covered with moss and ferns. Where we stood, however, the ground was unnaturally flat. Peering down the mouths of nearby animal burrows, and under the roots of blown-over trees, we could see the tell-tale white of sea-shells. Examining them closely, we could see that the shells were a meter deep in places….on a spot that was forty meters—one hundred thirty feet—above the beach. Dana opined that this may have been a refuge site, and that similar plateaus lower down on other bays were perhaps the home sites of families whose job it was to scan the waters for approaching warriors that might threaten the settlements below.

Though our tour of these elevated shell plateaus, Dana drove home her point that Lasqueti's middens were more than mere garbage dumps. Aboriginal people used their shells as building materials, and spent considerable time hauling them up Lasqueti's rocky headlands to build their home sites. Dana further opined that such large scale terraforming was much more extensive than would be expected at seasonal clam beds, and likely indicated year-round villages on the island. Villages that would attract raiding parties from other tribes, and need defensive lookouts and refuges on the mountains above. In Dana's estimation, Lasqueti's First Nations population was probably similar to its present-day level of several hundred people.

August 16, 1997

After several days of rising wind, we decided to end our summer stay a day early to make sure we could get safely across the Strait. Ken and I were both concerned and conferred several times on our plans. We'd decided to cross together so one of us could come to the rescue if something went awry.

Both of us laughed at our nervousness when today dawned quiet and calm.

After finishing my departure preparations, I sat down on a beach log to rest. On the rocks above the floathouse hunched the remains of an old cabin. Looking upon the pile of boards and beams that had been the home of Olsen's first settlers, I thought about their lives here so seemingly long ago.

Chapter 18
A Fisherman's Dream

The secret of life in the Northwest runs in packs of silver; as with most mysteries, it lies just below the surface, evident to anyone who thinks it is important enough to look.
—Timothy Egan, *The Good Rain*

Drawn by the salmon-filled waters of the Strait, white settlers arrived in the wake of early European explorers and their tales of abundance.

The early years of white settlement brought a number of fisher-folk who led nomadic lives on local waters and islands. Some lived on their boats while others camped on shore near their favorite fishing areas. They fished from rowboats and dugout canoes, and sold their catch to the roaming fish scows or traded them to island farmers for fresh produce.

During the late 1800s and early 1900s, several of the small islands around Lasqueti were seasonally inhabited by itinerant fishermen who came when the local fishing was at its best. As Elda Mason remembers, "One day in early March (1926) my father took Beatrice and I in a rowboat across to the Finnerty Islands. The largest island had a number of fishermen's cabins on it – a sort of village in a protected bit of harbor. We were curious and examined the shacks in and out ... as the spring gathered its warmth ... the islands became peopled with camping fisherfolk ... other fisherman lived in their boats ... none of these people remained permanently on the islands" (Mason 1976).

These out-island fish shacks were ingeniously pieced together from whatever materials the fisher-folk could scavenge: beach-combed lumber for walls, soles of discarded rubber boots for hinges, and empty jam cans for stove pipes.

One such fisherman was Charlie Higgins.

Harry Higgins, Charlie's father, had come to Lasqueti in 1873 as one of its first settlers. Charlie was born to Mary Ann Higgins, who had married Harry at the tender age of fourteen. Harry and Mary Ann were close friends with William and Maggie Rous, who lived at Rous Bay on Lasqueti's opposite end. In 1895, the two families exchanged spouses, each marrying the spouse of the other, "in a manner agreeable to all parties" (Mason 1976).

Charlie Higgins grew up on the waters around Lasqueti. Eventually he married and had children, and his family fell into the pattern of spending summers living on one small island or another as they pursued the season's salmon. At times they stayed on Olsen (then called Arbutus Island) in a driftwood fishing shack.

Charlie cruised these waters for years, chugging around their small islands and looking them over as he fished, searching for the perfect place to settle. With trolling lines stretched out behind, he leaned against the wheel and contemplated what he wanted in a home-site. And every time he passed by Olsen, he added to the growing list of reasons why it suited him.

Olsen was in the mouth of False Bay, on the edge of the local fishing grounds. Just offshore were underwater cliffs where herring schooled and attracted hungry salmon. Olsen thus made for a quick trip to where Charlie liked to set his gear.

This was a time when fisherman like Charlie couldn't afford radios. Olsen was a place where he and his family could signal each other if something went awry. His wife and kids could watch him while he fished, and know when he pulled his lines and headed home.

Olsen also lay adjacent to a labyrinth of sheltered between-isle passages. Charlie hoped his children could row through these to the False Bay School on days when the tide was right and the weather cooperated.

Wanting to explore Olsen and search out the best place to site his home, Charlie pulled into the small cove where the floathouse now sits. Living on the water and needing a protected place to land, he recognized this sheltered bite would be perfect at high tide. A house nearby would ease the chore of feeding his brood, as the cove's beach was filled with clams.

Climbing to the rocks above, Charlie found himself on a small point of land with a clear view of the waters where he fished. On this open spot he'd have light from dawn to dusk, and be free from the rot that leveled cabins in the woods. Below him was a natural defile in the rocks that could serve as a cellar beneath his home. Bridging it with timbers, he'd have a place to store his fishing gear right above high water.

Charlie had an eye for beauty, and once he had satisfied his practical needs, he recognized that he stood on an incomparable spot.

On one side of him were the waters of False Bay, with the Strait of Georgia and Vancouver Island peaks beyond. On the other side was the tiny cove, which led to the meandering pass between Olsen and Lasqueti. Little Olsen was a stone's throw away, and beyond it was a small bay with Higgins Island on its other side. A narrow channel lay between Higgins and Wolf Islands, which gave way to the receding silhouettes of Lasqueti and Texada Islands in the background. Billowing lichen-covered rocks were underfoot, and behind him was a mature forest.

It was a location Charlie Higgins chose from the many that presented themselves from the area's cluster of islands. It was at once practical and beautiful, a place to raise one's family and a spot of magical appeal.

After making his decision to settle on Olsen, Charlie set to work.

In fall "the Higgins family would have to anchor their ancient troller near a school and find a house for the winter ... Charlie would then work on the house which he was building on Arbutus Island in False Bay" (Mason 1976).

The cabin Charlie built was more enduring than the driftwood fishing camps that dotted the small islands around Lasqueti. It was entirely made of split cedar, except for the flooring. Even the two-by-four studs were cedar, hand split, and then planed. The shakes that formed the walls were fitted together so perfectly that no draft came through.

Charlie's house was essentially one large room with bedrooms partitioned off. Such homes were common on Lasqueti then, and were known as "shake shacks." They were built of cedar because of its resistance to rot and ease of shaping by someone using only hand tools.

In the early 1930s, Charlie and Hazel Higgins moved their family of six children to their home on Olsen Island, towing their belongings behind them on a cedar raft.

The children rowed themselves to school in False Bay in the family rowboat, and in the same way hauled water to Olsen from a spring on Lasqueti. When low tide and bad weather coincided, the kids stayed home. And when Qualicums blew up when they were at school, they overnighted at a friend's house on Lasqueti.

Elda Mason, the author of *Lasqueti Island*, told me that she overnighted in the Higgins' cabin on Olsen as a young girl. Writes Elda of the Higgins family, "When not staying in the house for some purpose such as washing or baking, Hazel Higgins went out with Charlie on his old troller. She helped to tend the lines, clean fish, steer, or do whatever tasks were called for. All the children were taken along on the boat; they were never left alone at the house ... In all the years the Higgins family travelled the coastal waters in their boats, they never lost a child by drowning. In fact it was something to be remembered if one of them even fell into the water" (Mason 1976).

Daughter Ruth Higgins lived with the family on Olsen during the Depression years, which she recounted to me as very hard times. No matter how bad the situation was, however, Islanders were generous with what food they had. "Salmon were scarce throughout the Depression and well-known cod reefs received considerable pressure, but one day Charlie Higgins happened on an unfished reef. He caught thirty-nine large lingcod. A waste? Not for Charlie. He took them home, built a smokehouse, and smoked the lot before sharing them with his grateful neighbors" (Mason 1976).

Indicative of how hard these times were was the use of "the ubiquitous flour sack." "These sacks were usually used for dishtowels, sheets, underwear, and even children's dresses, after the tenacious dye was removed by strong soap, boiling, and much rubbing with sore knuckles" (Mason 1976).

Newspapers we found stuffed in the walls of the Higgins cabin dated back to 1918. This confused me, as I was tempted to think they pinpointed the year of the house's construction. But Lasqueti elders assured me the house had been built years later.

Soon enough, however, I came to resolve this apparent contradiction.

Charlie built his home in the middle of the Depression, when both he and the fishing were poor. He was an itinerant squatter who coaxed food from the sea and shelter from uninhabited islands, and could only dream of owning the land he built on.

He scavenged his materials from the bays and beaches, and occasionally traded his catch with small mill owners on Lasqueti for lumber.

Newspapers of the time were valued not just for the news they brought, but also as insulation. If they were stuffed inside a wall, they could provide comfort from the icy fingers of winter gales. They had thus perhaps been stored for years by Charlie as he collected materials for his future house.

By the time Charlie finished building his family's home on Olsen Island, Vic Cramp had also built a small cabin there.

Vic settled near the island's west end. A stand of fruit trees, a rock-lined well, and an abandoned garden are all that's left of the Cramp homestead. Vic was a logger turned fisherman and lived on Olsen year-round when Ruth Higgins lived there. He had a sickly wife who abandoned the island after staying there for only one winter.

Another Charlie, Charlie Lundgren, came to Olsen after the Higgins family moved away. Charlie L. first lived on Lasqueti's Shumack farm, where he worked as its caretaker. From there, a short hike through the woods took him to the back pass separating Lasqueti from Olsen. Standing on the middens there, he surveyed the productive clam beds below. And when he'd dug his fill, he occasionally walked across the tide flats to Olsen and wandered through the abandoned Higgins home.

In the summer of 1944, recently divorced from his wife, Lundgren accepted a position as keeper of the Sisters Island Light Station. The Sisters lie about three kilometers west of Olsen, in the middle of the Strait of Georgia.

Charlie's marital problems may have come from his disregard for the niceties of housekeeping. Speaking of Lundgren's first stint as light keeper, Donald Graham writes, "He had brought an assistant and fifteen dogs with him, turning the dwelling at Sisters into a reeking kennel, hopping with fleas."

Elsie Tolpitt, the keeper who took over Sisters Light Station from Lundgren in 1945, had this to say about him: "Oh boy! What fun we're having along with the dirt, fleas, and old relics of furniture ... We can't even handle a thing but what our hands are covered with filth and grime; never in my life have I seen such a contaminated mess that those two partners made of this place. I'd like to string them up, especially the dog owner; every floor was stained from his dogs" (Graham 1986).

When Lundgren rowed back and forth from Sisters to pick up supplies at the Lasqueti store, he passed close by Olsen.

In good weather he'd row along its False Bay side. In bad he'd seek out the protection of the back pass. By February 1945, when he ended his term as light keeper, Lundgren knew Olsen well. Choosing a solitary life where he could indulge his habits of dogs and junk collecting, he moved into the Higgins house. With the money he saved from his term as light keeper, in 1946 he purchased Olsen Island from the Canadian government for $129.20.

Some referred to Charlie Lundgren as "Hard-luck Charlie," or simply "Old Hard-luck." Though he continued to periodically row to the False Bay store to stock up on canned food, he otherwise lived a lonely and spartan life.

In the winter, Lundgren did some trapping and logging—whatever he could to get by. He was also known as a sometime mechanic and full-time junk collector.

In the summer months Charlie L. was a "rowboat fisherman" in the tradition of many who came before him. These impecunious folk made their weights out of lead from old batteries and spoons from sheet brass, pounded into shape with small ball-peen hammers in yew-wood molds. In hopes of mimicking how a wounded herring swam, each fisherman tuned his spoons to his own fantasy of the perfect wobble. Since they were made of brass, they had to be polished before each day's fishing.

These fishermen cut "hootchies" out of old plastic rain coats, and purchased long bamboo rods for thirty-five cents if they could afford them. On these they used lightweight cotton line and fifty to eighty grams (two or three ounces) of lead, and sometimes a bell on the rod tip to signal the arrival of a fish.

They raked herring themselves and threaded them on small, long-shanked hooks, then trolled them behind as they rowed. Ruth Higgins remembers that if herring couldn't be found, she would cut a small piece from a salmon's throat to use for bait.

If the herring were too deep to be raked or the fisherman was simply mischievous, he might row to a nearby logging camp and fetch a stick of dynamite. After placing the dynamite in a capped can with a long fuse trailing out, he would tie the can to a piece of fishing line and lower it to the desired depth. After tying the line to a float and lighting the fuse, the fisherman would row for all he was worth. The subsequent blast would kill the herring and float them to the surface.

The most common tackle was the green cotton handline, which was weighted down with up to half a kilo (a pound) of lead. The line was tied off to the rowboat seat or the fisherman's leg, with perhaps a turn around the oar to give a little extra action as the fisherman rowed along.

These rowboat fishermen were an itinerant lot, using double-ended rowboats or canoes. With no overhead, even the dollar a day they might earn was worthwhile.

One colorful person pursuing this lifestyle was Red Edwards, "an old timer in the Gulf who lived out of a rowboat and stayed wherever he could find an unoccupied house on the beach. He was fond of telling stories of such marathon trips as rowing from Campbell River to Vancouver, stopping only to sleep while drifting in his boat. He was a skilled blueback fisherman and was credited by some old timers as being one of the first to rake and use whole herring for bait. Red's prized possession was an accordion that he carried with him in his rowboat and which he played at dances in small settlements along the coast" (Mason 1976).

Though Charlie Lundgren tried to support himself as a rowboat fisherman, he had difficulty trolling a living out of nearby waters. So when the job of light keeper at Sisters Island came open again in March 1947, "Lundgren, the detested dog owner, came back—" (Graham 1986).

Lundgren's dogs may have provided some diversion from the difficult times he endured during his two stints at Sisters.

In August 1944, he rode out a severe earthquake in the light station. The stationhouse started to "shake violent," dancing around on its foundation and breaking out all of its windows. Lundgren was jolted out of his slumber, and ran outside in his bedclothes. The light in the tower had been shattered and "som of the lens wher cracked," so Charlie climbed up to make temporary repairs. "I put in plase Aladdin lamps then 4:50 A.M. an other shock struck the house but not so violent ... I'd whent outside and it was 15 craks in the foundation and the plaster from the siding fell down onto the floor" (Graham 1986).

During his second duty at Sisters, the cargo hoist broke and its load crashed down on Charlie. Lundgren wrote to the lighthouse administrator, "Hoist wire rotten and broke and the Raof fell a topp of mi inured mi legs and left hand I have been crippled for a mont."

This calamity occurred during an extremely cold winter when Lundgren was having difficulty just keeping warm. He complained to the administrator that "If this violent cold don't stopp the coal box will be empty." Though he was stoking the stove with over two hundred pounds of coal a day, Sisters Rock remained "a iceberg ... a decrepart place to be in" (Graham 1986).

Glad to quit the light station job for the last time, Charlie returned to Olsen and lived there quietly. Then, as Lasquetian Pete Forbes told me, one day in the spring of 1953 Lundgren "went missing." When Charlie L.'s rowboat was found floating in False Bay, without Charlie in it, Forbes and friend Charlie Williams went out to Olsen to see if Lundgren was there. Looking through his cabin, they found it piled full of old tin cans. Said Forbes to me, "We found all sorts of junk out there when we went looking for him. He was a real collector."

Finding no sign of Charlie on Olsen, Forbes and Williams proceeded to search the area's waters for hours. But Komogwa, the malevolent god of the depths, had hidden Lundgren well. His body was never found.

Since Charlie Lundgren, "Frenchie" Madden and other drifters lived occasionally in the Olsen Island cabin that Charlie Higgins built. The pile of weathered boards we found on the rocks above the floathouse were the remains of this cabin. It was still standing when Larry and Millie Aites moved to the island in 1972, though in poor shape.

Grover and Carolina Forman lived on the island for several months in the summer of 1971, in a three by four meter camp near the west end. Grover built this cabin out of driftwood and lumber from the old

Schumack farm, then dismantled it after they left to "leave the place as we found it."

Merrick Anderson and Noel Taylor told us of a young couple who stayed for a while in Grover's cabin before he tore it down. One day in a strong southwest wind they attempted to rescue their boat as it began blowing away. In their haste they left their baby in a "jolly jumper" in the cabin. Tumbling into the boat, both parents were blown out to the Finnerties and pinned down by the wind. After a night of anguish they finally made their way back and found the baby crawling around inside the shack, hungry, but otherwise fine.

High winds also caught some friends of Larry and Millie as they attempted to make it from Olsen into False Bay to catch the ferry. Their canoe capsized and swamped, but luckily they all had life jackets on. Bobbing in the wind-blown waves, they were eventually rescued by a passing boat.

Pat Forbes told me of another couple who were in their canoe out near Olsen, trying to find shelter from rising winds. They capsized and swam ashore, waiting on Olsen until they were picked off by a fishing boat. Pat noted that when the winds are strong from the south, the waves and current near Olsen can literally suck a boat out into the Strait.

Chapter 19
The Floathouse

*Hank had a big floathouse with an outhouse on one end. Under the outhouse there was a long log that stuck out farther than the rest of the float logs and everything that dropped down from the outhouse collected on it. Percy noticed this and one day he went to Hank and said he could cut that log off with dynamite ...
Since the log was underwater, a saw couldn't be used so Hank agreed. Hank's wife Margaret was in the house at the time of the blast ... And thought the entire house was going to collapse ...*
— Alexandra Morton and Billy Proctor, *Heart of the Raincoast*

Larry and Millie Aites were among the hippies who migrated to Lasqueti in the early 1970s. In the tradition of the squatters who had built fishing shacks on Lasqueti's neighboring islands, they sought a life even more independent than could be found on Lasqueti. Our friend Allen Farrell suggested that they consider Olsen Island, so one day in 1972 they paddled there in their canoe. With every step over its rocks and through its forests they fell deeper under its enchantment. Watching a pod of whales play off the island's west end, they decided to spend the night, and ended up living there for thirteen years.

Larry started beachcombing materials for Olsen's floathouse shortly after they arrived. Although the island's owner told Larry and Millie they could build on the island itself, they chose the magic of the water instead.

Their first step was to build a cabin on pilings. Larry cut and shaped all of the shakes, boards, and structural lumber out of logs that he and Millie beach-combed. Each piece was hand-picked for its grain and appearance. As Larry said, "I put my heart and soul into every board. It was a labor of love—"

Once they finished the cabin, Larry and Millie began collecting cedar logs for their raft. As they never had a motor boat, they towed these logs into Olsen's cove with their canoe, either paddling or sailing. They built their float one log at a time, mooring it in front of their piling-house.

When the raft was finally finished, Larry jacked the cabin up off its piles and set it on blocks. Next he cut off the house's supporting posts below the level of the raft and put skids on top of them. Then he lowered the house onto the skids, spiked it to them, and pulled it onto the raft with a "come-along."

After failing at several attempts to catch sufficient rain-water on Olsen, Larry and Millie hand-dug a well on Lasqueti and lined it with wood. This fed a plastic pipe that ran across the back pass and trickled water into a tank on the beach near the floathouse. Larry hand-pumped this water from the beach tank to a holding tank higher on the island, which gravity-fed their sink and wood cook-stove's water jacket. This labyrinthian system allowed them running water and warm showers, which they took outside on the floathouse porch.

Larry never went far to go fishing, and did well for salmon and large rockfish in the waters just off Olsen. His top fish was an eleven-kilo (twenty-five pound) king, caught near Olsen's west end. Over the years they lived there, however, fishing gradually declined. As Larry told me, "I don't like to sound like my own grandfather. But back in the 'old days,' when we were having friends over, it was no problem to head out in the boat and shortly catch enough for our dinner."

The skids under Larry's house were two beams running front to back, angle-sawn on the ends so they could ride up over the uneven float logs. I'd noticed such skids under several Lasqueti cabins, and finally realized these homes had spent past lives afloat. When the owners decided to move ashore, they simply winched the house off its float onto its new island resting place

The original rafts under such homes were usually a single layer of logs. But as the water saturated the wood, the houses began to sink. While some owners then pulled their house onto a new float, others added additional courses of logs on top of the waterlogged ones, increasing the draft of such "floats" to as much as five meters.

Another menace to the buoyancy of float logs are toredo worms, which can perforate logs with holes the diameter of a little finger. Toredos are actually elongated clams, whose two ridged shells encase the clam's front end and are used to bore through wood. Known also as "shipworms" and "sea-termites," toredos feed on the wood they ingest and on plankton drawn in through their siphons, and can be over half a meter long. In time, toredos can completely consume the outer wood of a floathouse's logs, leaving only the knots uneaten.

To fight the toredos, floathouse owners occasionally resorted to dynamite. Sealing three-quarters of a stick in a can with a fifty-foot fuse, they pulled the dynamite under the float and lit the fuse. The shock of the resulting blast killed the worms if the amount of powder was right. But if the worm-hating owner used too much explosive, he risked blowing his house apart.

Life aboard a floathouse rose and fell with the tides and rocked on the waves. Views through windows depended on currents and winds. Water in the sink sloshed back and forth if the day was rough, and lanterns had to be steadied with guy-line to keep them from swinging into walls. Fresh-caught fish were placed into submerged "live boxes" attached to the float—loosely built crates where the fish would live until they were needed for dinner.

Houses were moved off floats and onto the land, or off land and onto floats. They were towed by fishing boats between logging and fish-buying camps, at times tied one behind the other. Outhouses were washed over-board en route, deep-drafted rafts broke apart on reefs, and occasionally the house itself was lost to wind and waves. But a floathouse had the ability to follow the meandering opportunities of the coast and afforded a life of ever-changing adventure.

CHAPTER 20
A LESSON FROM THE WIND

… the invisible, formless, capricious wind … is capable of tender caresses yet … has the power to arrive unbidden … and hurl us to the ground.

—Jan DeBlieu, *Wind*

August 1, 1998

We arrived at Olsen today for another summer stay. It's a testimony to the magic of our small isle that the whole family was perky and excited, even after the ten-hour journey to get here.

When we were putting the tent up for the kids, a nice six-point buck walked toward us and stopped close by to graze. We saw him again later, up by the outhouse.

Typical day one, cleaning and stashing. As usual the floaty's winter visitors had left it as they'd found it. There's no lock on the door, and by out-island tradition anyone in need is welcome to use it.

Over the past months Theresa and I had decided to sink deeper roots into our island. Though we were still charmed by the floathouse, we wanted to spend more time here. Substantially more time, in a bit larger abode. These desires spawned a new set of dreams, which introduced us to the drawn-out process of planning an island home.

Our intent was to work out the construction details while on Olsen this summer. But as we eventually realized, such ambitious winter plans easily melted away in the summer's heat.

August 2, 1998

Chris and I kayaked over to visit Ken and Claire on Lasqueti this morning, surfing the gentle swells. We showered in their outdoor bathroom, and had to scrub hard to clean off the layers of insect repellent we'd lathered on in our battle with this year's bumper crop of mosquitoes.

When the boys left with friends to go cliff-jumping in the Finnerties, Theresa and I cruised over to French Creek to bring across our second boat-load of gear. I knew I was living an islander's life when the highlight of my day was the "splash-bath" I took from the restroom sink at the French Creek Marina.

Though the waters around Olsen were pleasantly warm, I hadn't been swimming yet. For me a fresh water rinse is a must after a plunge in the salt water, and the tide hadn't been high enough for me to float in barrels of water to resupply our empty cistern system.

After sweating up a storm portering our gear from the boat, however, I was unable to resist the temptation of a refreshing swim. Diving in from the boat at anchor, I swam slowly to shore. The water was so pleasant that I went back in for another swim after standing on the beach and realizing how much I'd enjoyed myself.

August 3, 1998

As Theresa and I soaked up the morning sun on the floathouse porch, a pair of six-point bucks grazed nearby on Little Olsen. Our cove was glass calm, and the air perfectly still. Crow calls echoed from within the woods, and an occasional dog barked far away on Lasqueti.

After breakfast, Chas and I went out to catch some bait for the prawn traps. I caught several rockfish, and Chas got a dogfish that was pregnant with babies almost ready to swim away. Unlike most fish, which deposit eggs that develop externally, dogfish give birth to fully developed "pups" about twenty centimeters long.

When Chas was cutting the dogfish up for the traps, he found hooks in its mouth that he had lost earlier that morning. We can only get these dogs to the surface by using wire leaders, and at times even that gear isn't strong enough. Yesterday Ryan had one big dogfish bite right through the wire.

As evening approached, we went over to Higgins Island to join Ray and Eve for dinner. To our delight they had also invited Allen Farrell, who lives aboard the *China Cloud* in False Bay.

Allen is a legend in the Gulf Islands, having cruised among them his entire life on boats he built from beach-combed materials. He's still clear-eyed and spry in his late 80s, and always barefoot.

Allen told us of the days when Charlie Higgins called Olsen "Starvation Island" because the fishing was so poor. Allen knew Vic Cramp, "a rowboat fisherman like the rest of us. In the spring and summer we trolled with a handline and spoon, with a small chunk of salmon throat on the hook. In late summer and fall we'd switch to long bamboo poles and whole herring that we raked ourselves. Biggest fish I ever caught was a nineteen pound spring."

Motoring home in the dark, we found lots of phosphorus in our lagoon where the trees shaded it from the moonlight.

August 4, 1998

When I'd first examined the collapsed remains of the Higgins house, I was at a loss to comprehend how it could have deteriorated so completely. It had been a sturdy home on an exposed point, free from forest rot.

But it took only one storm to clear up my lack of understanding. In a serious blow, nature took control of the island again, inexorably tearing down anything man had wrought. It was only by persistent repair that an island home could be kept standing. Absent such attention, a house here was shaken apart and slid inexorably into compost.

With me acting as overseer, aka slave driver, today the boys cleaned out the site for our future boathouse. We'd decided to locate it in the natural basement that sat beneath the tumbled-down pile of weathered boards that remained of Charlie Higgins' house.

Our plan was to build our home above this boathouse, in the same spot that Charlie had constructed his house. As we reverently cleared away the debris of his forgotten dreams, I had mixed feelings about what we were doing. On the one hand I felt that we were disturbing something sacred, removing part of the island's past. On the other, I felt a kinship with the man who had chosen this spot to live, and knew he would approve.

When we'd buttoned up the island at the end of last summer's visit, we'd lugged our kayaks and ice chests up our wooden stairway to a storage area on the island. Despairing of doing the same with our beast of a refrigerator, we'd man-handled it to the floathouse porch, wrapped it in a tarp, and tied it to the cabin wall. Our hope was that it wouldn't tip off into the water during some nasty winter storm.

This summer we'd found our fridge safe and dry, and in the optimism of vacation laziness, decided to leave it where it was. Forgetting conveniently about its past gouts of flame, we crammed it full of food and lit it.

I'd been told our old propane fridge had to be level to work properly, and in this the floathouse's charm worked against me. Level the floathouse wasn't, and as a consequence the fridge wouldn't stay cold.

Feeling ingenious, I set a full bowl of water on the fridge's top. Alternately shimming different refrigerator legs, I tried to get the water level all around the bowl's rim. Squatting and sighting over the bowl, I was proud of my improvisation in the face of inadequate tools.

Unfortunately, the refrigerator remained unimpressed and stubbornly refused to cool.

Imagining that I was confronting a problem of significant complexity, I kayaked to Higgins Island to enlist the mechanical genius of my friend Ray.

When Ray arrived at the site of my failure, his first act was to point out the full-size carpenter's level hanging above the fridge, which had been right in front of me the whole time. Placing it on top of the fridge, he had it leveled and working in no time. I took this as a polite reminder that my evolution from ape-like ancestors had not progressed as far as I would have liked to believe.

August 5, 1998

As I am writing, a large buck has come down off Little Olsen and onto the beach in floathouse lagoon, and is walking right toward me. Close behind is another buck that prefers to stay behind the rocks, occasionally extending his neck to look at me and snort a cautious warning to the other. They seem to communicate by snorting back and forth, the shy one preferring to wade into the lagoon rather than come near the floathouse. These are the same two I've seen over the past few days, the bolder one distinguishable by his asymmetrical set of antlers.

An Osprey is diving in the shallows of the back pass and seals are slapping the water in False Bay. In the heat of the day, arbutus trees sound like crackling fire as their reddish outer bark splits to reveal new pea-green bark beneath.

***

Chris had heard reports of kings being caught over at French Creek, so the boys and I took off in search of a "smiley." A "smiley" is a big king salmon, so named because you smile when you catch one!

After a twenty kilometer run, we put our lines down on a hot and windless afternoon. Fishing was slow and all of us basked lazily in the sun.

I noticed a swell pick up, but thought nothing of it. A gentle breeze had started to burnish us, making the day's heat tolerable.

I have lived on the water since I was a child, but my countless hours in boats were spent on the sheltered waters of Puget Sound. I accordingly didn't know how to read the message the Strait was sending us through its swells.

Our languor was interrupted by a squawk on the radio. Theresa was trying to get through. We could barely hear her through the static, but we could pick out "white caps" and "windy." Looking north, we saw that the Strait was covered with white, all the way across from Vancouver Island to Lasqueti. Quickly pulling our gear, we set out for home.

Soon we were motoring through daunting swells, our boat lost in the troughs between them. While I usually cruised at over thirty knots, we could safely make less than half that speed. Some of the swells were breaking and we continually took spray over the top of our windshield. All of us were drenched, and I was nervous and highly focused.

The waves and wind continued to build as we proceeded toward Olsen, and I began to wonder if I should run for cover rather than for home. Big swells rolled all around us, forcing me to drop our speed lower and lower. I was humbled in my nineteen-foot Grady-White with its 200 horsepower Yamaha motor, supposedly designed for offshore fishing and heavy weather.

As we neared Olsen, I spotted Theresa standing on Lookout Point with binoculars, searching the waters for our return

When I was anchoring the boat after our retreat from the waves, a friendly chap motored up next to me and stopped for a chat. His boat was a wreck, kept afloat only through some secret ritual of magic. Its low gunnels had been beaten in and patched repeatedly, and the inside was littered with empty bottles and all sorts of other junk. Obviously inebriated, Captain Calamity offered me a bottle of hard cider as he clumsily rolled himself a smoke.

After drinking and talking for a while, he raised his arm in farewell as he took off into the wind and waves. He was headed for the back side of Lasqueti through several miles of rough seas in a wrecked fourteen-foot boat with a ten-horse tiller-steered motor. When I asked him about the wisdom of his plans to brave the maelstrom I'd just escaped, he told me of fishing up north in a twenty-two-foot boat in seventy-knot winds.

I was sober as a rock, captaining a seaworthy boat in excellent repair, and had just retreated from the Strait with my tail between my legs. He was drunk and piloted a boat that was floating only through sorcery or an incredible storehouse of luck. About to embark on the waters I'd just fled, he perhaps paused only because he knew it would be too rough out there to open another cider.

Inquiring of him later with my island friends, I could find no one who knew him. This made me wonder if he really existed, or was just a fantasy sent by the sea gods to mock my cowardly flight from our duel.

After making my way ashore, all of us hiked out to Olsen's windward side to watch the waves crashing on the rocks. Huge rollers broke on Olsen's west end, sending spray high on the rocky headlands. Yet all this came from a blow that I could hardly call a storm.

Our scare on the Strait today was another lesson about heeding the signs of the sea and listening to the weather forecast on our VHF radio.

The VHF's weather channel gives wind speed and wave heights for a variety of weather stations, as well as a forecast for the following twenty-four hours. It's a spliced recording of male and female voices, which I'm convinced belong to foreigners with speech defects who speak

English only as a second language. The broadcast is a continuous loop that repeats itself every five minutes, and though I listen just for the Sisters Island observations and Strait of Georgia forecast, I usually need to let the loop repeat itself several times to tease a clear picture from its marginally intelligible generalities.

Sometimes the forecasters speak through a storm of interference, requiring me to walk around with my handheld radio to find a clearing in the fog of static the report is lost in.

Complicating matters is the forecast's inaccuracy. Winds often arrive hours sooner or later than predicted, or don't arrive at all. Dinners are cancelled on the basis of what those disembodied voices have to say. Sometimes such cancellations are followed by sheepish shrugs, acknowledging that the evening's events could have proceeded as planned.

Today, it was windy enough to send impressive rollers into False Bay. Breakers smashed onto Olsen and shot high in the air. We could have had real problems if we'd been caught out in our kayaks, as indicated by a note we found in the floathouse: "As you probably have heard, Marianna and her sons tried to catch the ferry by going on the outside of Higgins. A Qualicum caught them and they were dumped from the red canoe. They managed to hang onto it (their life jackets floated away) until they were rescued. It was very close—hypothermia was a couple of minutes away."

In today's fishing adventure with the boys, we were caught by strong winds. But they fell far short of the savagery of our winter storms. The furthest reaches of the spray didn't touch the storm-tossed beach logs that rest high on Olsen's shores. The wind and wave gods had more in store for us, but they saved those lessons for later.

Chapter 21
The Birth and Death of Waves

The firmaments of air and sea were hardly separable in that all pervading azure ... the pensive air was transparently pure and soft, with a woman's look, and the robust and man-like sea heaved with long, strong lingerings swells, as Samson's chest in his sleep.

—Herman Melville, *Moby Dick*

August 6, 1998

The wind slept in Vancouver Island's mountains last night. As dawn broke over the Strait this morning, not a ripple marred its perfect skin.

I marveled at the calm water as I sat on the rocks above False Bay. Yesterday's waves were like forgotten dreams, lost to the sea's memory. Recalling the magnificent swells that blanketed the Strait a mere twelve hours ago, I realized that oceanographers and First Nations shamen had different explanations for how the waves could disappear so quickly and completely.

According to the oceanographers, there are two restoring forces that work to calm the sea. The first is gravity, which causes its bumps to flow into its hollows, literally pulling the water flat. The second restoring force is surface tension, which acts like a stretched membrane over the water, resisting surface curvature. The physical force of surface tension may be minute, but it keeps the sea level and it impairs the wind's ability to push up waves.

When I'd sought answers in my books on oceanography, these scientific explanations seemed compelling. But on a day like today, while the sea and the islands serenaded me, the powers of ancient gods made better sense.

***

As the wheels of the atmosphere began to turn, a breeze rose so gently that I barely noticed it. Only wandering heads of grass gave it away, for the waters of the Strait had not yet stirred.

Soon, however, the breeze began to tumble as it skidded across the water. In its turbulence, the vertical movements pushed small dimples into the water's surface.

As the breeze continued across the water it imparted its energy to the face of these dimples, creating capillary waves. This superficial crosshatch of ripples allowed the wind to grip the water's skin and push up small waves. Since the water's direction of least resistance was upward, as the wind pressed directly against the waves' steepening sides, small waves were pushed into larger ones.

Peering out across the water, I saw something odd happening in the bay's ripples. Though the breeze was steady there were shining trails of calm that meandered across the water, counterintuitive mirrors that suggested that no wind touched them.

These magical surface slicks reveal much about the waters that surround us. They are concentrations of a wondrous realm with its own unique residents and dynamics, whose personality is driven by mysterious forces from below.

There are permanent inhabitants living in the surface layer of the sea, in much higher densities than in subsurface waters. Some become strongly attached to the air-water interface through the forces of surface tension, while others feed on the organically enriched surface film or are trapped in its bubbles.

High concentrations of bacteria reside in the natural surface film, recycling its abundant organic matter. Dozens of species of microalgae live here, along with dinoflagellates, cilicates, protozoa, yeasts, molds, and tintinnids.

In the upper meter of water, perhaps a hundred species of larger organisms live, either floating or in association with seaweed. These include certain jellyfish, copepods, gastropods, nudibranchs, and crabs.

This surface layer also hosts many temporary inhabitants. The eggs and larvae of a large number of fish and invertebrates reside here during part of their embryonic and larval development. Cod, flounder, greenling, rockfish, and halibut all have surface-dwelling egg or larval stages, and some crab larvae concentrate here temporarily during midday.

English and sand sole release trillions of eggs that float on the surface until hatching occurs. Afterward, the buoyancy of their large yolk sacks causes the newly hatched larvae to float here upside down.

Although wind-mixing drives these creatures deeper, their concentrations in surface waters remains stable even in surprisingly turbulent conditions. Fish eggs are dispersed from the surface only when waves exceed one to two meters (three to six feet), and larvae and fry remain here even in three to four meter (nine to twelve foot) waves.

In days long past, whalers in extremis would pour oil overboard to calm the waters around their beleaguered ships. In a similar manner on the bay in front of me, the natural concentration of surface plants and animals forms a film that is a natural surfactant, acting like an elastic membrane that flattens the surface waters. The wind-resistant surface slicks I'd been observing were concentrated trails of this rich surface film. How they form is another story.

Just as fantastic as the communities of life on the surface is the unseen dance of the waters below, choreographed by tidally forced internal waves and areas of convergence and downwelling. This dance determines how things are dispersed on the surface above. For while surface dwelling organisms are present over the entire bay, they are concentrated into slicks by wind and subsurface currents. One of the mechanisms driving these concentrations is known as Langmuir circulation.

When the wind blows over relatively calm seas, it sometimes sets up underwater cells of vertically rotating water parallel to the direction of the wind. These currents can form quite quickly, and though they are seldom more than six meters deep, they can reach many kilometers in length.

In the north wind blowing this morning, Langmuir circulation acted like a series of rotating shafts stretching north to south just under the surface. Adjoining shafts of current rotated in opposite directions, and where their adjacent sides rotated upwards, plankton and other life got caught in the upwelling. This material concentrated in a series of streaks on the surface, where its natural wave-dampening qualities spawned the mirrored paths of calm in the bay's mantle of ripples.

***

Wave development outside surface slicks is affected by things other than just wind speed, and today I observed several of them. The width of the Strait allowed bigger waves to develop than would a narrower channel, and the day's lack of rainfall permitted the waves to build farther than they would in a heavy rain. On the other hand, today's heat reduced the wind's ability to push up waves, since warmer, less dense air has less impact and generates smaller waves than cold, concentrated winter winds.

Looking over the jumble of topography that surrounds False Bay, I beheld a myriad of demons spawning chaos in the growing waves. Cliffs allowed the wind to smash down from above, sending out waves in all directions. Irregular headlands created boils of wind, and small bays and peninsulas created backeddies in the flow. Gusts on the Strait blew up waves of different sizes, and the tide running opposite the wind pushed up steep, choppy waves that seemed to break upwards. Waves reflecting off Olsen's shore intersected incoming waves and doubled their heights, and waves refracting around the end of Lasqueti threw cross-waves into the flow.

All added their own unruly offspring to the pandemonium in the bay.

The growing swells in the Strait were actually the result of several wave groups moving in the same direction, which overlapped and passed over one another. Created by variations in wind speed, these different groups had different wave heights, lengths, and speeds. Looking at an especially large comber, I realized that its impressive size was the sum of several overlapping wave systems.

Given sufficient open water, or "fetch," for the wind to blow across, waves will increase in size until they reach the maximum dimensions possible for the wind creating them. The sea is then said to be in a "fully developed" state.

Although the waters of the Strait are expansive and its winds strong, its seas only get fully developed near Olsen in winds up to twenty knots. The open waters of the Strait extend no more than 125 kilometers (seventy-eight miles) north or south of Olsen, and these distances limit the wave's ability to grow. Only a twenty-knot wind blowing for ten hours over this fetch can fully develop its waves, where the highest ten percent will be about three meters tall and a few significantly higher. Further increases in wind speed won't push up any bigger waves.

While Olsen sees strong winds that raise waves of considerable size, they don't approach the sizes possible in areas with greater fetch. Our fifty-knot winter storms would produce waves averaging fifteen meters (fifty feet) if they could blow for seventy hours over 2,000 kilometers (1,243 miles).

Chapter 22
An Oyster Dare

It is hard to explain to those who don't do it by what strange impulse humans take these primitive creatures with their tiny hearts pounding and slide them down their throats.
—Mark Kurlansky, *The Big Oyster*

August 7, 1998

My lifelong friend Phil Kallsen flew in via floatplane today. Phil lives on Vashon Island, the scene of our boyhood haunts, and commutes via ferry to his architectural practice in Seattle. We'd invited him up to do some fishing and help us put together ideas for a house on our island.

After taking Phil for a hike around Olsen, we went out in search of fish. Jigging the Finnerty drop offs, Chas hooked into something big. But after giving his stiff halibut rod a workout, it let go and lived on only as a fish story.

As we pulled into floathouse cove on our way home, we ran into a boatful of friends coming to our place for dinner. I jumped ashore and got the barbeque going, and soon we were all eating on the floathouse deck. Then Ken pulled out his accordion and Merrick his guitar, and everyone joined together in song.

As we sang on the porch in the fading light, we watched Verner Schyleko cruise by in his kayak. He's an expert paddler, and moves his kayak along with a grace I can only marvel at. We see him stroke by frequently in his travels to and from the Finnerty Islands, where he squats in an old fisherman's cabin.

August 8, 1998

At once an adventurer and practical joker, Phil led our boys down to the beach for a lunch of raw oysters. The kids had never been fond of oysters either raw *or* cooked, but they were swept up in Phil's enthusiasm. They wouldn't be left behind when the men went out to play, and certainly weren't going to shrink from Phil's dare to participate.

As is well-known to his friends, Phil's seemingly innocent suggestions lead to traps for the unwary. Soon the boys had agreed to an oyster-eating contest, with Phil acting as judge and oyster selector. Though the bait had been delicacies the size of silver dollars, Chas was eventually gagging down a grandfather oyster the size of his shoe. The rules stipulated that the oyster had to be swallowed whole, and Chas actually managed to slide half of it down his throat. The rest hung out of his mouth like a dog's tongue, wagging back and forth as Chas struggled to control his gag reflex. Reflex eventually won out as the rest of us howled in laughter. Notwithstanding his defeat, Chas claimed the high ground among us, having gone where everyone else feared to tread.

If the boys had paused to consider what they'd plucked off the beach, they would have realized that the oysters they were swallowing were living animals with active nervous and circulatory systems. If they'd been shucked properly, their diminutive hearts would have been beating madly as our sons sucked them from their shells.

Oysters are ancient things, and the fossilized ancestors of today's oysters were filtering seawater as far back as 520 million years ago. Though tiny, these prehistoric oysters were survivors. They proliferated and grew in size during the Permian period when most marine species became extinct. Oysters continued to thrive during the Cretaceous period when the dinosaurs died off, and began developing into today's oysters about sixty-five million years ago. Though they were originally deep-sea animals, through hundreds of millions of years they evolved into creatures that thrived in the shallows.

The huge oyster Chas ate began as a fertilized egg mere thousandths of a centimeter in diameter, invisible to the human eye. But within hours, this diminutive egg developed into a swimming larva that propelled itself through the water by gracefully waving its threadlike cilia. Two shells formed before the oyster was a day old, and for the next ten days it swam around feasting on floating phytoplankton. Then some urge compelled the swimmer to dive to the bottom, where it started crawling around in search of a place to anchor itself. At this stage in development, its two matching shells resembled those of a clam, and like a clam it dragged itself along with its foot.

Before Chas's oyster was two weeks old, it found a suitable surface to attach to: another oyster shell, a rock, an abandoned boat anchor, or a frond of eelgrass. By secreting shell-like material from a gland it its foot, it bonded one of its shell halves to something on the bottom, and was never again capable of locomotion.

The clams and mussels that lived nearby had shells whose two halves were identical twins. But as our young oyster developed, its lower shell became decidedly deeper and curved, and its top shell relatively flat. If a shellfish scientist had observed it, they would have referred to its flat top shell as the "right" shell and the curved bottom one as the "left."

The Strait's warm, summer waters teem with food, and during this season the small oyster grew quickly. But as winter waters cooled and food became more scarce, the oyster's intake of nutrients slowed and its growth came to a halt.

When spring waters warmed again and food became more plentiful, the yearling resumed growing. It also started developing reproductive cells and became distinctly male or female, but unlike most other animals, its appearance gave no clue to its sex.

Spawned on our beach the prior May or June, the yearling was perhaps five centimeters (two inches) long and became fully able to reproduce. And when water temperature reached a certain point, an orgy of group sex commenced. Males were stimulated by eggs in the water, and females by sperm. The adult females on our beach were incredibly productive, each releasing from eleven to fifty million eggs in a single spawn and over ninety million in a single month.

There's an old myth that oysters should not be eaten in any month without an "R" in it (May, June, July, August). These are the months in which oysters typically spawn, and spawning oysters *can* be somewhat translucent and less than appealing. We harvest throughout these months, however, and find the oysters delightfully edible.

Through luck, Chas's oyster hadn't been eaten by a starfish, broken open by a crab, infected by a fatal disease, or buried under silt by a storm, and it had continued growing through all of its life. Though its growth rate was influenced by salinity, water temperature, and availability of feed, its age was the biggest determiner of its size, and it could have been over twenty years old.

Similar to most creatures in the waters around us, the more our oyster ate the faster it grew. By waving fine cilia that covered the surface of its gills, as an adult it could force twenty to fifty gallons of water through its shell on a summer day.

When the oyster was open under water, its most notable feature was the dark mantle between its shells. This mantle was covered by sensory nerve endings that alerted the shellfish to danger. When something stimulated the mantle's nerves, its muscle jerked its shells shut.

This mantle also created the oyster's shell, by combining calcium extracted from the water with carbon dioxide from respiration to form calcium carbonate. Throughout the oyster's life, its mantle continued to produce paper-thin layers of shell, each succeeding one inside and slightly larger than the shell before. Thus did the oyster's armor grow from the inside out, composed of layer upon layer of razor-sharp shell. As it grew, it conformed to whatever shape it rested against, and even healed itself when cracked.

We had found small white pearls in other oysters from our beach, but they bore no resemblance to the gem-quality pearls gracing necklaces and rings.

A pearl oyster builds the inside of its shell with succeeding layers of mother-of-pearl, and when a parasite gets caught inside the shell (not the grain of sand of popular lore), the animal coats it with the same lustrous material that forms its shell lining. When one of our local oysters encounters a parasite, it coats it with the same gray-white substance that forms *its* shell.

As I turned over the shell from Chas's oyster in my hands, one of the largest I'd seen on our beach, I was certain that its inhabitant had been all of twenty years old.

Looking up from this mammoth oyster shell, I eyed a midden on nearby Lasqueti. It was two meters deep in places, layered with butter clams, steamers, and mussels. But while the beach in front was covered with oysters, there was not a single oyster shell in the midden.

On the east coast of North America, the opposite is true. Although the aboriginal inhabitants of the east coast ate a wide variety to shellfish, their middens are comprised almost exclusively of oyster shells.

While the absence of clam and mussel shells from east coast middens still poses a conundrum to anthropologists, the lack of oyster shells in *our* middens is well understood. Very simply, oysters were not eaten regularly here by First Nation groups. While diminutive Olympia oysters were indigenous to the Strait of Georgia and abundant in certain areas, they were slow growing and subject to over-harvesting.

The descendants of our current oyster populations were delivered to western Canada by transcontinental railroads from the east coast and steamships from the Orient. Unlike other bivalves, oysters can survive for days out of water. When shipped cupped-side down, the natural fluids remaining in their shells keep them alive. Packed in barrels of seaweed, evaporation kept them cool during the long journeys from distant beds. These oysters spread prolifically through the Strait of Georgia after entrepreneurs planted them on a few of the Strait's beaches.

Though local harvesters like to name their oysters like hand-crafted micro-brews, most are biologically identical, belonging to the same genus and species, *Ostreidae Crassotrea gigas*. The fact that oysters from different bays vary in taste, color, size, and shape simply proves that oysters are like wine grapes; the most important factor is where they are grown. Temperature, salinity, seabed structure, available feed, and the relative amount of crowding all combine to determine an oyster's unique size, shape, color, and flavor. If the spat from the same parent oysters drift to two different bays, they may mature into significantly different oysters.

Notwithstanding Chas's reaction to the monstrosity he tried to swallow, Olsen Island oysters are delicious. They draw their essence from the wild waters of the Strait, clean and cold and teeming with life. Eating one is like swallowing a concentrated draught of the living sea.

Chapter 23
Dog Fish Guts, the Floathouse Fool and Phosphorus

Answer a fool according to his folly, lest he be wise in his own conceit.

—Proverbs 26:5, *King James Version*

August 9, 1998

In the company of their Lasqueti friend Tom Anderson, our boys have been boating back and forth between Olsen Island and Lasqueti. Tom is the son of Merrick Anderson and Noel Taylor, two of the Lasquetians we met when we sailed here twenty years ago.

When I emerged from the floathouse this morning, I found Tom's boat perched precariously on a big rock that sits in the entrance to floathouse cove.

Tom is a good boatman and has never hit this meter-high navigation hazard when entering our lagoon. But notwithstanding his diligence in properly anchoring his boat, it seems determined to find this rock and balance crazily on top when the tide goes out.

Theresa and I shake our heads amusedly whenever Tom spends the night here, as morning usually reveals his craft pointing toward the sky, with bow or stern meters in the air. Like a dog seeking out its favorite rug, Tom's boat appears most contented sleeping on that big rock. We're always amazed it doesn't swamp in the changing tides.

Regardless of where Tom's boat rests, however, it's a gag-inducing mistake to walk downwind and smell its rotting adornment of dogfish guts. The boys have been fishing out of this boat for days and catching a lot of dogfish. And as fishermen are prone to do, they practiced a bit of knife-work on their catch. Unfortunately for those who happen to pass nearby Tom's craft, this butchery was done *inside* the boat. And boys being boys, little attention was given to cleanup.

After breakfast, the boys and I spent more time cleaning up debris from Charlie Higgins' old cabin. My deal with the kids was one hour of hard work for one hour of boat time. Though they complained incessantly, I know that the story of these chores will serve them for the rest of their lives. Initially it will be offered up as an example of how ridiculously demanding their demented father is. Later in life, they'll tell it with pride to their friends as evidence of their part in building our island getaway. And finally, they'll share it with their children in an attempt to demonstrate their own work ethic and shush their children's complaints.

***

Allen Farrell rowed into our lagoon this evening in his usual fashion, standing up and facing forward, with his large oars resting in oarlocks fashioned out of forked branches.

After Allen beached his dory, we settled onto our beach logs to enjoy a campfire dinner. We started with oysters cooked on a grill over the coals, and then I barbecued halibut and yelloweye rockfish. These treats were accompanied by fresh beans, tomatoes, and cucumbers from neighbor Eve's garden. Our dinner pleased us all, especially Allen.

When I asked Allen his age, he replied impishly, "Can't smell, look like hell. Skin droopin', trouble poopin'!"

***

Ryan and Tom ended the evening by climbing into our hammocks for a sleep under the stars.

August 10, 1998

Ryan and Tom awoke early and retreated to the floathouse, seeking shelter from the rain that roused them from their slumber. I was grouchy without provocation, a human barometer responding to the weather change.

When I was cooking pancakes, Ryan tried to put an aluminum pot back on the rack that hangs above the cookstove. The pot fell and I caught it with no harm done, but I barked at Ryan for his lack of care.

Then *I* tried to put the pot up, and in the process knocked down a cast-iron skillet. The skillet crashed down on the woodstove, sent several pans and bottles flying, catapulted pancake batter all over the kitchen, and finally banged me in the ankle. I had to retreat outside and lick my wounds while everyone howled like hyenas.

My foot was still sore hours later, but hurt much less than my pride.

After breakfast, we all went our separate ways on the water. Chas went out with Allen Farrell for a sail, and Theresa kayaked to the store. Chris, Phil, and I went looking for our prawn traps, which we had left out through several days of rough water.

We found one set of traps filled with over a hundred prawns, and to celebrate our catch we went bottom fishing near one of Lasqueti's underwater cliffs. I had a vicious bite, followed by a strong run, and thought I was into a nice king. It turned out to be a lingcod that was brilliant green around the mouth and gills.

Savoring a refreshing dunk when we got home, I swam in from the Grady after anchoring it. A short while later, Ray and Eve arrived by rowboat, and Ken and Claire by kayak, looking forward to a sumptuous floathouse dinner. We didn't disappoint. Garlic prawns and chicken chili were the main courses, washed down with Eve's home brewed "Lyndorah Lager" and followed by peach trifle for dessert. The floathouse was packed with great food and good friends.

***

Sitting on the deck after dinner, all of us marveled at the phosphorus flickering in the lagoon.

I've called such underwater fireflies "phosphorus" ever since I was a child, though these light displays are actually produced by single-celled plankton called dinoflagellates. Their bioluminescence is usually blue-green, near the part of the spectrum that has maximum transmissions through seawater.

These dinoflagellates are also known as Pyrrhophyta, or "fire plants." The light produced by a chemical reaction within the cell is akin to that generated by fireflies. Dinoflagellates are highly sensitive to anything pushing on their cell walls, and it appears that the resulting bioluminescence performs a type of alarm function to protect the cells from predators. This sensitivity makes the dinos flash at any disturbance in the surrounding seawater.

Lying down outside after everyone left, I searched the dark sky for shooting stars. The night was calm, and the Milky Way out in all its splendor. Laying back on the chaise lounge and enjoying the magnificent heavens, I retreated inside only after the mosquitoes discovered me.

Chapter 24
Red Tide

*Animal species endemic to small islands are generally
unadventurous –
The adventurous genes have long since been buried at sea ...*
                                    —David Quammen, *The Song of the Dodo*

August 11, 1998

On today's low tide, Phil and our boys dug a quick five-gallon bucket
of clams at the entrance to the lagoon. They used traditional aboriginal-
style digging sticks, which worked quite well. The gravel was easy to
turn and the clams lay just under the surface.

Mussels, clams, and oysters frequently grace our table. We find these
delights in abundance just paces from the floathouse, and consume
them with about as much concern as we eat apples from our Minter
orchard.

On some of these evenings, as I luxuriate in melted butter and clam
nectar dripping off my chin, nearby boaters dig into their freezers and
canned stocks, shunning the shoreline's larder out of fear of paralysis
or death.

Their fear is not entirely misplaced, as Paralytic Shellfish Poisoning
(PSP) can cause serious damage. PSP may result from eating shellfish
that have consumed the microscopic plankton *alexandrium catenella*,
which produces an extremely potent nerve poison. As little as one
milligram of this quick-acting toxin can to kill an adult, and no antidote
has been found.

The early signs of PSP are tingling of the lips and tongue. If the amount of toxin ingested is significant, the symptoms may progress to tingling of the fingers and toes, loss of control of the arms and legs, and finally, difficulty in breathing. According to *The Waterlover's Guide to Marine Medicine (Gill, 1993)*, "You become dizzy, light-headed, and nauseated, your teeth feel loose, and you have a devil of a time speaking as paralysis sets in. You may become totally paralyzed and die of asphyxia, remaining awake and alert to the bitter end."

Less than fifteen percent of the reported cases of PCP have resulted in death, however. And since many cases go unreported, the actual incidence of death is relatively low.

If the victim is lucky enough to experience symptoms right after eating, there is hope. It is essential in such instances to immediately induce vomiting and use a strong laxative. The goal is to remove the shellfish from the digestive tract before further amounts of the toxin can be absorbed. If possible, the patient should be immediately transported to a hospital. If not, friends should prepare to administer artificial respiration—perhaps for hours.

Our shellfish are more likely to become poisonous in late spring, summer, and fall, when longer days and warmer waters result in larger populations of *alexandrium catenella*. These warmer waters also stimulate shellfish to pass water through their gills at much higher rates. Voracious feeding on toxin-carrying plankton can concentrate sufficient poison in the shellfish to make them perilous to eat.

Each cell of *alexandrium catenella* is equipped with two tiny whips that are used to propel it. At the end of their life cycle, some of the swimming cells drop their whips and develop heavier cell walls. These non-swimming cysts settle to the bottom and lie dormant in sediment through low winter temperatures. Some of these "resting cells" mobilize again when the water warms in the spring, producing another population of swimming cells.

These resting cysts, however, can be equally as dangerous as the swimming cells. If significant numbers of them become concentrated in the bottom sediments, clams and shellfish that ingest them can become toxic at any time of year. Hence the year-round closures in some areas, which may exist even in the absence of *alexandrium catenella* in the water.

All bivalve shellfish—clams, mussels, oysters, and scallops—may take up the toxins and pose a health risk, though these different species vary considerably in the rate they become poisonous, the total amount of toxin they take up, and where the toxin concentrates in their bodies. They also have their own unique rates of purging themselves of the poison.

In butter clams, much of the toxin becomes concentrated in the black tip of the siphon. Since it is retained there for long lengths of time, and as butter clams consume cysts in the sediment, butter clams are poisonous throughout the year on some beaches.

Mussels, by comparison, tend to take up and lose the poison rapidly. And if the mussels are located on rocks or pilings—out of the sand where cysts accumulate—they will generally be toxic only in a warm weather bloom. An exception can occur, however, if a storm stirs up bottom-dwelling cysts.

Low concentrations of *alexandrium catenella* have also been found in limpets, moon snails, and even Dungeness crab, though not enough to cause concern. In crabs, as with razor clams, the toxins are located in the digestive tract, which is typically not eaten.

A bloom of this poisonous plankton may leave a reddish tinge to the water, though this warning sign can be impossible to read in rough or cloudy weather. And in Washington and British Columbia, most of the outbreaks occur when there is no discoloration of the water, so water color must be ruled out as a guide to toxicity.

Neither can the look, taste, or smell of shellfish be used to determine whether they are poisonous. Nor is there a reliable test kit to use. "Sample and see" is like playing Russian roulette, as a single shellfish occasionally contains enough PSP to kill an adult. And even when the concentration in a single bivalve does not produce PSP symptoms, a whole meal can still harbor a potentially lethal dose.

Additionally, there is no known method for making toxic shellfish safe to eat. Cooking does not destroy the toxin, and discarding water they are boiled in only removes a small portion of it. While cutting off the black tips of butter clam necks does remove much of the poison, the rest of the clam can still contain dangerous amounts. Soaking live shellfish in water from a PSP-free area will slowly purge them, but this may take days to weeks, with no known consistent time period that results in a safe meal.

While many of the coast's maladies are blamed on pollution, over-fishing, or growing populations of white settlers, shellfish toxin was present long before any of these occurred. On June 15, 1793, one of the small boats off Captain Vancouver's *Discovery* was sailing in the waters north of the Strait of Georgia. According to Thomas Manby, one of the seaman aboard, they "stopt for breakfast in a small cove, that produced an abundance of Muscles, and in these they made their repast, without perceiving any difference, either in appearance or taste, to those we had always been in the habit of eating, since our arrival in America. In a few minutes, the whole were seized with convulsive pains, unusual swellings, and every other symptom produced by poison … one seaman died in an hour, and three others are brought to the ship, with scarce a hope of recovery."

(Manby, 1992)

Here are the phone numbers of west coast shellfish hotlines. Though I use them as a guide, my favorite way of determining what I should have for dinner is what I call the "healthy neighbor test." I just watch to see who is digging clams or picking oysters and give them a call the following day. If they are alive enough to answer the phone, I grab my bucket and head for the beach.

Washington	1-800-562-5632
British Columbia	1-604-666-3169
Oregon	1-503-378-4307
California	1-510-540-2605

Chapter 25
Wilderness Gardens

How much better when the whole land is a garden, and the people have grown up in the bowers of a paradise.
—Ralph Waldo Emerson

August 12, 1998

The morning toot of the Lasqueti ferry told us it was eight o'clock. Theresa and I were still reading in bed, having slept in after arising at 2:00 AM to lie outside in our hammocks and watch the night's meteor shower.

After a leisurely breakfast in the sun, Theresa, Phil, and I kayaked over to visit our Lasqueti friend Josie Martens. Josie is well-known on Lasqueti for the fruit and vegetables she grows, and when our food stocks are low, we boat over to replenish them from her larder.

Walking up the beach from where we tied our boats, we entered Josie's garden through a driftwood gate trellised with blackberries. This gate was a whimsical work of art, made of two curving beach logs that arched together overhead. The adjoining split-cedar fence was a mix of heights and widths and curves and straits, and it surrounded her garden with storybook charm. Though garlanded with blossoms and vines, it also kept the deer at bay. Just inside was a low set of wires staked above the ground, which when charged with electricity from Josie's solar panels not-so-politely informed raccoons that Josie's garden of delectables was strictly off limits.

After harvesting our way through Josie's profusion of vegetable beds, we enjoyed a cup of tea sitting on a bench among her fruit trees. When we finally made our way back to the beach, we were laden with fresh produce.

Kayaking our way home through False Bay, we saw two police helicopters flying toward Lasqueti. Thus began the bane of all Lasqueti marijuana growers—Raiding Day!

In their usual pattern, the helicopters flew a grid over Lasqueti looking for pot gardens in the bush. Son Chas was over on Lasqueti when the copters first swept in, and said the island phone-tree rang into action. People called friends to let them know a helicopter was overhead, provoking impromptu harvests and a migration of potted plants deep into the woods.

If this year's law-enforcement agenda follows those of years past, the police will arrive on-island in the next couple of weeks. After pulling up the plants they mapped from the air, they'll burn the offending crop and then depart. As long as the growers don't make their ownership obvious there will be no arrests.

Meanwhile, there will be a lot of work to do. While the temptation to let plants bud out a bit further will still exist, all local pot farmers will remain vigilant for the expected arrival of police.

To the amusement of local growers, the same government that sends in the police also provides advance notice of their arrival. Official regulations prohibit anyone from carrying gas on the Lasqueti ferry, and islanders scrupulously refuse to sell the police gas for their on-island car. When the police contact local boatmen to have them haul barrels of gas to Lasqueti, the word goes out that the police are shortly expecting to do a lot of driving. A flurry of island gardening is done by lantern-light that night.

Lasqueti's pot growers are just a few of the island people that love to dig their fingers deep into this remote soil. Many islanders reverently carry on the Canadian tradition of the wilderness garden.

While Lasquetians' vegetable gardens sprout from their desire for self-sufficiency, their ornamental glades grow out of the sparkle in their eyes. Perhaps this is inspired by the natural beauty that surrounds us. Whatever the muse, it has given birth to some incredible gardens.

Wanting to tour Phil through the gardens of our Lasqueti friends, we set out to visit John Cantrell. Far up a dirt road, an elaborate Oriental gate gives way to John's acres of parkland. Though his cabin is the same size it was twenty-five years ago when Ken and I helped John pull thistles from the surrounding clearing, through years of patience and dreaming John has transformed his wilds into meandering expanses of lawn and flower beds and ponds.

John's cabin looks out from a small rise, nestled among rhododendrons and a few ancient firs. Terraced flower and vegetable beds give way in front to acres of lawn. An orchard to the right hugs his bath house, and across the lawn a stand of white birches catches the morning sun, brilliant against the backdrop of dark forest.

Bidding John farewell, we walked dirt roads and trails to a small point where Brian and Colleen Pitt live in a charming house that looks like it grew out of the rocks and trees. Leading us down paths that curve around the shore's irregularities, Colleen showed us hidden bowers that revealed themselves only gradually. Weaving through carefully tended flowers of every hue, we marveled at Colleen's collection of colored grasses and budding shrubs.

Colleen's garden is a secret place known only to island deer and friends, nestled between moss-covered plumes of basalt surrounded by aged arbutus and fir.

After bidding Colleen adieu, we kayaked over to Higgins Island to visit Ray and Eve.

Within Ray and Eve's deer fence is their year-round garden of vegetables and flowers, where fruit trees and grape arbors surround a pond graced with water iris and papyrus. A riot of blooms flowed in and out of the vegetable beds, and hummingbirds flitted by us as we inhaled their exotic scents.

While we walked through their garden, we came upon Ray's "Bucket O' Death," his homemade mousetrap comprised of a bucket full of water with a hinged "teeter-totter" attached to its rim. In its resting position, the on-ramp of the teeter-totter serves as a convenient walkway leading from ground to rim. This allows a greedy fur-ball to see a dollop of peanut butter on the board's far end, toward which it scampers. Gravity working as it does, the balance-board tips the mouse off into water, where it swims around in little rodent circles until it drowns.

No doubt some city dwellers might have their sensibilities ruffled by the pile of mouse skeletons next to Ray's "Bucket O' Death." Most islanders, however, break into smiles.

In a raised frame covered with fish net, we found Ray and Eve's bumper crop of island strawberries, carefully protected from hungry raccoons. After stuffing ourselves with these sun-sweetened delights, we walked to the beach and kayaked over to our dinner date with our old friends Merrick and Noel.

Merrick and Noel's house is full of the Lasqueti charm we hoped Phil could design into our home. They built their house themselves and succeeded in creating a rustic retreat that invites friends in to relax. Relying totally on wind and solar power, they feed themselves out of their large garden.

We can reach Merrick and Noel's home only by a path that wanders through deep woods. The trees give way to a meadow, which rises occasionally into islands where Merrick tends his produce and flowers. Apple trees encircle the house as the forest surrounds the meadow. The isolation is such that Merrick mows the lawn in the nude, and young island maidens lounge there topless in the sun.

Merrick also uses their garden to keep his freezer well-stocked with meat. When the spirit moves him, he'll "accidentally" leave the gate open. Going about his chores with an eye on the gate, he appraises any game that enters. If it's a sinewy old sheep or gamy island buck, he'll herd the animal out. But when a tender lamb or delectable doe wanders in, Merrick quietly closes the gate behind them. At his leisure, he ambles to the house to fetch his gun.

In this and other Lasqueti gardens, swamps have been drained and springs channeled to fill ponds. Deer have been fenced out and seaweed brought in. Berry vines cover old stumps, and paths follow natural contours of the land. Straight lines are hard to find and whimsy abounds. Driftwood benches invite admirers to sit and share special views.

These bush gardens are hewn out of rock and forest through years of slightly crazed dedication. They are the creations of dreamers in a wilderness that inspires dreams.

August 13, 1998

Theresa, Phil, and I sat in our boat jigging for cod as we waited for the seaplane that was supposed to pick Phil up. In between fish, Phil sketched ideas for our new home.

We finally called the seaplane base when the plane was several hours overdue. "Fog problems this morning ... he'll be there in fifteen minutes." Two hours later we called again. "Mechanical problems, call tomorrow morning." Though Phil had an important meeting in Seattle first thing in the morning, he was less than heartbroken at not being able to leave.

We celebrated Phil's extra night on the island with a great dinner of linguine with fresh prawns, garlic, smoked salmon, and dried chanterelles. All of us scraped our plates clean.

Evening brought a very high tide, which isolated Phil's campsite on Little Olsen. I took the kayak for a paddle around our island as sunset faded into night.

CHAPTER 26
KOMOGWA

To grope down into the bottom of the sea ... to have one's hands among the unspeakable foundations, ribs and very pelvis of the world; this is a fearful thing.

—Herman Melville, *Moby Dick*

Among the earliest forms of human self-awareness was the awareness of being meat.

—David Quammen, *Monster of God*

August 14, 1998

Today's sun rose into a cloudless sky. The wind gods were still asleep, their breathing so soft it left the bay a perfect mirror for the heavens above. I lay languidly in my hammock, my mind drifting through day dreams of the waters offshore.

On such a day in 1973, Maurice and Maralyn Bailey were sailing from Panama to the Galapagos Islands, enjoying a relaxing morning on their voyage to the South Seas. "Before us lay the beautiful and wide Pacific Ocean—warm, blue and peaceful—promising everything that we had dreamed about ... It was glorious sailing, over placid seas" (Bailey 1992).

Gazing out over the feline sea, they were about to encounter its tiger heart, and learn the truth that the Sirens seek to distract us from—that even on such calm days, unspeakable perils lurk.

As Maurice Bailey recalls, "I had barely roused myself when we felt a jolt on the port side which shook the boat with a report like a small explosion. 'It's a whale,' Maralyn cried ... I reached the deck to see the monster threshing wildly off our stern leaving a red trail of blood in the water ... 'We'll have to abandon her,' I concluded. Sitting in the life raft, we felt sick at heart and stupefied watching everything we had worked for sink slowly until the tip of the mast disappeared beneath the waves with fearful finality" (Bailey 1992).

In the aftermath of this encounter, the Baileys spent 117 days drifting across the Pacific in their life raft, surviving on what they could catch of rainwater, turtles, and fish.

In 1820, the crew of the whaleship *Essex* met a similar fate. They watched in horror as a giant sperm whale charged their ship, ramming it with such force that it knocked men off their feet. After lying quietly next to the ship and recovering from the collision, the leviathan cruised slowly away. Then it became increasingly agitated, snapping its jaws and thrashing about in the water. In the words of First Mate Chase, it was "as if distracted with rage and fury" (Philbrick 2000).

Holding its huge, battering-ram-shaped head halfway out of the water, the whale beat the ocean into a wake of froth as it again charged the *Essex*. Swimming at full speed, it smashed into the ship's bow with a tremendous crash. With its tail pumping furiously, the creature drove the ship backward with such force that water surged up over the transom.

When the whale finally disengaged itself from the hole it had made below the waterline, the ship began to sink. Within ten minutes, she filled with water and rolled onto her beam, floating her masts on the ocean's surface.

Though the crew made it off the sinking *Essex*, they had not yet escaped the denizens of the deep. In the middle of a dark night, a killer whale slammed into one of the whaleboats and then took a big bite out of it. After "playing" with the boat, batting it around with its head and tail, the killer whale attacked again. As the whale churned up the surrounding water, the men repeatedly punched it with wooden poles until it at last swam away. With a split stern, the boat began to swamp and the crew had to climb into the other boats so that their own could be repaired.

This crew's odyssey of survival spanned three months and three thousand miles. Failing in their attempts to draw sustenance from the sea, the men finally resorted to cannibalism to stay alive. In the end, only eight out of twenty survived.

An entirely different type of attack from the sea beset Orde-Lees, one of the members of Sir Ernest Shackleton's 1914 expedition to the South Pole.

When the expedition's ship *Endurance* was crushed by pressure ice, the crew moved onto the floes and was obliged to hunt seals to eat.

As Orde-Lees returned on skis from a hunting trip, a sea-leopard sprang from the water and chased him across the ice. When it had almost caught him, it unaccountably wheeled and dove into the water. Apparently tracking Orde-Lees' shadow under the ice, it exploded out of the water in front of him and lunged at him with bared teeth. The sea-leopard only gave up its attack after crewmember Wild shot it repeatedly with his rifle.

Two dog teams were needed to drag the carcass into camp. It measured four meters (twelve feet) long, was estimated to weigh over 450 kilograms (a thousand pounds), and sported a jaw that measured twenty-three centimeters (nine inches) across. That night Worsley observed in his diary, "A man on foot … would not have a chance against such an animal … they attack without provocation, looking on man as a penguin or seal" (Lansing 1959).

***

Kayaking out to the Finnerties today, I was sobered as a 500-kilo sea lion rose near my boat. It eyed me over, cocking its head from side to side, whiskers bristling and nostrils flaring. The size of its teeth did not escape my gaze, nor did the power of its meaty flippers. With one thrust of its powerful tail it could heave itself over my flimsy cocoon of fiberglass, breaking it in two and driving me under water.

As my stroke quickened, a sweat broke out on my forehead.

The sea lion slid backward beneath the waves, only to surface again minutes later, closer behind. It was following me! As this game of cat and mouse continued, I judged the distance to the nearest island. Fishing had been poor this summer, and I wondered if the sea lion had gotten enough to eat. Venturing onto the deep, had I become part of the food chain?

When I launched from Olsen at the start of today's paddle, I'd peered down and seen the island drop away into underwater darkness. Stroking outward, I was keenly aware that I was passing over the lip of the abyss.

A few boat lengths from shore, I was in waters thirty meters (a hundred feet) deep with the bottom still dropping. Harboring 300 meter (900-foot) depths, the Strait of Georgia weighs heavily on the sea floor, with pressures up to thirty atmospheres. That's enough weight to crush a man's rib cage and rupture his guts.

The world of these depths is one of dark shadows, of black silt that swirls in the currents. Things are more felt than seen, gliding and slithering and appearing suddenly out of the gloom.

The seafloor below me was where I set my shrimp pots. From these baited traps I'd been allowed titillating glimpses of odd creatures that inhabit the depths: spiny crabs, crawfish with impossibly long pinchers, prawns with whip-like antennae, and an occasional octopus. It was not lost on me that all of these were carrion eaters.

I knew that juvenile octopi three meters (ten feet) in diameter lived in the shallower waters closer to shore, and that in the depths below me prowled much older and craftier specimens. Gliding over the bottom with arms spreading over nine meters (twenty-seven feet), they searched like blind men for their dinners.

Their beaks could rip me apart in no time.

"Two-Gun" Brown told Billy Proctor about a night of dog fishing near the north end of Vancouver Island, when "as I was pulling the gear aboard, a giant octopus leg came waving over the side and it was followed by another and they just kept comin." Brown recounted that he snatched his knife and sliced off the legs as they grabbed onto him, fearing all was lost to the endless creature. Billy himself saw "deep knifecuts in the rail all the way around the cockpit and the chunks of octopus legs six inches across that lay everywhere. Sleep was a long time coming that night as he thought about the terror of being dragged overboard by such a monster" (Morton and Proctor 2001).

Sharing this gloom is the giant squid, an even bigger cephalopod. Seldom caught or seen, these squid only show themselves when a decomposing tentacle washes ashore.

To the area's First Nations peoples, these occasional body parts spoke of a watery underworld ruled by creatures of mythical power and proportion. A Tlingit story tells of a giant "devilfish" that destroyed a whole fishing village. Lured from the deep by the red color of drying salmon, it extended a single mammoth tentacle and swept the whole fish camp into the sea, smashing canoes and gorging itself on the people.

To the Indians, the Strait was a place of food-rich summer camps and abundant salmon runs. But it was also a place of deep waters close to shore, a place that allowed occasional glimpses of large and powerful creatures of the depths.

Here reigned Komogwa, the Master of the Sea, ruling fickly from an underwater palace of beaten copper. Represented by the Indians as a fat man with see-all, protruding eyes, he could manifest himself as any of the animals or perils of the sea: an octopus or killer whale, a wave or a whirlpool. He was malevolent and greedy, a plutocratic lord of oceanic disorder.

It was Komogwa's doing when a canoe was lost to a whirlpool or swamped by a surfacing whale. If a valuable stock of blankets toppled overboard, it was destined for Komogwa's treasure chest.

The insatiable Komogwa was a favorite character at Indian dances. Dancers played the part wearing masks painted green for the sea and black for the hidden depths where Komogwa dwelled. Many Komogwa masks showed his bulging cheeks adorned with suckered octopus tentacles, whose slimy embrace welcomed the unfortunate visitor to his underwater realm.

Komogwa's arms had reached out to grasp prior residents of Olsen, such as "Hard-luck" Charlie Lundgren. Was Charlie knocked out of his boat by a wave, or pulled in by a slithering tentacle? Did he slip and hit his head? Or did he merely tumble in while taking a pee—the most common cause of fishermen falling overboard and drowning?

Is Charlie sleeping in the oyster beds, nestled in a comforter of eel grass as the crabs comb his hair? His grave marker, the sea, bears no inscription that tells.

All of us living on the islands know that some sort of blood sacrifice is necessary to earn the right to live here. The only thing that matches its certainty is the inability to predict when Komogwa will demand it.

CHAPTER 27
DUSTS AND SCENTS

The dust we tread on was once alive.

—Lord Byron

August 15, 1998

As we sat on the floathouse deck last night cleaning prawns for dinner, we tossed the heads into the shallow waters before us. After dinner we sat in the deck's odd assortment of chairs to watch small crabs and fish feast on this underwater buffet. Feeding the lagoon's swimmers and crawlers has become a pastime for us whenever we have food scraps from the sea.

Crabs piled on top of each head, working dozens of legs and claws as they mined the banquet we'd provided. Poggies lifted the crabs off the bottom when they swam away with a piece of meat that a crab clutched tight in its pinchers. Chas and Chris put a tiny hook on some light line, baited it with a minute piece of prawn, and were actually able to catch some of these diminutive fish.

Poggies and crabs were already in the lagoon this morning, at it again, with all of us looking on. White, green, red, and speckled crabs, sometimes fighting, and occasionally one crawling all the way inside a cleaned-out prawn carapace.

As we were watching this flea circus, Ken stopped by with an amusing report. This morning his prawn traps had seemed unusually difficult to pull in. When he got his traps to the surface, tangled in them was the buoy from the trap he'd lost two weeks ago. As he pulled in that trap line, it too was surprisingly heavy. When he got to his trap, he found another buoy snagged in his gear with my name on it. He then pulled in the traps I'd lost a week earlier, loaded with over two hundred prawns!

***

My new punishment for the kids is to banish them to the outhouse. Chas got the first such sentence, but I found him hiding behind rather than sitting inside. This got him extra time on the seat.

To "sweeten" the growing pile in our outhouse, after each use we sprinkle in some duff from the forest floor. We keep a bucket of this in the outhouse, and scoop out the desired amount with a rusty can. When I found the bucket empty today, I walked into the woods to refill it.

On my knees among the trees, I scraped up the compost I was seeking. Curiously this brown layer of humus was only inches thick. Below it I dug into gray soil containing a variety of rounded granite rocks. Given that the islands rock was angular black basalt, I paused to consider where this cap of foreign soil and rocks had come from.

Thinking back on the island's past, I came to realize that the gray silt and granite stones came from last ice age and its aftermath. Rocks and fines had been carried overhead in the mile-thick ice that blanketed Olsen, and slowly settled out as the frozen massif melted. When the sea level rose, and the island was left a hundred meters underwater from where the glacier had pushed it down, marine sediments accumulated in the thousands of years it took for Olsen to rise to its present elevation.

To me, our island dirt was thus anything but mundane. Yet, further research revealed that its lineage was even more exotic than I had imagined, bestowing on it some very unusual ingredients.

While the air of our Northwest coast is some of the cleanest in the Northern Hemisphere, it still contains over a hundred particles of dust per cubic centimeter. These have been accumulating on our island since it was scraped clean by the last ice age and included a plethora of foreign material.

Some of the motes were microscopic bits of the historical world. When Columbus first set sail, the settling dust might have contained soot from an Indian campfire. At the birth of Christ, the wind may have delivered the skin flakes of a grizzly bear scratching on a remote mountain side and, at other lost times, undoubtedly the ash from one of our now-dormant volcanoes.

Other parts of our soil come from even more remote sources. Storms in the desert regions of central China gather tiny fragments of everything in their path: prayer flags, fossilized dinosaur bones, and braids of drying garlic. When the weather gears of the Pacific turn, within days an atmospheric river of such dust reaches British Columbia. As they pass, the winds sift out their delicate burdens onto the islands and waters below.

Even rarer than such Asian treasures, but just as certainly among the motes that settled, are the remains of extraterrestrial bodies. Space dust has been drifting down around us at the rate of one speck per square meter per day. Some was boiled off recently visiting comets. Other particles were knocked off asteroids that collided eons in the past. Most precious of all are small space diamonds and sapphires. Some of these date to before our planet's creation, remnants of the explosive deaths of primordial stars.

***

It was a bit breezy tonight, and the floathouse creaked as its logs settled and adjusted themselves. The night sky was perfectly clear, the Milky Way strewn across it. Shooting stars imitated phosphorus in the lagoon, winking this way and that, teasing me to stay and gaze a while longer. I finally retired to bed from the chaise lounge on the porch after seeing a long streaker leave a trail across the sky.

August 16, 1998

As the afternoon heated up, our crew kayaked over to Ken's to float the channel leading to Johnson's lagoon. This narrow entrance resembles a river as the tide rushes in and out, and it starts just down the beach from Ken's house. Our goal was to hitch a ride on its flow at maximum flood.

Donning masks and snorkels, we floated in the current over fields of waving seaweed. Crabs scuttled, starfish glided, and shells gleamed as we drifted by. On the beach above us gravity ruled like a tyrant, caring little for dreams of floating or flying. But the flume cared not for this single-mindedness, glibly repealing gravity's laws as it swept us over a world of undersea delights.

After hiking the beach back to Ken's, we cooked up a dinner of oysters, sockeye salmon, fresh prawns, and blackberry cobbler.

At the end of another perfect day, we kayaked home in the dark under magnificent stars. Phosphorus lit up each paddle stroke and illuminated the turbulence of our wakes. Inside the floathouse lagoon, Theresa and I stopped to stir up the underwater lightning bugs, plunging our paddles deep into their magic world.

August 17, 1998

The world's breathing was slow this morning, so gentle that not even grass blades were disturbed. The gods of water and sky slept together likes spoons last night, and today they awoke from common dreams. Lying peacefully in one another's arms, their chests moved only imperceptibly.

When the first gods roamed the Old World, they set up waystones to mark special places for the humans that would arrive later. I'm convinced our island was one of these, and that the gods sprinkled it with treasure chests full of their favorite things.

One of these was Olsen's smell: a smell of black rocks baking in the sun, of ripening juniper berries and drying grasses, of peeling arbutus bark and fir trees oozing sap, a delicate odor of drying seaweed and beach logs turning grey on the shore. A smell sweetened by the breathing of a thousand crickets and seals offshore and eagles in the trees. Today the smell is of calm water, a summer smell that is complex and savory and perfectly delicate. It is an incense smell that evokes glimmers of exotic religions, the smell of a wild place at rest, dozing in the sun.

✳✳✳

Our rocks and trees dream most of the time, not in weariness, but in contemplation of deeper mysteries. Their sense of time embraces untold thousands of years, and the highlights of our days fail to even ripple their consciousness. I am convinced they think of things slow and huge, thoughts known only to scientists and priests.

CHAPTER 28
KOMOGWA CALLS

Quickly the one who haunted those waters,
who has scavenged and gone her gluttonous rounds
for a hundred seasons, sensed a human
observing her outlandish lair from above.
So she lunged and clutched and managed to catch him
in her brutal grip...
Then once she touched bottom, that wolfish swimmer
carried the ring-mailed prince to her court ...
and a bewildering horde came at him from the depths,
drones of sea-beasts who attacked with tusks
and tore at his chain mail in a ghastly onslaught.

       —Seamus Heaney (translator), *Beowulf*

August 18, 1998

Theresa and I kayaked out to the Finnerties today, where we explored passages little more than a paddle-length wide. Through the clear water, we could see oysters blanketing the bottom and starfish clinging to the rocks. It was so calm that I put my lunch of bread and cheese on my kayak deck and ate it at my leisure as I paddled along.

But today's weather report warned that a Qualicum would beset us late in the afternoon. And sure enough, just as our family was leaving for dinner at Ray and Eve's, we could hear the wind start to moan through the trees tops. Out in False Bay the swell had already arrived, though there was no wind on the surface yet.

While warning bells began to clamor in my mind, I was lulled into denial and chose to ignore the discomfort of returning from Higgins Island through a Qualicum. All of us were looking forward to an evening of merriment with our friends, so we climbed into the Grady and headed out.

After the short ride to Higgins, we tied our boat next to Ray's much larger one. Aware of the rising wind and swell, we put our entire stock of bumpers between the two hulls.

At the end of our climb to Ray and Eve's home, we could see white caps on the bay below. The wind, however, was not yet stirring the branches around us. As we stood on their deck in the calm, however, the onslaught finally hit us. Suddenly, we were in thirty knots of wind.

Seeking to escape worries about our ride home, we went inside and lost ourselves in laughter and hors d'oeuvres.

Theresa and I had promised each other we'd leave before darkness fell, but we were lured to stay by a sumptuous dinner. When we finally made our way down to the beach, we got a sobering look at what we had been avoiding all evening.

Huge rollers steamed into the bay, heaving about all the boats anchored there. Peering through the dark, we could see our beautiful Grady-White smashing against the side of Ray's steel-hulled cargo boat. And worse, we could hear it, our fiberglass gunwale splintering in the thudding collisions.

Frantic to stop the carnage, we clambered into Ray's skiff. In our rush we neglected to put life jackets on, and had foolishly left our head lamps at home.

After making our way out through the swells, we paused to consider how we might get safely aboard. No easy solution presented itself, so in surging seas we jumped from Ray's skiff to our boat, which continued to collide with the much larger one next to us.

At my urging, son Chris leapt onto the bucking deck of Ray's workboat, fighting to get us quickly away. In an instant, he slipped and fell between our boats, bouncing his head off our gunwale as he tumbled. Then he was gone beneath the waves, down between the colliding hulls.

There was no sign of Chris in the black water beside us. He had passed through the entrance to another realm, which closed seamlessly behind him.

Time slowed and I moved as in a dream. While my senses were painfully sharp, my arms and legs felt like lead. Though my mind shrieked at my arms and fingers to grab for him, moving to help Chris seemed impossible.

While my mouth was open, no sound came. I felt the cold air eddying around my teeth, drying the top of my tongue.

The boats ceased their crashing, suspended impossibly in the air. The waves of the sea were frozen, but revealed nothing of what was below. I knew that in their depths moved my son, trapped in a struggle with unseen foes.

I found myself in a long hallway in Komogwa's underwater palace, lined with a series of seaweed doors. I knew that behind each door I would find the treasures of a hundred sunken ships, but that each cache would be empty of the son I sought.

Yet, I could hear Chris crying out to me. He was yelling in a tinny voice that wavered in and out of earshot, horribly distorted as it passed between incompatible worlds. I tried to lean forward, straining to sort out the warbling sounds.

When Chris was swallowed by the waters between our crashing boats, Komogwa grabbed his ankles and drew him deep, towing him toward the entrance of his underwater lair.

But always a fighter, Chris struggled to the surface, breaking free of Komogwa's grasp. The curve of our bow out away from Ray's boat allowed him to escape being smashed in between. In a split second, I had his hand and pulled him sputtering on board.

Sleep eluded me that night as I tossed and turned, reliving Chris's disappearance beneath the waves. I failed in my efforts to keep my mind from following darker endings to his mishap.

Dozing fitfully, I half-dreamt of a sulking Komogwa. Peering at the floathouse with hooded eyes and unsated hunger, he was determined to deny us a second chance at escape.

CHAPTER 29
ISLAND FALL

The fog comes on little cat feet. It sits ... on silent haunches and then moves on.

—Carl Sandburg

October 22, 1998

Up until now, our trips to the island had been summer jaunts. But as we came under the island's spell, Theresa and I longed to experience life there in all seasons. Accordingly, we set off to visit Olsen in late October.

The French Creek Marina was totally fogged in when we arrived, and through the hour-long ferry ride to Lasqueti we couldn't see a thing until we nosed into the False Bay dock. Ray met us there and whisked us off to Higgins Island for conversation and tea. The fog lifted as we chatted with Ray and Eve, giving way to an afternoon of brilliant fall sunshine.

But the fog was jealous of the afternoon sun, and soon it was back. We sensed it return before we saw it, and though it came on padded feet, all of us knew it had arrived. Gently absorbing the usual sounds of the forest and shore, the fog flowed in like some great white river, smothering us in quiet. Nearby Lasqueti dimmed in the filtered light, now glimpsed, now gone.

Sliding gracefully over the calm bay, it stole our islands away to a white universe where even nearby trees disappeared. I would not have

146

known they existed except for the gentle rain that dripped from them, dew skeined from the mist by their network of boughs.

Though the foghorns on Sisters Island suggested that there was an outside world, I remained unconvinced inside our womb of white.

Taking our leave, Theresa and I borrowed Ray's dory for the trip to Olsen. Both of us manned a set of oars, and while rowing in the deep fog we ran aground on a midchannel rock. T and I laughed at our folly as we rocked ourselves off, and then proceeded blindly toward home. In the middle of the pass behind Olsen, we couldn't see a thing beyond the tips of our oars.

As we closed on the shore, trees and rocks materialized as hazy silhouettes. The mist was so thick that I half expected to see lingcod lurking in Olsen's forest. Catching a muted flash out of the corner of my eye, I was sure that a school of herring had just flitted out of view, swimming away through the fog. I imagined that when the sun finally chased the suspended water out of the air, I might find a salmon stranded on our deck.

Sniffing at us in suspicion that we were insubstantial, the fog tried to digest us in its gentle stomach. But it had the impatience of a wraith, and after tarrying, moved on.

After finding our way into Olsen's protected lagoon, we discovered that Dick had left us a special present: a fire in the floathouse cookstove. We moved in snug and happy as dark settled around us. The evening sky cleared for a while, with water so calm we could see constellations of stars reflected in the lagoon. Then the fog returned and chased them away.

Our problem this evening was not being too cold, but too hot! The wood cookstove turned the one-room floathouse into a sweat lodge, and we had to open the door and windows to cool it down to a comfortable level.

As we lay in bed, we were serenaded to sleep by the high-pitched foghorn of Sisters Island lighthouse, counterpointed by the deep-base bellows of ships passing in the night.

October 23, 1998

I awoke this morning from a sound sleep. After the floathouse had cooled down to where we could snooze without sweating, it had stayed reasonably warm all night.

Our first duty was to get a fire going in the cookstove. After savoring a breakfast that only a woodstove can produce, we noticed Dick canoeing into our cove. Phil had completed the design for our island house and we were ready to get the project started.

Given Dick's experience on remote projects and his impeccable craftsmanship, Theresa and I knew he would be the perfect person to put in charge. He was here today to help us plan the infrastructure needed to support our dreams.

The water system was our first priority. After several months of devouring all the information I could find on catching and storing rainwater, I'd conferred with Dick and he got things moving.

First, he barged in two 3,000-gallon storage tanks. After landing them on the beach at high tide, our crew rolled them up through the woods to the top of the island. Muscling them into a rocky defile screened by trees, they sat them on a base of gravel hauled up from the beach.

Dick then built a stout watershed around the tanks to shelter them from the sun and falling limbs. We designed this out of big cedar beams—big to resist the winds that scour the island, and cedar to last forever.

With our island's annual rainfall, I'd calculated that a five-by-six meter (fifteen-by-eighteen foot) roof would be sufficient to catch the six thousand gallons of water we were going to store. As long as we continued our scrupulous water conservation, this would be more than enough to supply us through the dry summer months.

We covered the roof with prepainted metal, avoiding cedar shakes because of the things that tend to grow on a wood roof. Our gutters were screened to keep fir needles and bird feathers out of our water supply. The gutters drained into roof-washers, which were supposed to remove all of the bird droppings and other treats that would wash off the roof with each rain. After making its way through the roof washers, clean water would run into our cisterns.

As we realized when we were left alone by Dick's departure, the islands at this time of year were completely different places than in the busy summer months. Lasqueti's population dropped by half, and there was much less boat traffic in the Strait.

Rafts of birds were fishing the bay, and new collections of beach drift had been added by unusually high tides. Starfish had moved onto deeper underwater rocks to avoid beatings from winter storms. Our woodpile was used rather than built, and our friends' pantries were visited more often than their gardens.

Social gatherings on the outer islands shifted from dinners to breakfasts and lunches, as everyone preferred to avoid boat rides in the dark through potentially dangerous winter seas.

This evening, however, a calm bay and bright moon allowed Ray and Eve to join us for our evening meal. I made pasta with a sauce of salmon I'd smoked and chanterelle mushrooms I'd picked. Our table was graced by a bouquet of Eve's flowers, which had been waiting for us in the rowboat the day we arrived. All this was topped off by Eve's apple pie for dessert—an incredible meal for such a remote place.

October 24, 1998

After a woodstove breakfast and several games of cards, Theresa and I rowed out to the Finnerties. Flocks of gulls and terns worked schools of bait beside us, crying the whole time. Seals slid off the rocks and followed us around, and a sea lion came close enough that we could hear him breathing. A big dogfish cruised across our wake on the surface in perfectly calm water as four eagles wheeled above.

On our way home, we picked up an old hatch cover I'd previously discovered on a Lasqueti beach. We threw this in the dory on top of a nice length of rope we'd beach-combed on the Finnerties. Our plan was to make the hatch cover into a table for our new home, and the rope would go into my growing collection of "things that someday I'd surely need."

When walking through the woods back on Olsen, Theresa and I found the fallen remains of our eagles' nest, which had been blown out of its tree. These nests are enormous. They can be up to three meters in diameter and weigh a thousand kilograms (two thousand pounds).

Eagles add onto them for years, flying in branches sometimes as thick as my wrist. The nest we found made a compressed pile of debris two meters across and one meter high. The eagles are perching in the same tree where this nest used to be, though they have not started rebuilding yet.

Eagles pick particular trees to sit in, where they feast and survey the surrounding waters. These are typically the tallest trees in the area, chosen for the views they afford. Often they have a snag at the top, which makes for easier landing.

From the ground we can pick out these "eagle trees" by the white spattering on the underbrush, and we've often found animal skeletons scattered nearby. No doubt these are the remains of prey the eagles brought home to eat.

Given the number of eagles we regularly observe, we weren't surprised to learn that over twenty thousand of the world's seventy thousand bald eagles live in British Columbia. Most of this population is concentrated on the B.C. coast where the birds flourish on abundant fish.

The waters around Olsen teem with feed that attracts other birds as well. When we rowed to Ray and Eve's for dinner, we passed raft after raft of gulls and terns and ducks and cormorants, all working bait-balls and chattering up a storm. A din of bird calls hung over the calm waters of the bay.

As we rowed home later in the dark, pools of glowing phosphorus marked each dip of our oars, and a shimmering carpet of brilliance lay in our wake. Fish darting under the boat left luminous trails behind them, small shooting stars in the depths.

CHAPTER 30
WINTER WINDS

Oh passengers, may God preserve you! Run for your lives, leave your gear, and hurry back to the ship to save yourselves from destruction. For this island where you are is not really an island but a great fish that has settled in the middle of the sea, and the sand has accumulated on it, making it look like an island, and the trees have grown on it a long time! When you lighted the fire on it, it felt the heat and began to move, and it will soon descend with you into the sea, and you will all drown. Save yourselves before you perish.
—Hussain Haddawy (Translator), *The Story of Sinbad the Sailor,*
The Arabian Nights II

February 19, 1999

I arrived at the French Creek boat harbor just after sunrise, en route to Olsen to decide how to site our new house. Though I'd heard a forecast for gale to storm force winds, all was quiet so far.

After an easy ferry ride across the Strait to Lasqueti, I jumped into Dick's boat and motored over to Olsen to begin work. Dick had laid out some boards in a rough outline of our house to help us visualize how it would sit on the island. We moved it, spun it, and did our best to nestle it in the rocks.

As we were working, an eagle cried in a nearby tree. Dick says he's seen a pair building a new nest in a big fir near the floathouse.

***

Our rainwater catchment system has collected about three thousand gallons in the last two and a half months, filling our cisterns half full.

One of the satisfying parts of living "off the grid" has been figuring out how we can get water and power for the comforts we usually take for granted. Simple things like a shower or electric lights don't occur naturally on a remote island. Having completed our arrangements for water, we were now working on our solar power system.

This too involved many hours of self-education, which I had pursued through the fall. As solar power is common on Lasqueti, we had no problem finding a local electrician to supply and install the necessary gear.

Mere weeks after giving the go-ahead, I now looked delightedly at eight gleaming photovoltaic panels mounted on our island-top. These fed into a bank of twenty-four-volt batteries, which in turn were wired to an inverter. The inverter's job was to turn the battery output into regular 110-volt current, which it did nicely. We'd put the system in early so we could run the construction power tools on solar power rather than a generator.

After finishing our day of work on Olsen, Dick ran me over to Higgins Island, where I spent the night with Ray and Eve.

February 20, 1999

As I awoke from a contented sleep, the moans of immense winds disinterred the bones of nightmares from my youth. Pulling myself out of the straight jacket of my imagination, I reached over and turned on my handheld weather radio. Its disembodied voice informed me it was blowing fifty knots at the nearby Sisters Islands. The wind rose further as I lay in bed visualizing the swells that were surely breaking over the Sisters. Anxiety closed in, prowling around me like a hungry predator.

The Sisters lie three kilometers west of Olsen, in the middle of the Strait. In *The Keepers of the Light* (1985), a history of British Columbia's lighthouses and their keepers, Donald Graham describes the light station on Sisters Island as "little more than a dwelling clinging limpetlike to a barren wave-swept rock ... The spray ... pretty well carried over the roof in high winds."

Sisters' lightkeepers have told grim tales about the weather that haunts these waters:

> *With waves constantly washing up and over the rocks, launching a boat and hauling it back up its ways was always a perilous venture. Walter Buss went out ... and was unable to land on his return. A fish boat was wrecked on the rocks around 7 PM that night and the crew cowered in the dark, screaming for help as the tide rose and heavy southeast swells tried to wash them off ...*

> *... The awareness of living just beyond the sea's reach ... [was] ... quite literally brought home to Jonathon Fleming during Christmas week 1932 ... "The following is a list of the damage done by the storm," the keeper wrote in a still-shaky hand: "Boathouse wrecked and most of it washed away ... boatways washed away and boat damaged ... oil house was saved but was shifted on the foundation and sides and floor damaged. Outside walk of engine house badly damaged, and drain pipes leading to water supply tanks broken and washed away. Toilet, sidewalks and platform all wrecked and washed away. Pipe guard rail round dwelling twisted out of shape and broken. During the storm I could not get away from the dwelling as heavy seas were breaking over platforms."*
> —Graham, *Lights of the Inside Passage*

Other lighthouses in the Strait have suffered through similar nightmares. Speaking of one storm that thrashed the East Point Lighthouse, in his book, *Lights of the Inside Passage*, Graham relates that "... 100 knot winds ripped out all communications between Saturna and the mainland ... For three days and nights the seas rose forty feet up the rocks, enveloped the house in spray, washed through the windows to flood the living room and ran down the eaves troughs into the freshwater cistern" (1986).

In another storm, a lightkeeper from the Chrome Island Lighthouse, "was unable to go up the tower to put out the light as sheets of sea spume washed over the rocks deluging the place and making it unsafe to struggle against it" (Graham 1986). As he watched helplessly, the waves picked up Chrome's boat house and carried it away.

Merry Island Lighthouse was also unable to escape the fury of the Strait. "A hurricane force gale sheared off their chimney, tore up the boardwalk, scaled shingles off the tower, hoisted the roof off the paint shed and splayed it flat" (Graham, 1986).

Such are the horrors delivered by the Strait's weather, and Dick and I were painfully aware of the dangers that threatened us this morning. After he picked me up from the beach at the foot of Ray's path, we were thrown about in the waves as we discussed the wisdom of our intended crossing. Fifty knots at Sisters meant fifty at Olsen. Though we knew that the narrow passage between Wolf and Higgins Islands would protect us for most of the journey, both of us were aware of Don Dempster's near-swamping there. Over-confident of the pass's shelter from the winds that were pounding False Bay, he ran it fast with his bow in the air. Savaged by an unexpected gust, he had his bow thrown sideways to his direction of travel. When his gunwale slammed down into the waves, his boat's momentum nearly rolled him over. Had Don not been holding on with both hands, he would have been catapulted into the frigid waters.

But Dick and I had made it to Olsen in such winds before, so with a nervous laugh we set out.

Though we were able to sneak through the pass, when we reached the open waters near Olsen, the wind hammered us with awesome power.

In an odd twist, when I peered through the spray, I could see our island more clearly. For in winter winds like these, Olsen revealed its true nature. It is a wild place, a place I could better understand during the harshest weather.

As I walked the island in summer, its rocks and wind-swept junipers seemed strangely alpine, scoured things that belonged on mountain peaks.

In winter, however, when the island was lashed by horizontal rain and soaked by crashing waves, the anomaly of its appearance was blown away by the wind.

In winter storms I could see how our eagles' nest wound up on the forest floor. I watched as logs were tossed impossibly high ashore and juniper trees were pruned into their tortured shapes.

In winter, Olsen revealed itself with brutal honesty. Rising as a monolith from storm-tossed waters, it took its place in the natural order of things. Its bare shores were part of the storm, a tumult frozen into place. Things grew only where the sea couldn't reach, and junipers bore scars from approaching the island's edge too closely. As Dick and I landed, we were gripped with the anxiety of interlopers, of animals hoping to survive.

***

I'd hoped to catch the 1:00 PM Lasqueti ferry back to French Creek after our morning work on the island, but it was cancelled due to high wind and seas. Dick believed the wind and seas weren't what caused the cancellation, but rather the captain's fear of mutiny. Such mutiny broke out a couple of weeks ago on an especially violent crossing. Passengers pushed their way into the wheelhouse, which is strictly "crew only," and tried to force the captain to abandon the voyage and return to Lasqueti.

This trip across the Strait can be a leisurely one. On calm crossings, the captain sits in his helm chair nursing a cup of coffee and chatting with the mates.

But everything changes in a blow. Then the captain stands the whole way across, bracing himself against the shuddering impact of the waves. He leans forward from the waist, trying to peer through spray-lashed windows. It's not lost on him that all of our beach logs are heaved up by these storms. In such winds, the waves hide these floating battering rams from view, helping them attack rudders and props.

Often the captain steers only by feel, blind from water flooding the windows. Wipers are of little use and may be torn off by the tons of cascading green.

In a storm, the ferry's normally straight trip mutates into a contorted journey. The captain constantly works the wheel, less steering a course than picking his way through a chaos of toppling waves. Instinct born of experience takes over, guiding him through the continually shifting hills and valleys. Without warning, he spins the wheel to one side, rolling the ferry on its beam as he struggles to avoid a wave judged too dangerous to hit head-on.

At times, the captain is denied the luxury of seeking the least abusive route for the passengers, many of whom are retching. Instead, he must deal with issues of safety and whether it would be wiser to keep going or turn back.

As I stood on the dock with others who'd wanted to make today's crossing, I listened to their storm stories of past ferry rides. Some of these epics had lasted for hours, and as the tales got more gruesome, I was unashamedly glad that this morning's run had been cancelled.

I was confident that the islanders I was commiserating with felt the same. All activity on our local islands revolved around the Strait and the boats that crossed it, and this had bred humility in us all. In today's storm stories, no one mentioned bravado or conquest.

Everyone had been out in a blow and had a boat or motor fail. All had been surprised by the sudden onset of Qualicum winds. Each one of us understood how it felt to arrive safely after a wide-eyed crossing. Few thus sat in judgment on a neighbor's failure in preparation or equipment. We'd all been there ourselves.

The wind dropped a bit in the late afternoon, allowing us finally to depart. The ferry heaved up and shuddered down the whole way across, sending spray high above the bridge and down its entire length. A full complement of pukers lined the stern rail.

I got to the Nanaimo ferry late, but the boat was still loading due to wind-forced cancellations of earlier sailings. The purser told me that the swells they encountered in the Strait a week ago were so severe they herded passengers to the rear of the ferry, where some donned life jackets. This on a 150 meter (490 foot), 15,000 horsepower super-ferry.

CHAPTER 31
LASQUETI

It is true here, as elsewhere in the West, that the tightest, most intimate communities were also the most isolated and scattered.
— Jonathon Raban, *Passage to Juneau*

May 1999

On our way to Olsen this spring, we found the Lasqueti ferry loaded with the necessities of island life: coils of pipe, blue tubs full of groceries, bags of mail, a new fruit tree, bikes, lumber, much personal baggage, and a hand truck carrying four cats stacked in their travel containers.

Standing next to me on the ferry's back deck, blissful in the sun and salt air, was a man to whom dirt and poverty were obviously of little consequence. I moved upwind to escape the slipstream of stale sweat and wood smoke that eddied around him. This bath of fresh air would be the closest he came to clean, and he smiled contentedly as the breeze blew through his knotted hair and beard. I imagined small creatures taking refuge in his locks, burrowing and nesting in their depths.

The 1960s brought big changes to Lasqueti Island, which until then had been populated by loggers, fishermen, and the odd boat builder. In the middle of the Strait of Georgia, Lasqueti was remote and fiercely independent. It offered wild coastlines, abundant harvests of salmon and shellfish, and beautiful forests. The climate was benign, the soil rich, and the population sparse. With no interference from government or police, it was a hippie's dream.

These free spirits started arriving in the 60s, settling in an odd coexistence with the self-sufficient men and women who previously claimed "the rock" as their own. Though the two groups followed almost comically different lifestyles, all agreed on one overriding goal. Everyone was committed to keep Lasqueti out of time, buffered from the changes that "progress" had brought to much of the coast.

By common assent, the ferry was set up to serve only foot-passengers, and wouldn't sail on Tuesdays or Wednesdays. Its days of service and schedule at odd hours were designed to keep Lasqueti from becoming a bedroom community for commuters.

Though it's only fifteen kilometers across the Strait, Lasqueti locals still refer to Vancouver Island as "The Other Side," recognizing the great divide that the Strait puts between them and the outside world.

Whatever they are when they first arrive, all islanders experience a "sea change" when they sink into island life. All are forged into someone new by the hot summer sun and the thunderous waves that hammer our anvil shores. They are pruned like island junipers by the predatory wind, and have their cares washed clean by serene calms.

To make one's home on the islands is to pass between one life and another. Aboard and ashore, ours is a compressed and humble existence. Man's ambitions have long had their spines snapped on these isles.

Life on the water has taught us all that while attending properly to charts and forecasts is one thing, survival can be quite another.

For the canny sea and aloof island resist the intentions of each one of us. The effect is not predictable and touches each of us differently. On some they carve the lines of our character deeper. Others are driven to excess, foolishness, or sloth that leads surely to the grave. You never know the result, but there always is one.

***

A small fleet of old boats rests permanently a shore above the False Bay dock, their corpses slowly decaying in the sun. Such graveyards of derelict hulls are found in many of the Strait's old fishing settlements, relics of a bygone age of wood boats.

Many of the homes on local shores have no road to them. Houses like Dick's aren't even served by proper paths, and skiffs and canoes are the way their owners get about.

There are no police, no speed limits, and no building codes. When a resident gets too far out of line, a self-appointed delegation of locals might pay the offender a visit to set things right. If their advice is ignored, more extreme measures may be employed. When a past school principal proved unresponsive to citizen input, a disemboweled deer was placed in his car.

Most homes are still heated by woodstoves and they regularly burn to the ground from chimney fires and lack of quick fire protection. The next day a collection is taken for the recently displaced and life goes on.

Some of the islanders enroll their children in the "alternative" curriculum at the Lasqueti School, in which even reading is optional. As a result, there are fifteen-year-old island kids who still can't fathom a book.

Most of the island is "open-range," where it is the homeowner's responsibility to fence *out* wandering goats, sheep, and cattle. Some of these are branded and claimed by particular islanders, others are wild and casually taken by anyone when need dictates.

Lasqueti is a small community where months have the effect of years. Residents seem to have known each other for lifetimes, and newcomers are either quickly absorbed into the island community or remain strangers forever.

Local stories grow like the rich coastal forests, becoming tangled and dense as they spread over the island telegraph. Penetrating the underbrush of these tales, groping through them to find a clearing of truth, is an explorer's task.

Each islander has their place in the island's mythology. Their personal tales, retold until they are larger than the people themselves, are like the stories of gods and demons. These individual myths are known by all, offered up as a means of introducing newcomers to folks they haven't met.

Perhaps because of this attraction to mythology, the wisdom of old people is sought and revered. Lasqueti is a place where the passing of old ways is drawn out and attenuated. Island socials involve people of all ages, and everyone is the richer for it.

While poverty and slovenliness have been pushed into hiding in more settled places, where ugliness and deformity are being bred out of our species, this isolated island accommodates everyone. The demented and disfigured are our neighbors here, fully integrated into the community. Living with them all the time makes us forget what makes them different.

Lasqueti is at once a place of poverty and abundance. There are few jobs, but the environment provides. The cult of self-sufficiency is alive and well, and people heat with the wood they cut and eat the food they grow or preserve. Residents take pride in the self-imposed hardships of their lives, wearing them like sashes of honor for all to see. These are people who believe in the redemptive power of a wild environment.

A witch runs the local gift shop and the natural foods store has all but shuttered the Lasqueti Hotel's feeble attempt at competition. Ultimate Frisbee is the main sporting event and hitchhiking is the most common way of getting around.

There are only dirt roads and heaps of worn-out cars pile up until they are periodically barged off the island. The bakery operates just three days a week and people smoke pot openly at Community Center functions. Environmental consciousness is high and so is drunk driving.

Deer are plentiful and make devastating raids on island gardens, to the point that people either surround their gardens with tall fences or give up altogether. This may be why islanders love the taste of venison, devouring it with a victor's grin.

Here are a few articles and ads from the monthly Lasqueti newspaper, *Our Isle and Times*, which capture some of the charm of life on Lasqueti.

1. Ferry News (always on the front page).

2. New Library is Open: The Vancouver Island Regional Library has given us a Book Deposit Station to supplement the Books by Mail Program. It is housed in the church, and has 1,000 books … hours, 2:00 PM to 4:00 PM on Thursday afternoons.

3. Found: Cake plate, two plastic food containers at the Solstice gathering.

4. For Sale: Washable, snap fastened, terry and flannel, locally-made menstrual pads. Cotton and colourful. An easy choice you can feel better about. Check out the bleed now, pay later plan.

5. Wanted: Could whoever borrowed tools (3/4" drive socket set) from my shop, please call me.

6. Lemon-Aid: We are having a fundraiser, and this is how it works ... we will be selling numbered lemons. When all the lemons have been sold, we will release them into the wild waters at the mouth of False Bay, where they will race each other in an attempt to be the first lemon to wash up on shore. The owner of the first lemon to be returned to me at the Internet Centre will win a treasure trove of groovy prizes.

7. Dear Deer: There is an orphaned fawn that hangs out with me at the Teapot House. She has been my companion since September and eats kale and apples from my hand and likes a good scratch behind the ears. She is often around the front gate grazing before she enters. She is not all that traffic savvy, not understanding this human contrivance called a road. So, please be aware of her and any animal, in your travels. I'd like her to live a long life.

8. True Story: This is the transcript of the actual radio conversation of a US Naval ship with Canadian Authorities off the coast of Newfoundland in October 1995. (Radio conversation released by the Chief of Naval Operations on October 10, 1995.)

Canadians: Please divert your course 15° to the South to avoid a collision.

Americans:	Recommend you divert your course 15° to the North to avoid a collision.
Canadians:	Negative. You will have to divert your course 15° to the South to avoid a collision.
Americans:	This is the Captain of a US Navy Ship. I say again, divert YOUR course.
Canadians:	No, I say again, you divert your course.
Americans:	THIS IS THE AIRCRAFT CARRIER USS LINCOLN, THE SECOND LARGEST SHIP IN THE UNITED STATES ATLANTIC FLEET. WE ARE ACCOMPANIED BY 3 DESTROYERS, 3 CRUISERS, AND NUMEROUS SUPPORT VESSELS. I DEMAND THAT YOU CHANGE YOUR COURSE 15° NORTH, I SAY AGAIN, THAT'S ONE FIVE DEGREES NORTH OR COUNTER MEASURES WILL BE UNDERTAKEN TO ENSURE THE SAFETY OF THIS SHIP!
Canadians:	This is a lighthouse. Your call.

9. Lasqueti Christmas Bird Count: Here is a list of the birds, and the numbers of each, seen on the Christmas Bird Count. If you'd like more information call Marti Wendt or Peter Johnston. If you'd like to come birding with us some day, phone and say so.

Common Loon 3

Pacific Loon 32

Spp. Loon 6

Western Grebe 3

Red-necked Grebe 10

Common Murre 151

Marbled Murrelet 11

Ancient Murrelet132

Spp. Murrelet 4

Rhinoceros Auklet 5

Horned Grebe 2

Spp. Grebe 5

Double-crested Cormorant 48

Brant's Cormorant 5

Pelagic Cormorant 6

Spp. Cormorant 12

Great Blue Heron 15

Trumpeter Swan 6

Mallard 10 Pileated

Ring-necked Duck 2

Lesser Scaup 1

White-winged Scoter 1

Surf Scoter 2

Harlequin Duck 3

Longtail Duck 358

Barrow's Goldeneye 105

Bufflehead 108

Common Merganser 395

Red-breasted Merganser 9

Hooded Merganser 13

Spp. Merganser 6

Virginia Rail 2

Black Oystercatcher 25

Black Turnstone 66

Rock Sandpiper 2

Surfbird 9

Mew Gull 38

Thayer's Gull 15

Glaucous-winged Gull 1,823

Spp. Gull 1,250

Bald Eagle 30

Sharp-shinned Hawk 1

Osprey 1

Merline 1

Peregrine Falcon 2

Belted Kingfisher 11

Northern Flicker 10

Downy Woodpecker 1

Woodpecker 15

Northwestern Crow 147

Common Raven 31

Chestnut-backed Chickade 137

Brown Creepe 8

Red-breasted Nuthatch 7

House Wren 1

Winter Wren 28

Bewick's Wren 5

Golden-crowned Kinglet 204

Ruby-crowned Kinglet 6

Varied Thrush 26

American Robin 80

European Starling 16

Hutton's Vireo 2

Rufous-sided Towhee 24

Song Sparrow 32

Dark-eyed Junco 91

Fox Sparrow 6

Pine Siskin 103

Purple Finch 5

10. Firewood Social: We've got three trucks of logs at the Community Center that need to be bucked into firewood. Please give me a call so we can set a date to get together with our chainsaws. Some food would be welcome too!

11. Island Driving: If you loan your vehicle to visitors, please inform them of the extreme danger of going too fast on a gravel road. Tell them how awful the dust is for walkers, bikers, and homes on the road. Tell them that *none* of the side roads comfortably hold two cars. Thanks.

12. The Book Depository on Lasqueti is now closed. Please return all borrowed books. We gave it a good try over a three-year period, but use doesn't warrant the number of hours the volunteers put in. Thanks to all the volunteers for their wonderful dedication.

13. Hang Onto Your Teeth: The marine dental clinic, the *Daemon*, will not be arriving this summer, as we are in the process of selling the boat. We're hoping to have another boat so we can come next year.

14. Butterflies: I've become interested in butterflies and would like to hear what's been seen on Lasqueti this summer. If you see something special and can let me know, I might be able to come look. If you find a dead one, I'd like to see it.

15. Around Together: I'd like to have as many of us as possible spend time paddling, rowing, or sailing around the island together. Anyone who has an extra boat that's suitable, or space for another person in their boat, please let me know. I encourage everyone to spend some of the day at the shore, and if they stay ashore, attract boaters by song or signal.

16. Free: Propane fridge that sort of works.

17. Energy, Clarity, and Focus: Curative Massage, Hyperspace Healing, and Transformational Breathing.

18. Free Jazz Concert on the Dock: On August 5, our own Ken Lister will be performing an evening of jazz on the False Bay dock. Come by boat or inner tube, and groove on the waves. Bring your lawn chairs and picnic on the beach and dock, relax and watch the moon as the band plays on. It's Free! To cover the cost, a raffle will be held through the month.

This protective, frontier spirit enfolds Olsen in its arms, keeping it wild and undeveloped. We were lucky to find it thus, kept out of time with Lasqueti.

Chapter 32
Our Construction Crew

Imagination is more important than knowledge.
—Albert Einstein.

May 1999, Continued

Construction on our new home is in full swing, replete with the rewards and challenges of building on a remote island.

Virtually everything we've needed has been taken off a truck, loaded onto a barge, boated across the Strait, unloaded onto the shore, and hand-carried up over the uneven rocks to our homesite. In hopes of easing the burden that this portage puts on the crew, Dick and Ray have come up with the idea of building a wooden road from the water to the project. A winch at the top would pull a farm wagon up the roadway, which could be piled high with the endless implements of torture that the crew now humps up on their backs.

Everyone working on the house is ecstatic about the relief this system will give them. They'd rather put their energies into creative work than backbreaking labor.

This crew reflects the unique character of Lasqueti Island, and Theresa and I look on with appreciation and amusement as their creativity is expressed in our emerging house.

Sylvain Lieutaghi is a Frenchman in his mid-thirties. Thin and energetic, Sylvain is a nonstop torrent of enthusiasm and creativity. After seeing some photographs of work he'd done, we hired him on the spot. He's been building rock steps, paths, walls, hearths, and fireplaces for us ever since. Talking rapidly in a heavy accent that I can barely understand, he often convinces me of something with his twinkling eyes and infectious smile. Sometimes I'm not exactly sure what I've agreed to, but give the go-ahead out of trust for his judgment and appreciation for his spirit.

Art Housten is Sylvain's helper. In his mid-forties, he outworks men half his age, lifting rocks and carrying mortar all day long. He recites lines of classic poetry and discusses European history with detail and insight, but after work each evening he rolls up a joint and retires to the tavern to drink the night away.

Alex Bain arrived in the hippie invasion of the early seventies and still holds true to the values that brought him to Lasqueti. He still has no refrigerator in his home, keeping perishable items in an ice chest on his back porch. Alex can work on a few shingles for hours, philosophizing about their placement and making sure their shape is in harmony with nature. Though he drives Dick and me nuts with the pace of his work, his craftsmanship is impeccable. Alex is a gentle soul, brilliant in a completely undisciplined way, and cares deeply about the spiritualism he weaves into his work.

Richard Bauer makes whimsical furniture that is sold in Vancouver Island galleries. He has laughing eyes and an artistic touch that graces everything he does.

Shawn Cindrich has hair halfway down his back and lives in a tree house. He works himself into a sweat for days on end, hustling through tough manual labor that others shun, and then misses a few days when something more interesting beckons.

Mike Chan has a cabinet shop in Nanaimo and is a hard-driving perfectionist. Taking a break from his normal life, he moved onto his sailboat and anchored it in a Lasqueti cove for the duration of our project. Mike is a hugely talented craftsman, well-suited to solving the myriad of technical conundrums that our unusual design is presenting.

Dick is the mother hen who keeps this team on track. Few are used to steady jobs, and none are among the regular workmen employed by Lasqueti's homebuilders. Dick himself chose the island for its alternative lifestyle, and he picked a crew who shares his philosophy. He has a massive crown of curly hair, a huge beard, and is endlessly considerate of other people. He shows up at Lasqueti parties in drag, and will do anything to help a neighbor in need.

This crew commutes in a comical assortment of kayaks, canoes, and motorized craft, including Dick's old motorboat *Rosenante*. *Rosenante* embodies all the humorous defects of this odd flotilla, the boat equivalent of Don Quixote's comic nag that she was named after.

Rosenante would make a better bathtub than boat, as her rounded bottom causes her to wallow in even the slightest waves and pushes her bow skyward whenever the throttle is advanced. This places a wall of dirty fiberglass across Dick's field of vision, obliging him to steer a zigzag course to catch glimpses of what lies ahead.

Rosenante also resembles a bathtub in that she is often awash with water. Her seams have been sprung open and fiberglassed shut so many times that they resemble the arthritic joints of an aged fisherman. Scars and age spots mottle her yellowed skin, reminders of her protracted losing battle with Lasqueti's rocky coast.

It's a testimony to Dick's impish sense of humor that he refuses to abandon this caricature of a boat. For what *Rosenante* lacks in grace, she makes up for in personality and the ability to amuse.

On calm days, the work crew arrives one by one: Mike in his kayak, Shawn and Art in a canoe, Sylvain and Richard in a double kayak, and Dick in *Rosenante*, ferrying Alex and whoever else happens to be helping at that time. But when the wind and waves are up, when the passage out to Olsen would be tough on the paddlers, the crew ties their canoes and kayaks end to end behind *Rosenante* and Dick pulls them out through the blow.

This is the way our crew begins their days, and they incorporate the sights of their passage into what they build. Shake lines on our outhouse roof meander like waves, and dormers curve like the Strait's swells. Paths flow around obstacles the way currents flow around our shores, and the rock walls of our boathouse resemble the rocky borders of False Bay.

***

After the crew left for the evening, I walked to the island's west end to watch the sun set. Looking across the Strait at Vancouver Island's snowcapped peaks, I thought of Captain George Vancouver's feats exploring this rugged coast.

George Vancouver was made captain of the *HMS Discovery* at the age of thirty-four, and shortly thereafter he embarked on a four-and-a-half-year, 65,000 mile voyage of discovery. Sailing into uncharted waters at a time when scurvy still claimed many sailors' lives, he managed to bring both of his ships and almost all of his men home. En route, they charted over 1,700 miles of coast, including some of the world's most complex and potentially dangerous coastal geography. In doing so, he disproved the myth of the Northwest Passage, which had obsessed European powers for years. Through his dealings with the Spanish explorers who'd arrived before him, he solidified British claims of sovereignty on North America's west coast. And by cultivating the favor of Hawaiian monarchs, he laid the foundation for British governance of Hawaii.

But unfortunately, for all his accomplishments, George Vancouver was not an inspiring man. Short, bald, and fat, he sweated copiously and had bulging, thyroidal eyes. His exploding temper was known only too well by his crew, some of whom believed that he descended into insanity in his darker periods.

Though he possessed every technical skill, Vancouver was devoid of either charm or humor. Rising on his own merits in a time when British aristocracy held most important command positions, he was forever living down his mangled Dutch name, originally van Coeverden.

Captain Vancouver made life miserable for his crew. Devoted to the lash, he handed out punishments that were excessive even in the 1790s. Though the *Discovery's* log books were lost, Peter Puget copied some of their entries into his own journal. If the frequency of floggings recorded there speak reliably, Vancouver ordered beatings several times a week: "20 lashes for insolence … 12 lashes for disobedience of orders … 36 lashes for neglect of duty." These were administered with a cat-o'-nine-tails, which was kept in a red, blood-soaked bag.

Wracked by a persistent cough, his health steadily deteriorated over the course of the voyage. He became "white-faced, withdrawn, monosyllabic, and thought likely to explode at any moment" (Raban 1999). He was intensely disliked by most of his crew, and respected by very few.

Returning from his epic voyage at a time when Napoleon's exploits were absorbing Britain's attention, Vancouver was repeatedly slandered by a young nobleman he had humiliated aboard the *Discovery*. Instead of being recognized for his accomplishments, he was lonely and penniless, "shunned, humiliated and driven to an early death by anxiety and worry" (Bown 2008). As often happens, his legend and accomplishments loom larger than did the man.

CHAPTER 33
ISLAND CONCRETE

A laugh is a mighty good thing.

—Herman Melville, *Moby Dick*

July 30, 1999

We depart for our summer stay on Olsen tomorrow, and I think all is ready.

Preparation for island life is an art itself. Throughout the winter, I think back to things that broke last year, and forward to this year's projects. I plod through my summer plans from beginning to end, time after time, considering each screw, tool, and piece of line I will need. I think through our daily lives, weekly routines, and nightly wanderings, each with its own requirements. I consider likely repairs and religiously catalogue everything potentially needed.

As I think through all this, I write everything down on a collection of lists. I keep these lists from year to year, repeatedly scrutinizing them with the thought that I've surely forgotten something. Walking around our piles of gear, I wonder what island necessity I've failed to consider, and fret as I doubt that all the gear will fit into our car and boat.

For those of us on remote islands, good gear is like a drug that convinces us that we're ready for anything that nature might throw our way.

The studying and buying of this gear is hugely satisfying in and of itself, inspiring almost giddy self-confidence. Its presence alone seems to deter rough weather and equipment breakdowns. Reviewing and reorganizing such gear calms anxious stomachs when conditions start to deteriorate.

Coils of line, extra props, and boxes of tools all make us believe that our homes and boats are equal to nature's challenges, and that we ourselves have moved beyond close calls of the past.

All of us on the out-islands have a kit for every emergency. After being repeatedly blindsided, we've become zealots in our pack-rat mentality. Our pilgrimages are to chandleries and hardware stores. Our state of grace is that of being prepared for every contingency. Our prayers are embodied in our piles of equipment: "We'll be fine … just look at all the stainless steel shackles we have!"

Through the winter, I have stockpiled our island gear in special drawers and cupboards, in hopes of assuring nothing will be left behind.

As departure approaches, however, additional concerns besiege me. Will the trailer bearings freeze up? Are the kayaks tied securely? Did I remember the binoculars?

Theresa and the boys help contain my anxiety, snarling back at my outbursts.

Then we make the leap of faith into the peace of knowing that we will live with what we have, unplugged from trips to the store. If we break it, it stays broke. If we forget something, we do without. If we deplete our stores, we live off the memory of abundance. Life is simplified as material desires are quenched by the impossibility of their fulfillment. I thus smile when I step off the dock and into our boat, into the world of island life.

But that step will come tomorrow, and meanwhile I've got to deal with these piles of gear surrounding me.

August 1, 1999

Our Chevy Suburban resembles the old truck that carried the household goods of the Beverly Hillbillies. It is packed to capacity, and on top is a four-foot-high pile of boxed gear tied together under a blue tarp. Our trailered boat is also stuffed to overflowing, with odd shapes pushing through its tightly stretched cover.

Shoehorned into the car with me are Theresa, Chris, and Ryan, and their friends Bobby Gauthier and Patrick Jackson. Stacked around us are food and clothes for two weeks, tents, sleeping bags, air mattresses, fishing gear, building materials, two surf kayaks, one regular kayak, three ice chests, two crab traps, a new fishing net, two portable CD players, more food, the floathouse rug we brought home to wash, and boxes and bags of who knows what else.

It took the four boys and me over five hours to cram the Suburban full and secure the boxes on top with a rat's nest of crisscrossed ropes. I'm sure we'll win the "Most Sophisticated Guests" award at the Seattle wedding we are attending on the way up. The blue-tarped load on top will no doubt be the clincher.

August 2, 1999

We spent our first morning on Olsen unpacking and discussing various construction details with Dick. Then we boated across False Bay to Ken's for a swim, followed by a warm water rinse from his solar shower. This was simply, and ingenuously, just a hose bib on the end of a coil of black plastic pipe that heated up in the sun.

Dinner in the floathouse was followed by a rousing game of "spoons." I had an early lead on everyone, only to go down in defeat. This earned me the loser's obligatory plunge into the lagoon, accompanied by the catcalls of all.

Waiting for sleep in the floathouse loft, I shook my head at how complicated construction was here. One thing I found particularly amusing was how we made concrete.

First we talked with Sailor Johnson, who runs an oyster farm on Lasqueti. We needed to find out when he was taking a batch of oysters to French Creek, so we could arrange to have him bring a load of materials back for us on his return trip.

Then we called our supplier and made an appointment for them to meet Sailor's barge. After Sailor had unloaded his oysters, the supplier's boom truck backed down the launching ramp. Parked crossways with its rear tires in the water, it lifted pallets of bagged sand and cement onto the bow of Sailor's vessel. These bags were then hand carried to the rear of the barge to keep it from nosediving under the waves.

Sailor next made the run across the Strait to Olsen, where he lowered his bow-ramp onto the rocks below our wooden roadway. All bags, of fifty kilos each, were hand unloaded onto the rocks, and then carried to and stacked on the farm wagon on the roadway.

The "roadway" was composed of two tracks of Lasqueti-milled two-by-twelves, one track for the wheels on each side of the cart. The two-by-twelves were secured to a series of yellow cedar logs, which acted like railroad ties. These logs, which were collected from the beaches around the island, were spiked to the uneven rocks below.

The winch and cart was an ingenious system that only Ray could have designed. Its heart was a surplus marine winch powered by a cast-off rototiller engine and controlled by the power steering mechanism out of an old truck. The large metal spool of the winch was fitted with a length of used galvanized cable; this pulled the farm cart up the wooden roadway.

Three people were needed to run the winch and wagon system. One person kept the cart on the curving roadway by managing the wagon tongue, another worked the hydraulic control lever that operated the winch, and a third overrode the governor on the rototiller engine to keep it from stalling. If the tongue-man took his eyes off the wheels, the wagon ran off the roadway. If the engine operator didn't mind the throttle, the strain of the load stalled the motor; if he forgot to use a small stick to manipulate the throttle, he burned his hand; and if the hydraulic-control specialist didn't depress the hydraulic control lever, the winch wouldn't turn.

After the threesome winched the wagon-load of cement and sand up to the house, the bags were unloaded and hand-carried to the cement mixer. This ran off our bank of batteries, which were charged by our solar panels.

Water flowed down from the rainwater-filled cisterns at the top of the island. Sand, cement, and water were then blended by hand and carried in buckets to where the resulting mix was reverently poured into its final resting place.

August 3, 1999

Today our Grady's motor started coughing and belching white smoke. As we were preparing for a fishing trip to Nootka Sound on Vancouver Island's remote west coast, I recognized that these motor problems could not be ignored. So the twins and I ran our boat over to French Creek and then trailered it to a boat shop, begging for quick repairs.

Thankfully, they obliged.

After we'd collected out boat and were getting ready to depart for Olsen again, I was standing in the French Creek Marina when a crow dropped his ballast on my head. The boys laughed until they cried as I pondered possible symbolic meanings of this humbling event. Was this possibly an omen, or payback for some slight I'd given one of the Strait's totems?

When we arrived home, I found that Chas and Alex had finished our new smoker. But as I was admiring it, I realized it was a bit cocky to build a large smoker in anticipation of a big catch on our Nootka fishing trip. Was this just good planning, or conceited thinking that would bring bad luck?

Son Chas and his friend Matt Peterson had joined our work crew in early June, and set up camp in a tent on the island. I'd had a good laugh when I'd helped them load their baggage onto the ferry for their trip up. Zipping open the impossibly heavy duffle bags they'd lugged to the dock, I'd found them stuffed with cans of beef stew, ramen noodles, macaroni and cheese, and more canned stew. Though the boys are now fit from their month of construction work, I doubt they've had a mouthful of fresh fruit or vegetables the entire time.

***

Ken and his son Aaron joined us for dinner tonight. While talking of our Nootka plans, we grilled our dinner over a bark fire in the barbecue. I grew up eating dinners barbecued over bark fires, and still relish the special flavor that their smoke imparts.

Investigating some chirping noises, we found that a nice catch of sparrows had built up in our empty prawn traps that I'd stacked on the logs by the floathouse. Like the prawns the traps are intended to catch, the birds found their way in but not out. We had caught several in each trap, where they fluttered around seeking escape. This delighted eight-year-old Aaron, who laughed as they flew away when he opened the trap doors. They reminded me of the temple birds Theresa and I had bought in Thailand, which we released from their cages as offerings to the gods.

August 4, 1999

I was up early to enjoy the peace. The sun was just rising, and there was no construction crew or kids around yet.

When the day's beehive of activity got into full swing, Theresa and I sought escape in a kayak trip to the Finnerties. Just as we were about to leave, our good friends Cheri Grant and Sue Schoonover arrived in their boat. Every year since we started coming to Olsen, these two adventurous women had boated all the way from their Fox Island home to spend time with us. Though we'd extended invitations to numerous friends, the women and Phil were the only ones who'd accepted. Many of our friends loved to bathe in the romanticism of our island life, but few were willing to make the journey to share it.

Here I should mention that Fox Island lies some 250 water miles south of Olsen. These miles are traversed via a meandering route down channels, around islands, and through passes so narrow that they are safely run only at certain tidal flows. All this is properly navigated only with a tide book, current tables, marine chart, and constant attention to one's position.

The ladies commandeered the kayaks for the trip to the Finnerties, so the boys and I went to the Fagan Islands in the Grady. The kids fished while I beachcombed for some cedar logs for our house. All I found was an afternoon of treasure hunting on a deserted island, which was a treasure in itself.

Around dinner time, when the boys were skinny-dipping off Little Olsen, Theresa and I paddled out to our friends' boat for some wine and cheese. We spent a very pleasant evening aboard, admiring the setting sun reflecting off glass-calm waters.

As we were enjoying the evening, Verner kayaked by on his way home to the Finnerties. We've seen him many times paddling through the protected waters behind Olsen.

Verner lives a rugged life on the island he has chosen to call home. Where Olsen is wild, the Finnerties are wilder. While we are partially protected by Lasqueti from the rages of the Strait, his island has no shelter, and is lashed by the full force of the Strait's gales. We live in a floathouse with beautifully wood-worked charm. He lives in a shack in the woods. Our kayaks are supplemented by a motor boat, whereas all Verner has is paddle power.

Verner's cabin can only survive because it is hidden in a protected spot among the trees. If it were on an exposed point like our home under construction, a good storm would tear it apart. Persistent wind would force its way through the cracks in the walls, shredding the Tyvek that Verner stretched to protect himself from the elements. Horizontally driven rain would invade his sanctuary, soaking him and his belongings. Like a toy in the mouth of a dog, the cabin would be shaken until its rusty nails failed. As a pile of rotting boards, it would join the islands' other old fishing shacks.

Notwithstanding his humble abode, Verner is no bum. He is a very educated man and a talented artist. Presently, he is doing a set of illustrations to be published in a new printing of the classic, *A Thousand and One Nights*. He has just chosen a very private life in a very wild place.

CHAPTER 34
NOOTKA SOUND

When the gods are with you, the wind and the sea conduct you onward, like thistledown blown from wave to wave.
—Jonathan, Raban, *Passage to Juneau*

August 5, 1999

Today we left for Nootka Sound, a remote fishing spot on the storm-battered west coast of Vancouver Island. After traversing the Strait in our boat, then trailering it across Vancouver Island, we launched at the Sound's inland terminus. Our plan was to run out through Nootka's forty-eight kilometers (thirty miles) of twists and turns to our destination on Nootka Island, and then pitch our tents just inland from where the Pacific breaks on the island's western shore.

Navigating through the inner reaches of Nootka Sound proved easy enough as we matched the shoreline to our charts. But when we got to where the sound opened up at Bligh Island, we entered a heavy fogbank.

When canoeing in fog or at night, coastal First Nations People shouted and listened to the echoes of their voices bouncing off surrounding land. The quality of the echo told whether they were close or far away—whether the shore was a vertical clay bluff or a gentle slope of trees. Combining their knowledge of shoreline topography with the echoes from regular shouting, they painted a mental picture of where they were.

But I had no such skills, and neither did any of the boys.

Looking at each other with questions in our eyes, we all realized that we *hoped* we were at the tip of Bligh Island. Since the fog deprived us of almost all references, we couldn't be sure where we were. We finally came upon a small navigation light on the shore, whose surroundings seemed to match the coast depicted on our chart. I must have looked back and forth between chart and shore twenty times in a vain attempt to convince myself that I was confident of our location.

As we bobbed in the slight chop at the edge of the fogbank, I was reluctant to let go of our umbilical tether to the rocky piece of uninhabited land. In front of us were miles of open water blanketed by deep fog, which would reveal nothing of the shrouded coast until we were hard upon it. We had no radar or GPS, and thus were effectively blind.

We were headed for the southern tip of Nootka Island to rendezvous with Ken. A course too far to port would take us out through the mouth of Nootka Sound and into the Pacific Ocean. Next stop, Japan. A course too far to starboard could land us on the rocks off several small islands, which could send us to the bottom.

I managed to raise Ken on the radio and found that he was fishing near our desired landfall. At his suggestion, we turned off our motor and listened for the foghorn at Friendly Cove. After hearing it and estimating its direction, we conferred with Ken on our desired compass heading.

Finally, I shrugged my shoulders, fired up the motor, and headed off into the unknown. After thirty minutes of cruising through grey soup, land began to materialize in front of us. We followed it southward to Friendly Cove, our temporary island home.

August 6–8, 1999

Our Nootka campsite was just above the beach at Friendly Cove, on the site of the native village that existed when the first European explorers arrived here. Today only two families remain, caretaking an old church filled with totem poles and masks.

A gathering of First Nations People was in progress when we arrived, most of whom had come by canoe. Some had paddled from as far away as Alert Bay, a journey of over 400 kilometers, much of it through the ocean off Vancouver Island's weather-beaten coast.

Some of the canoes were carved out of cedar logs and beautifully painted with traditional designs. Their bows were decorated with beaded eagle feathers, cedar-bark ropes, and wreathes of cedar branches. The paddles themselves were works of art, hand carved and decorated with feathers and painted figures.

Nightly chanting and drumming around a beach fire lent additional mystery to the celebration.

Captain Cook visited Friendly Cove in 1778, and it was here that his crew made the observations of First Nations life quoted in chapter thirteen of this book. It was also where John Jewitt was enslaved by the local Indians from 1803–1805, after they killed all but two of the crew of the trading ship *Boston*. Jewitt's account of his years as a Nootka slave is chronicled in his excellent book, *White Slaves of the Nootka* (1994).

Though salmon fishing at Nootka was slower than expected, bottom fishing was full of action. Chris caught a monstrous snapper, the biggest I'd ever seen. On two different occasions, Ryan reeled up lingcod that had grabbed onto a rockfish that he was fighting. Greedy unto death, they wouldn't let go until Ryan tried to lift them from the water.

One of Ken's friends lost a big halibut right at the boat. We caught plenty of ocean perch, cabazon, mackerel, greenling, and other miscellaneous bottom fish. Everyone smiled as their rods bent repeatedly toward the water.

August 9, 1999

Just after dawn on our first morning back on Olsen after the Nootka Sound trip, son Chas stumbled into the floathouse rubbing sleep from his eyes. When I asked him what brought him in so early, he remarked that he'd been awakened by a pod of killer whales blowing just off Olsen's shore.

Climbing up on the rocks, we saw the pod making its way across False Bay. In the middle was a mature male, distinguished by his towering dorsal fin. We watched the whales until they disappeared around a far point. In the morning quiet, we could hear them blowing kilometers away.

When we kayaked over to the Lasqueti store a bit later, we found that the visiting killer whales had prompted local fishermen to believe that salmon were schooling nearby. This in turn spawned a lot of fishing talk and reports of big fish being caught. But these reports were all vague, with no names attached. Were the salmon really schooling in the bay, or just in the depths of our imaginations?

Lifetimes of fish stories were brought forth from the dusty memories of the patrons in the pub above the dock. Patched up and polished, they were shared with anyone who would listen. Which was everyone, for nobody would interrupt a fish story. These were stories we all wanted to believe, and experiences we all wanted to live. These tales were molded into thousands of silver-sided salmon which we released to join a growing school of dream salmon in the bay.

Walking down the dock, I found myself repeatedly looking into the clear waters below. With each glance I expected to see shadowy flashes that would confirm that all plans should be broken and the day spent fishing.

CHAPTER 35
SMOKED SALMON

*And heaved and heaved, still unrestingly heaved the black sea,
as if its vast tides were a conscience; and the great mundane soul
were in anguish and remorse for the long sin and suffering it had
bred.*

—Herman Melville, *Moby Dick*

August 10, 1999

Today dawned hot and sunny. Seduced by morning heat, I walked to
the small grove of juniper where our hammock hung and surrendered
to its depths with my book. Crickets lulled me into a comforting stupor
as I ghosted past distant suns in the science fiction tale I was reading.
Though I'd had a full night's sleep, I found myself close to dozing. Sweat
dripped slowly from my brow.

Perplexed by a gradual chill, I emerged groggily from my lethargy.
Looking out at the bay, I found a stout breeze blowing up whitecaps.

Sluggish and stupid from all the sun, I was forgetting things that
were usually second nature. Though unsure of why the rising waves were
important, I was nagged by some vague feeling that they were.

When a fishing boat chugged close by Olsen en route to False Bay,
I raised my hand to wave hello. After two more fishing boats and a
yacht came in from the Strait, it finally dawned on me that they were
seeking refuge. The mackerel sky and fleeing vessels were a sure sign of
an approaching storm.

After jogging back to the floathouse, I fetched the Grady and triple-secured it in the lagoon. Though the two anchors off its bow and stern line to shore might have been overkill, they would allow me to sleep that night. The anchor-dragging disappearance of our boat several years ago is indelibly imprinted on my memory, as are the storm tales of my island friends. Now I simply can't relax until I've taken proper precautions for a coming blow.

I'd come to know that the sea doesn't tolerate mistakes. As we had learned firsthand, Komogwa needs just one slip or oversight. Our roofer Wayne told me that his father drowned after a long life on the water as a commercial fisherman. Though he was protected by instincts honed over a lifetime, he perhaps grew inattentive for just a moment. In that instant, his years of experience on the sea counted for naught. Komogwa hovered just below the surface, and dragged him down to an underwater grave.

August 11, 1999

Though yesterday's wind built into a midnight gale, by morning it had blown itself out. After a leisurely breakfast, Theresa and I went over to visit Allen Farrell on the *China Cloud*. With beautiful lines and sturdy construction, both boat and Allen are very well-preserved. We all took our blood pressures and heart rates, and eighty-seven-year-old Allen's matched T's and mine.

Allen said he never felt old until his wife died three years ago. Allen and Sherie had spent a lifetime together cruising the waters of the Northwest and Pacific, loving each other and their life afloat. After her death, he lost weight and started feeling like an old man.

Allen is an accomplished artist, his paintings admired by all. He said he'd paint us a picture of Olsen's floathouse, but wouldn't take any money for it, informing us, "I'm not like that."

Later, on our way over to dinner at Ray and Eve's, we stopped by the *China Cloud* again to drop off some of our freshly smoked salmon. I'd been brining and smoking the fish since our return from Nootka.

For reasons rooted deep in their primitive biology, some fishermen guard their smoking technique as if it were a secret fishing spot. The following recipe is adapted from Tom Piscitelli's, who will have fits of apoplexy when he finds I've released it. This produces the best smoked salmon I have ever tasted, with a wonderfully sweet flavor.

1. Cut filleted salmon into 4" wide chunks. Where fillets are more than 2" thick, lightly cross-score them with a knife. This exposes more of the flesh to the smoke and brine.

2. Prepare a "brine" in multiples of the following, in sufficient quantity to completely cover the fish.

    2 cups brown sugar
    ½ cup salt
    3 tbsp Worcestershire Sauce
    2 tbsp liquid smoke
    Crushed garlic (several cloves)
    1 tbsp ground pepper
    1 tbsp tabasco sauce
    2 tbsp white vinegar
    2 tbsp balsamic vinegar
    Juice squeezed from 2 fresh lemons

    This should form a grainy goo, with a consistency like thick pancake batter. If more liquid is needed to get this consistency, add a dash more vinegar or lemon juice or a shot of white wine.

3. Put the fillets into a bowl and rub the goo all over them. Make sure it gets into the scores on the flesh.

4. Refrigerate for twelve to twenty-four hours, depending on how thick your fillets are and how dry you want your smoked fish.

5. Wash brine off the fish and pat dry with paper towels. Rub slime off the skin. Air-dry for twelve hours in a place where your cat can't get at it. I put my fillets skin side down on my smoker racks to allow the air to circulate around them.

Tom puts his on paper towels (skin side down) on top of newspaper, which helps draw the moisture out. Do this drying at room temperature.

6. Rub brown sugar all over the flesh of the fish after it has air-dried for twelve hours.

7. Smoke for three to six hours, again depending on how thick your fillets are and how dry you like your finished product. I continually add more alder as it ceases smoking.

8. Vacuum pack and freeze for a winter of delighted guests.

August 12, 1999

I awoke this morning to hard rain and wind, and was not at all happy about how uncomfortable these conditions would make the first leg of our journey home to Minter Creek.

The wind blew the boat around as I tried to maneuver in the confines of floathouse cove, making landing and gear transfer frustratingly difficult. Loading the boat in driving rain, we decided it would be safest and driest for Theresa and Ryan to go on the ferry with most of our load. So I ran them and the gear over to the False Bay dock before entering the Strait.

I initially considered following the ferry across, but Chris was game to give it a try on our own. So we cinched down the hoods of our rain coats and headed out into the waves.

The wind was about twenty-five knots, there were big swells and many were breaking. We had to keep the boat off a plane to avoid beating it apart. While our course to French Creek allowed us to quarter the waves and soften the ride somewhat, we took a lot of spray into the cockpit, and one wave came over the side and into the boat.

Chris and I enjoyed the challenge of the big waves, and were completely drenched by the time we reached French Creek. Monitoring Emergency Channel 16 on our radio, we heard of one vessel in need of assistance.

Olsen Island

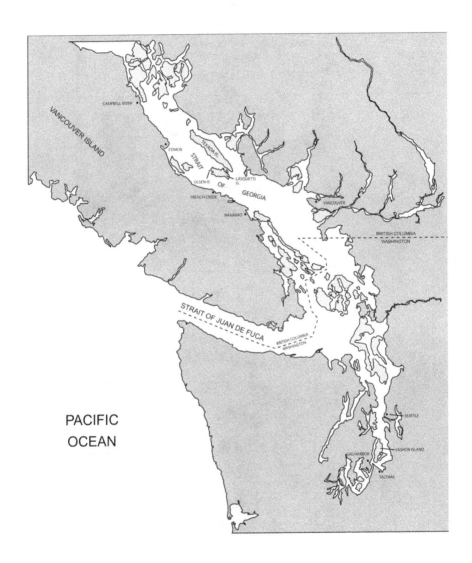

CAMPBELL RIVER

VANCOUVER ISLAND

TEXADA IS.

COMOX

STRAIT

OLSEN IS.

LASQUETTI IS.

FRENCH CREEK

OF GEORGIA

NANAIMO

VANCOUVER

BRITISH COLUMBIA
WASHINGTON

STRAIT OF JUAN DE FUCA

BRITISH COLUMBIA
WASHINGTON

PACIFIC
OCEAN

SEATTLE

GIG HARBOR

VASHON ISLAND

TACOMA

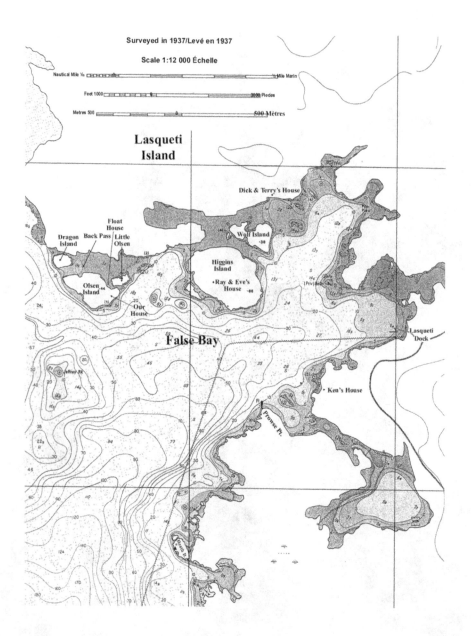

"Reproduced with the permission of the Canadian Hydrographic Service"

"Not to be used for Navigation"

Ryan, Charlie, Chas, Chris & Theresa on the floathouse at low tide

Our Original Outhouse

Fishing at the Finnerty Islands

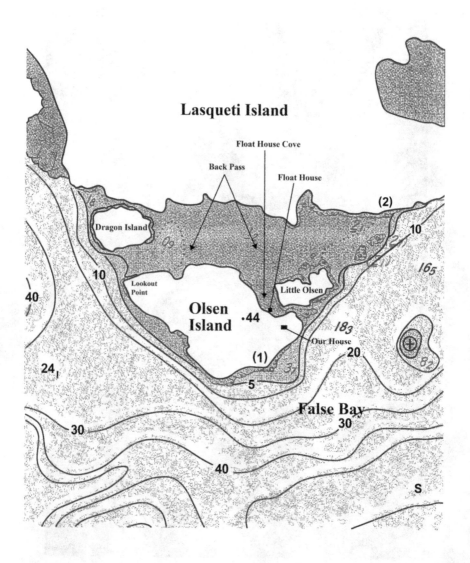

Ken & Charlie

Terry and Dick coming over for dinner

Ray & Eve delighting in their first s'mores

Dick's morning commute in *Rosenante*

Phil, Ryan, Chas & Chris on the floathouse porch at high tide

The *China Cloud* with Allen Farrell at the tiller

Theresa sailing in her kayak

Charlie & Phil with a load of prawns on the bar-b-que

Party Goers arriving at Olsen aboard the *Argent*

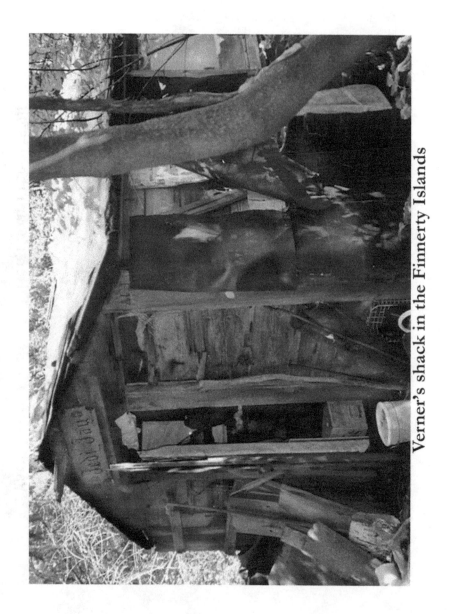

Verner's shack in the Finnerty Islands

Kirsty in *Rosenante*

The Lasqueti ferry bucking through light chop

Peter and *Little Wren*

Carlos and Theresa on Olsen's Floathouse in a very high tide

Aurel Girard - Citizen of the Year

Unloading building materials on Olsen Island.

Charlie & Theresa

CHAPTER 36
OUR BOAT GETS SWAMPED

However baby man may brag of his science and skill ... the sea will insult and murder him, and pulverize the stateliest, stiffest frigate he can make.

—Herman Melville, *Moby Dick*

September 24, 1999

Theresa and I arrived at Olsen on an overcast fall afternoon. The wind was out of the southeast, and built to about forty knots in the evening. We were glad to be safe and warm in the floathouse. Our new homestead stood partly built on the hill above us, but wasn't even close to being habitable yet.

September 25, 1999

What a night! The throaty roar of the wind made it sound like the gods themselves were snarling at us.

Sometime after dark the wind shifted 180 degrees, lashing us with fifty-knot gusts. Though we managed to sleep in the rocking floathouse, in the middle of the night we were jolted awake by a loud crashing noise. Theresa thought it was a big tree coming down, and I was convinced our new house was blowing apart.

In my grogginess, I mistook moonlight for dawn, but when I went out to examine the destruction, I realized it was only one in the morning. Peering up at our new house, I saw that a large tarp, which had been stretched over our recently built fireplace, had ripped loose at one end. New and hard, it let forth streams of machine gun reports as it snapped in the windstorm. Concluding that there was no way to secure it without being blown away myself, I went back to bed.

We awoke in the morning to find our aluminum boat swamped next to the floathouse. The shifting wind had blown it against the float logs under the overhang of the deck, and the rising tide had gradually forced one gunwale under the water. While still in my pajamas, I bailed out the boat and gave the motor a hopeful pull. Luckily, it started on the first try.

As I stared at the waves, which were running completely opposite to those I had seen yesterday evening, I realized I had to secure our boat against all possible winds, not just the one blowing when I tied it up.

By then, the flapping tarp had been beaten soft as a chamois and was fairly quiet.

***

As neighbor Ray says, we live in "the No Bullshit Zone." Last night's wind wasn't even storm-force, but big things can happen here in our sustained winds and the seas they push up.

To get some perspective on the area's weather and sea conditions, I sought out the tales of Frank Barker, who had spent his life on tugs doing marine construction. Barker worked year-round on Northwest waters for thirty-eight years, through days and nights in all kinds of weather. He built docks, dredged harbors, and laid submarine cables. He worked twenty-four-hour shifts on the Strait of Juan de Fuca in "heavy weather and swells," and rebuilt the Hood Canal Floating Bridge after it was blown apart in a storm.

As recorded in a family record of Captain Barker's exploits, he encountered some daunting storms that tested both him and his boats.

"During one tow to Seattle with 2 barges, Captain Barker and his deckhand Brett Barker encountered sustained winds of 60–78 mph. The *Ruby 6* started having engine problems and ... was starting to lose headway when the 135-ft. *Hunter* came to their assistance. The *Hunter* came close enough for their deckhand to toss Brett a line. Brett had tied himself on so he wouldn't be washed overboard. He caught the line, secured the barge, and the *Ruby 6* continued for 14 hours to ride out the storm in Elliot Bay" (Olsen 1998).

On another job, Captain Barker was working in Bellingham Bay near another company's barge of materials. "The 220-ft. barge was tied for the night on the buoy, when the seas got so rough that the barge broke loose and landed on the breakwater. Captain Barker and Larry Olson floated a line to the barge and pulled it off the beach in 72-mph winds" (Olsen 1998).

Though these experiences were harrowing, Captain Barker indicated their challenges didn't match those found on the Strait of Georgia. Describing one job in the Strait, he noted that it was the "Toughest job ever worked due to large swells and wind about 75% of the time" (Olsen 1998).

Chapter 37
Beachcombing

Treasures landed on our doorstep every day ... of all the pleasures of island living, beachcombing is by far the most exciting and rewarding pastime.

—David Conover, *Once Upon an Island*

November 12, 1999

This morning I embarked on the ferry out of French Creek on gray water under grayer skies. The Strait was smooth and shiny under soft clouds that reached down to hug the distant islands.

I spent most of the day working on the house with contractor Dick. While absorbed in some construction detail, I occasionally looked up and drifted away into the world of water and sky. Then I shook myself and plugged back into the project.

After dinner with Ray and Eve on Higgins Island, I came back to an unheated floathouse, but it was time for bed so I felt no need to make a fire. The floathouse was cold, though not unbearably so. In my sleeping bag with my socks and pajamas on, I was as warm as fresh toast.

I put the fluorescent lantern in my bag with me to see if I could warm it up enough to stop its flickering. When this failed, I stood the propane lantern on a cook pot next to me so I could read in bed.

November 13, 1999

I slept soundly and awoke when it was still dark. I was cozy and warm, though the temperature inside the floathouse was about four degrees Celsius (forty degrees Fahrenheit), the same as it was outside. Just my face was cold where it poked out of my sleeping bag. An eagle cried nearby in the gloom, letting me know I wasn't alone in braving the morning chill.

Last night had been as black as a raven's wing. When I came home from Ray and Eve's, I found it difficult to pick out the silhouette of Olsen and keep off the rocks. I couldn't even see the entrance to the back pass until I was hard upon it.

My head lamp had been no help until I was very close to shore. Even then it was more of a hindrance, as it blinded me when it lit up my steaming breath.

***

After breakfast I went over to visit Allen Farrell on the *China Cloud*, which was anchored in the protected waters of Mud Bay.

At age eighty-seven, Allen still lives on the *China Cloud*, a sailboat he built out of beachcombed wood. A lifelong hunter-gatherer, he has lived off what the land and sea provided.

As we shared a leisurely morning of tea and talk, Allen gave me a guided tour through two books of paintings he'd done. These were created out of two old novels someone had given him, each page patiently gessoed white before he began his work. He also showed me some of his recent larger paintings, which he'd painted on scavenged tar paper.

Theresa and I had scratched our heads trying to figure out what to give Allen in return for the floathouse painting he's doing for us. Allen cooks in a battered old aluminum pot that floated in on the tide, and he takes pride in the fact that he found it. His dishes are old castoffs from the free store, and that's why he likes them. We could give him a pot or dishes, but they'd just be nice things, not found or salvaged, and thus totally lacking in interest.

Our solution was to get him some acrylics, a sketchbook, and some canvases. But then we had to invent a ruse that would make the gifts acceptable to him. "Bought them at a garage sale—almost for free!" I thought about squeezing some of the paint out of the tubes, so they'd look used, and thus perhaps be more enchanting to him.

All worked out well, however. Allen's eyes sparkled when I unwrapped the painting supplies, and he rubbed his hands together in joy when he saw that I'd also bought six burlap bags of wood for his boat's stove.

When I had previously given Allen the canvas to paint our picture on, it had been part of a two-pack. The second canvas had been a gift for him.

Apparently I didn't make this clear. True to his generous nature, Allen had painted *two* pictures of the floathouse. On the spot, I decided to send one down to Larry Aites, who'd hand-built the floathouse out of wood *he'd* beachcombed. Allen had introduced Larry to this area and educated him in the fine art of beachcombing, and I knew the picture would bring back fond memories of Larry's years on Olsen Island.

***

There was a lot of drift in the bay today from unusually high tides and the previous week of wind. A miles-long "tide line" snaked north along Lasqueti and into False Bay, then through and beyond the Finnerties. Formed by the collision of two currents, this floating junkyard was a collection of eelgrass, stray logs, frayed rope, old boards, and innumerable other debris.

I was drawn by the occasional spot of color in this tangled mass, which more often than not was a piece of Styrofoam or discarded oil container. But my search was also rewarded with several treasures.

I found a nice commercial prawn-trap float, a net float, a blue seat cushion, and a black buoy with a crab trap hanging below it. All this from an afternoon in my boat, poking around in False Bay, baycombing rather than beachcombing.

My affection for scavenging the waters and shores reaches all the way back to my Vashon Island childhood. There I loved walking the beaches in search of agates and arrowheads.

Phil and I, together with friends Rob Williams and Scott Jones, were known as the "Beach Rats." At our favorite beach we'd spend hours leap-frogging one another down the shore, trying to be the first to arrive at patches of unsearched rocks. While hunting we'd talk reverently of special agates we'd seen in legendary Vashon collections. Occasionally, one of us would break into a short run in the certainty that such a jewel would be poking out of the sand just ahead.

My favorite beachcombing days at Olsen are in the late fall or early spring.

All summer long, boaters and fishermen forget to tie on fenders, cut loose buoys with their props, break nets, knock cushions off their decks, or simply have their possessions washed overboard. People living on the beach lose their belongings to the rising tide. This scattering of goodies inevitably comes to roost on the miles and miles of uninhabited shore bordering the Strait of Georgia.

The first major blows of fall are always accompanied by atmospheric lows, which allow high tides to bulge up higher than normal. These surges float the beaches' accumulation of lost articles. Drawn off the shore by receding waves, this flotsam is blown northward by prevailing winds until it washes into the rocky arms of an island. In my case, these arms are the shores of the Finnerties, which lie north of many miles of open water.

In the aftermath of a good fall storm, I return to my boat from beachcombing with arms full of bounty.

During my fall visits to the Finnerties, I have never seen another person there. I take extra care clambering over rocks and logs, since part of the lure of beachcombing is not telling anyone where I'm going. It could be days before someone might find me if I fell and were seriously hurt.

Spring can also be a great time to beachcomb. If I am lucky enough to find a small island that has seen no visitors over the winter, I can raid its storehouse of accumulated treasures.

***

Though I'm always excited by my beachcombing finds, they're rather mundane when compared to the tantalizing artifacts that have fetched up on our coast.

In 1979, the *Beaufort Sea* "was bottom-dragging about 15 sea miles off the mouth of Juan de Fuca Strait when something became tangled in the vessel's net on the ocean floor, at a depth of about 90 fathoms. Skipper Mike Tyne ordered the net hauled back up, and in it were several shards of wood and a large urn, which was later identified as Asian and probably about 300 years old" (Glavin 2000).

In 1956, a boy on Saturna Island found an Asian earthenware head, believed to be 2,000 years old, and in 1961 a fisherman walking the beach near Cape Cook found a Korean burial urn.

On October 25, 1882, the *Victoria Colonist* reported the discovery of thirty Asian coins in northern British Columbia. Experts believed that these brass coins were some 1,500 years old.

These, and similar finds, are evidence that wreckage from the Orient has been landing on the Pacific Coast for thousands of years. To First Nations People, such treasures were evidence of an alien world with vastly superior technology. In the Tlinglit story describing the origin of copper, it was said to come from the sea in the form of a canoe.

Doubtless such wreckage reinforced the aboriginal belief that god-like beings lived beneath the waves. If a wreck floated up, Komogwa had torn it apart, and its missing cargo and crew would be found in his underwater palace.

Yet more than just exotic wreckage has found its way to our coast.

On September 26, 1985, Kazukio Sakemoto set out fishing from his home in Owase, Japan. The wind came up, and he never came back. Eighteen months later his boat, the *Kaza Maru*, drifted ashore in the Queen Charlotte Islands.

George Quimby, a researcher of such occurrences, has concluded that over 180 Asian boats washed up on our coast in the thousand years before the first Europeans sailed here. "Bad storms … could easily disable coastal merchant and fishing vessels. Once a junk was helplessly adrift … the North Pacific Current destined the vessel for a trans-Pacific voyage" (Glavin 2000).

Amazingly, a few of these Asian craft arrived on our coast with some of their crew alive. In 1782, the survivors of a shattered Japanese junk were picked off the Aleutian Islands by Russian fur traders. While the American *Forrester* was cruising off the entrance to the Strait of Juan de Fuca in 1813, she encountered a dismasted junk that had been drifting for eighteen months. Three of the original thirty-five man crew were still alive. Three years later, the *Forrester* spied another dismasted junk off Santa Barbara, California. Incapacitated in a Japanese storm over a year earlier, it had drifted across the Pacific. Several of its crew peered up hollow-eyed at their rescuers when the *Forrester* came alongside.

In 1832, a Japanese ship lost its rudder and mast in rough seas. Carried by the currents for fourteen months, it eventually washed ashore near Cape Flattery, where the Makah Indians salvaged its remains. Three of the original fourteen-man crew survived this crossing and were eventually returned to Japan.

Even more intriguing is the evidence of *intentional* medieval Asian visits to our coast. "In the oral traditions of coastal peoples, there are a variety of stories that hint of the possibility of 'pre-contact' Asian voyagers. On Vancouver Island's West Coast, there were stories of mariners in ships preceding white people who were said to eat 'maggots,' which has led to speculation about [visits by] rice-eating sailors" (Glavin 2000).

These visitors may have come from China, which had developed an oceangoing fleet and transoceanic trade long before Columbus set sail. This fleet was substantially expanded by emperor Zhu Di in the early 1400s, as part of his audacious plan to "'sail the oceans of the world and chart them, impressing and intimidating foreign rulers, bringing the entire world into China's 'tribute system'" (Menzies 2003).

The heart of this fleet was its treasure ships, immense junks that were specially designed for extended ocean travel. Each ship contained sixteen watertight compartments that would keep the ship afloat even if some were breached. The junks' prows were reinforced to smash through the fiercest ocean storms, and channels were placed on both sides of the bow to funnel water to internal compartments, whose alternating filling and draining helped dampen the ships pitching motion in rough seas. Adjustable side keels could be raised or lowered to increase stability, and above them semisubmersible sea anchors were mounted, which could be pitched into the water to soften the ship's rolling.

Setting sail under the command of Admiral Zheng He in 1421, these ships appear to have fulfilled emperor Zhu Di's globe-spanning dreams. For according to many accounts in official Chinese history, which seem to be supported by physical evidence found on our continent, parts of Zheng He's Chinese fleet reached the Americas long before the first Europeans.

Though traditional Eurocentric histories herald Columbus, Magellan, and Cook as the first to chart the Americas and the world's oceans, these places are shown on a variety of maps that *predate* these explorers' sailings.

The Pacific coast of North America, including Vancouver Island and the Queen Charlottes, is clearly depicted on a chart made in 1507 by Martin Waldsemuller. This is striking in that the first European to explore this coast was Hernando de Alaicon in 1540.

At the times these charts were made, prior to European exploration of the Pacific, Europeans *were* traveling to Calicut (modern Calcutta) and other ports where the Chinese traded. And in the writings of these European traders, there are descriptions of Chinese ships with the type of detail that could only have been observed by being aboard. In his book *1421–The Year China Discovered America* (2003), Gavin Menzies proposes that the Chinese had previously explored and charted much of the world and shared their maps with the visiting Europeans, who then conveyed the information home to European cartographers. According to Menzies, these mapmakers incorporated this Chinese knowledge into the charts carried by the first European explorers.

Zheng He's fleet was immense, and as would be expected in the exploration of unknown waters, many ships were lost en route. Though Chinese wrecks on the west coast of North America might be explained by transpacific drifting of disabled ships, such wrecks have also been found in Mexico, Peru, Chile, the Caribbean (found by Christopher Columbus himself), and the eastern US state of Virginia, places where they could not have reached by accidental drifting.

One west coast wreck in particular seems to harken from Zheng He's fleet. Resting in a sandbank of the Sacramento River over a hundred miles inland from the open sea, its location indicates purposeful up-current sailing. Its dimensions are similar in shape and size to those of Zheng He's trading junks, and fragments of wood extracted from the wreck have been tentatively identified as coming from a conifer native to China. These fragments have been carbon-dated to 1410, easily within the construction period of vessels in Zheng He's fleet, and rice brought up from the wreck has been identified as indigenous to China and unknown in the Americas at the time of the ship's demise.

Besides these ships, there is a variety of other evidence suggesting fairly intimate early Chinese contact with our coast.

When the first Europeans arrived in Mexico, they found lacquerware flourishing in several Mexican states. This Mexican lacquerware was produced using highly complex and specialized processes that were suspiciously similar to those utilized in China.

The teaching of such complicated processes took time, indicating at least temporary stays ashore. And as the Chinese and local peoples grew to know to one another, they exchanged more than ideas. "Recent DNA evidence shows conclusively that local people in Mexico, Panama, Columbia, Venezuela, and Peru share Chinese DNA" (Menzies 2003). This DNA is of a different character than that coming from the original Asians who crossed the Bering Strait and spread throughout the Americas.

When the Chinese set sail from our coast to continue their journey, they took indigenous plants with them, as indicated by the variety of native plants from the Americas that had been introduced to the east before the first Europeans arrived. On their voyages of discovery, European explores found papayas, tomatoes, and sweet potatoes on Easter Island, sweet potatoes in Hawaii, and maize in the Philippines and China, all plants that were indigenous to the Americas. Stone tools used to grind maize were found in the wreck of a junk in the Philippines, considered to have foundered there about 1423, consistent in both time and place with the return voyage of the Chinese fleet.

In the *I Yu Thu Chih*, a book whose title roughly translates to "The Illustrated Record of Strange Countries," the author-artist documents the people, plants, and animals known to the Chinese in 1430. Included are animals indigenous to the Americas, including a jaguar, armadillo, and llama, all probably encountered during Zheng He's voyage of discovery.

According to Menzies, "A mountain of evidence—wrecks, blood groups, architecture, painting, customs, linguistics, clothes, technologies, artifacts, dye-stuff, plants, and animals … points to a pervasive Chinese influence the length of the Pacific Coast of Central and South America—" Though such evidence is not as pervasive in the coastal Northwest, there are sufficient remains here to indicate that Zheng He's fleet spent at least some time in our area.

In Haida lore, there is a tale of an alien people sailing in from the west. The Italian mapmaker Antonio Zalta labeled the Queen Charlotte Islands "Coloma dei Chinesi," indicating a considerable legacy left by the visiting Chinese. This is further suggested by the forty Squamish and Chinese words that appear to have common roots. The oral histories of British Columbia's Squamish Indians tell of Chinese trading visits that preceded the first Europeans, and as has been detected in other indigenous American peoples, post-Beringia Chinese DNA has been found in people of the Queen Charlotte Islands.

A surprising amount of Chinese artifacts have turned up on the British Columbia coast, including a pre-Columbian Chinese lamp, sacks of Chinese coins, vases, storage jars, statues, votive offerings, urns, and carved-stone position markers. When considered with the other evidence, they suggest at least some purposeful contact with the Orient preceding the arrival of the first Europeans.

Chapter 38
A Scare in the Dark

Our fear of monsters in the night probably has its origins far back in the evolution of our primate ancestors, whose tribes were pruned by horrors whose shadows continue to elicit our monkey screams in dark theaters.

—Paul Shepherd, *The Others*

... A voyager will encounter things that are not supposed to be there.

—Terry Glavin, *The Last Great Sea*

February 8, 2000

On another winter trip to work on our emerging home, today I pulled up to Olsen on calm waters. Idling slowly toward shore, I saw that as our crew had moved into the "finishing" stage of the project, their imaginative craftsmanship had become more apparent.

Sylvain has been inspired in his rockwork, finding perfectly angled stones for corners and weaving in curved juniper trunks over windows. The stone steps he laid from beach to house followed the curves of the natural rock they abut.

Ray had mounted huge bronze portholes salvaged from a sunken tug in each of our boathouse doors, and affixed large marine cleats to serve as door handles.

I was glad when Dick told me that Verner would be doing our interior painting. With his artistic touch, Verner will hopefully be able to achieve our goal of making the interior look like weathered driftwood.

When we landed in the lagoon, I tossed my gear onto the floathouse porch and went to work at the homesite above. Coming down off the island later for a break, I saw a raven fly guiltily away from my bags with something brown in his beak. Perhaps "warily" would be a better word to describe his departure, as I'm sure that ravens feel nothing like guilt.

I knew something was amiss by the way the raven looked back at me as he flew, and by the unusual thing that he carried, which was not something you'd find on the beach. I finally realized it was one of my bagels! Stop thief!

This was a problem, as I had purchased my food sparingly with a plan for every meal. I had just seen tomorrow's lunch fly off into the sky.

The raven had made short work of the grocery bags I'd left on the porch. I found the rest of my bagels on the beach full of peck marks, though luckily they didn't get wet. I wasn't sure if ravens carried disease, or if their beaks were fouled from picking through garbage and carrion all day. Concluding that hunger was worse than any disease I'd catch, I decided to eat the bagels anyway.

I shared my raven tale that night over dinner at Ray and Eve's, where everyone at the table had a crow or raven story.

In an experience like mine, Ray surprised a raven that had pecked its way through a cardboard box and was robbing him of his groceries. On another day, two ravens sat on his garbage can. They grabbed the edge with their claws and beat their wings until the can tipped over and the lid fell off, disgorging their sought-after meal.

Last spring, Ray went to a grocery store in Parksville and beheld a crow flying around inside. It had come in through the doors that morning and had been searching for an exit ever since. Arriving at the checkout counter, Ray said silently to the crow, "If you go to the window, I'll let you out." Immediately the crow flew over and perched on a nearby window sill, whereupon Ray walked over, picked him up, and carried him outside.

Allen Farrell told of a time when he and Sherri pulled into a marina after a good day of fishing. He set his fish on the dock and covered them with newspaper, then went to a nearby boat to chat up a friend. Immediately a crow flew over, removed the newspaper, and began pecking the fish. It was unfazed by people walking close by, but the minute Allen turned his head to look, the crow flew away. When Allen again turned away from the fish, the crow returned to them. Allen alerted his friends to what was happening, and then played this game of cat and mouse several more times for their amusement.

An acquaintance of Allen's died some years back, and a friend went over to clean out the dead man's house. Crows are well-known for their pilfering, and in Indian lore are considered tricksters. When Allen's friend went into the house, a crow hopped in behind him. It stayed inside the whole day, left only when the movers went home, then came back the next day and did the same thing. It made no attempt to take anything, just watched all that went on. Allen noted that his dead friend was an irrepressible jokester, and proposed that the crow was watching over the spirit of one of his departed brethren.

Morgan told of a friend who had become very frustrated with the cawing and dive-bombing of a crow. Intending to scare it away, he got his gun and fired an unaimed shot into the air, whereupon the crow tumbled from the sky and came to rest on the man's feet. Filled with guilt and disbelief, he stared at the unmoving crow and bent over to pick it up. The crow opened its eyes, cocked its head, stared at the man for a long moment, and then got up and flew off. According to the gunman, there was no evidence the crow had been shot.

Ravens are larger than crows with thicker beaks. Crows are often found near urban settings, while ravens typically live in more remote terrain. Crows and ravens are found in all parts of the world, from the arctic to the tropics, except South America.

A group of crows is called a "murder of crows." This name probably evolved from their association with battlefields, execution sites, and cemeteries, where in the past they scavenged on human remains. In England, a tombstone is still sometimes called a raven-stone.

Crows are very effective urban scavengers, and their numbers are soaring along with the Northwest's human population. They feast on french fries spilling out of dumpsters, roadkill on highways, and earthworms on lawns.

The average life span of crows and ravens in the wild is seven to eight years, though in captivity they have lived for thirty years.

Crows and ravens are among the most intelligent animals around us, with excellent memories and clear problem-solving skills. They may use a sharp stick to help them dig insects out of the ground, and know just when to jump out of the way of traffic as they feast on roadkill.

In Seattle, crows drop sea snails on waterfront streets, wait on the phone lines overhead, then fly down to eat the snails after their shells have been cracked open by passing cars.

In his studies of crows and ravens, University of Washington wildlife biologist John Marzluff has come to appreciate their uncanny memory. They can pick Marzluff and his researchers out of the 30,000 students that throng the university campus, and will not go near the baited traps they set. Says Marzluff, "If men had wings and bore black feathers, few of them would be clever enough to be crows."

***

After the last of the crow stories, I bid my friends goodnight. Closing the door on warmth and light, I stepped into a granular dark that absorbed the glow from Ray's house the way sand soaks up water. Standing quietly on the porch, I could sense that the clouds hung low, shuttering out the moon and stars.

The night yawned deeply beneath the trees, revealing stump molars and bracken serpent tongues. In gloom that was too still, I stopped breathing for a moment as my stomach twisted inside me.

The woods closed in around me as I felt my way down the path to the beach. Though my rational mind told me there was nothing to fear, the rest of me wondered what predators lurked among the sullen trees I stumbled through.

The path was rutted and muddy and roots reached out to trip me. Momentarily, I saw forest eyes that were quickly gone. Shapes shifted in the underbrush and shadowed me down the trail, betrayed by an occasional cracking branch. The out-buildings along the trail were not in their usual order, and the path seemed much longer than I remembered it to be.

Clambering down the steep bank to the water, I found that a small stream ran over the rocks where I sought my footholds, coating them with slime.

After seating myself in my dew-covered boat, I pushed off into the black bay. Rocking silently, I felt vastly alone. In the deep silence that shrouded the bay, I strained my ears to catch some hint of what lay before me. Failing utterly to pierce the gloom, I felt my imagination take flight. Breathing shallowly through dilated nostrils, I smelled either some terror's rancid breath or the stink of my own fear.

Vainly trying to stare tunnels through the dark, I was as blind as some cave fish whose sightless ancestors had swum deep underground for untold generations. In an odd reversal of the ways of light and shadow, I had entered a deeper darkness when I left the woods and put out on the water.

Making my way through the gloom, I was convinced that ancient things glided below me. The currents themselves seemed troubled, whispering of unseen turmoil beneath my keel. Peering through eyes distorted by fear, I suddenly pushed the tiller hard away from something big and black in front of me.

Shuddering in the certainty that I had disturbed something better left alone, and instantly unsure of what I'd seen, I jerked the motor the opposite way to avoid a collision.

Tentacles of giant squid slithered through my panicking mind as breaching killer whales tore through the surface of my imagination. More troubling was my certainty that these monsters rode remora-like on the back of some huger presence that would drive the bay skyward when it breached. Primitive emotions washed over me, scuttling forth from the part of my brain I share with lizards and frogs.

As I tried to calm myself, I reasoned that perhaps I'd only seen some reflection on the waves. My heart raced as I pointed my boat toward home with the throttle at dead slow.

I leaned forward in my seat as I approached Olsen, fruitlessly plumbing the gloom. Though I knew the island was ahead, I couldn't tell whether it was ten or a hundred meters away. Was I headed into the back passage, or onto the rocks next to it? The black against black gave me no hint of outline or distance.

Turning on my headlight to search for the shore, I recoiled from the apparition of my own breath, a squid-like wraith that sought to wrap its tendrils around my head. Frightened and blinded by the steam, I quickly shut it off again.

When I closed on Olsen, I saw something crouching at the water's edge, moving slowly back and forth. But in a moment this animal became my buoy, bobbing in the waves offshore.

As I tried to tie a bowline in the dark with my frayed rope, my fingers were clumsy with cold. While balancing between the boat and rocks, I knew I was courting trouble. The safety of my boat depended on that knot, and *my* safety depended on not falling in the water.

Once inside the floathouse, I hurried to get the propane lantern going. Peering out into the gloom, I shuddered as the night's scares jumped back into my mind.

I knew these fears were ancient things, survival instincts from the dawn of our species. When early humans passed their nights on Africa's plains, the ones that lived were the ones who stayed awake in fear. Rattling the spear, stoking the fire, talking to the dark—performing rituals to keep the night's beasts away.

This ancient blood coursed through my veins. The night was dark, deeply so, and I was afraid.

Chapter 39
Verner Meets Komogwa

To an Islander, the greatest of all hazards are at sea.
                    —David Conover, *Once Upon an Island*

April 29, 2000

Today dawned grey and calm, with a sky that sulked and brooded. Though its anger was hidden for the moment, there were signs that a weather change was coming.

Neighbor Verner awoke in the small cabin he was housesitting on Jenkins Island, which lies south of our island off Lasqueti's western shore. After relieving himself in the woods, he walked to the island's weather side. Standing on the rough rock of the shore, he looked across the Strait toward distant Comox, where friends were expecting him the following day.

Verner's plan was to kayak across the Strait to Flora Islet, a small, uninhabited gem that huddles near Hornby Island. He would camp there for the night and leave for Comox the following morning. As he had told friends, however, he might stay at Flora for two nights if the weather was especially nasty.

This trip wasn't a necessity, but Verner didn't want to disappoint those waiting for him. He had no phone or other way of notifying them if he decided not to come.

Years before, Verner had paddled from the US to Lasqueti, though he never officially entered Canada. As he said to our friend Dick Grinnell, "I never saw any sign telling me to stay out!"

Since then, Verner had lived on different islands near Lasqueti, and spent the last few on one of the Finnerty Islands. Staying in an old fisherman's cabin that was up a discreet path from the beach, he led a squatter's life that was an area tradition, but had been legislated out of existence years ago. Our friend Ray described this home as "more hovel than cabin, really just a pile of rotting wood."

Verner's home was one small room that he had to stoop to enter, heated by Ray's cast- off woodstove. Light came from kerosene lamps, and water from a plastic swimming pool that caught the rain. To keep things dry from the showers that streamed through the roof, Verner had covered the inside with scavenged scraps of plastic sheeting.

Verner's kayak helped him catch dinners of fish, and was his only means of contact with the outside world. He had paddled in all types of weather as he headed back and forth from his home on the Finnerties, and knew the dangers of life on the sea. He had told his girlfriend, Reine, that he felt he would die on the water and would not fight when the sea reached out to claim him.

In hopes of helping Verner survive such a nightmare, Reine had given Verner a Mustang exposure suit, a full-body floatation garment designed for extreme immersion events.

Verner made the twenty-kilometer crossing from Jenkins to Flora Islet, enjoying calm waters under steely grey skies. He was a man who treasured his solitude, and this was solitude at its finest. After nosing ashore on Flora, he carried his kayak up to the logs at the top of the beach and made camp in a small clearing overlooking the Strait.

April thirtieth dawned ambiguously. After crawling out of his sleeping bag, Verner stretched and searched the sky and water for clues to the day's weather. Though nothing of any consequence had been predicted, a moderate wind was blowing. A wind that could blow itself out over the course of the day or grow into something more ominous.

Verner considered his options as he stood on the beach with the wind ruffling his grey hair. A strong man in his mid 50s, he was an experienced paddler. Experienced enough to evaluate the possibilities carefully when there was a chance of building weather.

The most direct route from Flora to Comox would cover twenty-six kilometers, most of it through the open waters of the Strait of Georgia.

A more protected route lay through the channel between Hornby and Denman Islands. But the wind was out of the Southeast, and Verner knew he would have to paddle through beam seas to reach this inside passage. Chop in the channel would be aggravated by the wide, shallow shelves around the islands, and currents there would be more pronounced. This route would mean extra hours of travel and potentially rougher conditions. Yes, he thought, its protection was only illusory. A course through the open waters of the Strait would be safer.

Verner donned his exposure suit and broke camp. After stowing his gear aboard, he carried his craft down the beach to the water. Uneven rocks crunched under his feet and small crabs scurried to find shelter as he passed.

As a safeguard in case the wind did blow up, he tied his sea anchor to the kayak's stern and tucked it inside his spray skirt.

When Verner paddled into the open water of the Strait, he felt the wind freshen behind him. His hair began to whip into his eyes, causing him some small irritation. Soon, however, it was wet with spray and bothered him no more.

By then he had other things to worry about.

The first real indication of what was coming was the arrival of a low swell. Verner knew that such a swell raced out in front of the wind producing it, and he began to weigh his options.

Pushing back upwind to Flora would be a battle and paddling beam to the swells to Hornby Island would be foolhardy.

Thus, Verner continued his downwind course, stroking quicker and harder as he tried to outrun the coming gale.

The wind increased steadily to twenty-five knots and gusted over thirty, which pushed up big waves on top of the underlying swell. The resulting peaks frequently toppled over, throwing thousands of kilos of water forward in an avalanche of froth.

Verner now had several pressing challenges to deal with, and the most worrisome was his growing speed. The big waves were rushing forward at over ten knots, and when they were in phase with the swells beneath them, they lifted up his kayak and threw it forward in an uncontrollable surge.

What Verner feared most was a broach, for as his kayak planed forward on the wave faces, it lost its track in the water and slewed sideways. Only by steering aggressively was he able to keep it from turning broadside to the breaking waves.

In an attempt to slow his progress, Verner somehow managed to deploy his sea anchor. Though this held his stern into the wind and waves and minimized the chance of a broach, it also pulled him under the breakers that overtook him and severely compromised his maneuverability.

That afternoon, a salvager from Cortez Island was making his way across the Strait between Marina and Cortez Islands, far to the north of where Verner had been paddling. From a lifetime of experience on these waters, the salvager knew that southeasterly winds blew a floating bounty northward. If he was lucky, he'd find some logs washed out of the protective booms of a passing tug.

At 1:19 PM, the salvager spotted something that brought a scowl to his face. In the distance, he saw a red kite blowing around in the wind, held back by an object it was dragging through the waves. Approaching closer, he realized that he'd come across something he didn't want to find.

At the end of the kite's line was a kayak full of water, with no one aboard.

After some tricky maneuvering in the wind and waves, the salvager hauled the kayak onto his boat. Searching through it, he found a small collection of personal effects: a pair of glasses, a toothbrush, a notebook, and some camping gear.

In the grim realization that the kayak's owner was probably in the water somewhere to the south, at 2:19 PM the salvager called to the Coast Guard on Emergency Channel 16.

The Coast Guard and its Search and Rescue Team flew into a whirlwind of action, as chronicled in the feverish entries from their Marine Incident Log:

"2:31: Task *Point Race* and *Manyberries* to Marina Island.

2:36: Task Labrador Helicopter by telephone.

2:40: Task 442 Helicopter. Search 3 mile radius around point where kayak found, then area boxed in by adjacent islands.

> 2:42: Task *Mallard* to search around Savory, Hernando, Mittlesuatch Islands.
>
> 2:48: Task *Haida Spirit*, search Viner Point to Center Islet, through Uganda Passage to E. Side Marina Island, if safe.
>
> 2:54: Task *Ricker.*
>
> 3:06: *Bonnie May* at Twin Island offers help."

Within thirty minutes, five Coast Guard boats, two helicopters, and a handful of civilian vessels had joined in the search. The "Prime Area" was identified as the waters surrounding the point where the kayak was found, and those to the north where its occupant was expected to drift. As the vessels and helicopters completed their assigned searches without success, they were directed to other parts of the prime area, sometimes repeatedly.

The Coast Guard didn't know who the person in the water was, when he'd been dumped overboard, or where he had been paddling. All they had was the call from the salvager and the location where the kayak was found.

The wind at Cape Mudge was now blowing thirty knots from the southeast, and the only clues to the location of the person in the water was the kayak itself. The waters around it and to the north seemed the logical places to scour. They hoped their guess was correct, as someone's life hung in the balance.

What they didn't know was that Verner had been paddling far south of where they were looking for him.

By about 3:40 PM, the Coast Guard had made a preliminary review of the contents of the kayak and concluded that the person on board was "Art Ways, of General Delivery, Lasqueti Island." "Art Ways" was a false identity that Verner used in his dealings with Canada's officialdom, and his quest for anonymity now worked against him. For when the Coast Guard called the Lasqueti Hotel and the proprietor checked the bar to see if anyone knew Art Ways, he was answered with only blank stares. The crowd of regulars included some who knew Verner well, but not one of them had ever heard of Art Ways.

Verner was an eccentric man who valued his privacy, and piercing the veil of his identity took time. But with his body temperature dropping by the minute, Verner had precious little time to spare.

As the helicopters and boats were directed to search further north, the Coast Guard scoured the notebooks from the kayak. When they came upon several phone numbers, they called them all in a hurried hunt for information. Luckily, some of the numbers were those of Verner's close friends.

By 5:00 PM, the Coast Guard determined the kayak belonged to Verner, but it took another hour and a half to discover where he'd been paddling.

That knowledge momentarily stunned the rescue teams to silence, as they soberly realized Verner had been kayaking fifty kilometers south of where they'd been searching.

With dogged determination, officers at the rescue center shifted the search south. Hurriedly feeding data on Verner's route into the search and rescue computer, along with information on tides, wind, and sea state, they plotted several "drifts" for a loose kayak and a person in the water.

While the search teams now had something specific to pursue, they realized this critical information had probably come too late. As they soberly noted in their search log that the survival time for a fifty-year-old male was a "maximum of six hours," all knew that it had been over five hours since the salvager spotted Verner's kayak. And worse still, that the kayak had probably blown empty for several hours before it was found.

With dimming prospects of performing an actual rescue, the search team directed their efforts to the shorelines of Lasqueti and other nearby islands. All hoped that Verner had somehow made it to a beach, soaked and cold, but still alive.

Verner's kayak was swamped when it was found, with the kite aloft, the paddle jammed firmly in the cockpit, and the sea anchor deployed. Although there was no evidence of a collision with the kayak, officials later reported that Verner had a knot on his head from something striking him there.

It is safe to conclude that Verner had made it part way from Flora to Comox, where a breaking wave caught him, and drove his kayak down into a broach and over. After a quick and futile attempt to roll himself upright, Verner no doubt pushed himself out of his craft, holding onto it with one hand. In his other hand, he held tight to his paddle. In the melee, another wave must have smashed his head against the kayak. Though his boat was full of water, its internal flotation kept it from sinking. After rolling it back cockpit-side up, Verner jammed his paddle into the opening.

Now holding on with two hands, Verner had time to think. He attempted to bail the kayak out, but the waves continued to break over the boat and fill it. In the rough seas, weighted down by his water-filled boots and exposure suit, he found that reboarding was impossible.

It seems unlikely that Verner would have had his kite up in a thirty-knot gale. In winds of that strength, the kite would have aggravated problems of control. The fact that his kite was found aloft suggests that Verner launched it while in the water, hoping to drag himself to shore.

Positioning himself in the water amidships, Verner sought to maneuver the kayak at an oblique angle to the wind. First by muscling it, and then simply by being towed along in the water beside it, he tried to steer his kite-powered boat to the nearest island.

At best, if he could have somehow managed to sail across the wind, he might have had only a few kilometers to travel. At worst, if he was simply pulled in the direction of the wind, the distance could easily have been fifty kilometers. A journey which might as well have been to the other side of the Pacific in terms of Verner's ability to survive it.

Verner was far from the nearest land, in a wind-driven sea, holding on to a swamped kayak that he couldn't re-enter. The water was cold, and he realized that the biggest threat didn't come from drowning.

It came from hypothermia.

The affect that the cold water had on Verneer is grimly illustrated by the experiences of some unlucky Alaska fishermen.

Keith Richards was a young crewman crabbing on the *Golden Pices* when he was knocked overboard by a shifting crab pot. The skipper was able to position the boat to rescue him within minutes, but the cold Alaskan water had already numbed Richards to the point that he was unable to lift his arms to grab hold of a life ring when it was thrown next to him. Recalled the skipper, Richards had become "completely immobile, like a sack of potatoes" (Walker 1991).

When the 158-foot scalloper *St. Patrick* began to founder in November waters off Kodiak, her entire crew abandoned ship to take their chances in the storm-tossed sea. Over the next two days, Wallace Thomas watched crewman after crewman succumb to the effects of hypothermia, notwithstanding that they were clad in cold water "survival suits."

The last to go was Vanessa Sandin, whose steady deterioration left her totally dependent upon Thomas for survival. She was unable to move her legs and had lost all feeling in her arms. Her lips were dark blue and her face the color of blue chalk. When a Coast Guard helicopter roared by overhead, she could barely raise one shaking hand.

Thomas himself fought a desire to close his eyes and doze. Paddling numbly, he shuddered and throbbed with cold. At times, his legs were so stiff that he was convinced he could no longer use them.

As Thomas came down off the peak of a passing wave, he saw something huge floating near him in the darkness. First he thought it was a buoy splotched with seaweed, so he paddled toward it. Then he recoiled in fear, believing it to be a giant whale.

Eventually, he realized that what he feared was actually a nearby point of land. When he was finally thrown ashore by the waves, he was unable to stand, and had to pull himself up the beach with his hands (Walker 1991).

***

When Verner first plunged into the water, his body involuntarily began its own fight for survival. The instinct against breathing underwater is so dominant that it overwhelms even the agony of starving for air. A drowning person will not inhale until he is on the brink of blacking out, for only at that moment do the chemical sensors in the brain detect such high levels of carbon dioxide in the blood that they trigger an involuntary breath.

When Verner hit the water, his peripheral blood vessels constricted, reducing heat loss through his skin and preventing cooled blood from returning to his body's core. Simultaneously, his heart rate and oxygen consumption slowed, and his blood pooled in his heart and skull where it was needed most.

While Verner tried to regain control over his kayak, his vigorous movements kept him somewhat warm. But as he gained the chance to pause and think, his skin quickly numbed.

Towed through the icy water by his kayak, Verner was beset by a steady deterioration of his physical and mental condition. He shivered violently as his body attempted to generate heat through frantic muscle twitches.

When his core temperature dropped to 35–36°C (95–97°F), probably within the first half hour, Verner was covered with goose bumps and felt deeply cold. His hands were numb, unable to even tie a simple knot as to secure his kite to the boat. He must have done this shortly after he entered the water.

After perhaps an hour or two, Verner suffered from moderate hypothermia, with a core temperature of 33–35°C (93–95°F). He still shivered intensely, and was alert but confused. Merely holding on to the kayak was an accomplishment, and his movements were increasingly slow and labored.

Verner shivered for possibly another hour, until his store of muscle glucose was depleted.

Hypothermia progresses slowly and surely, just as the earth turns inexorably from daylight into darkness. If Verner was knowledgeable about hypothermia, he would have attempted to crawl at least partially on top of his kayak. Even getting his chest out of the water would have helped. Water's heat conductivity is thirty-two times that of air, and removing his torso from the water could have added hours to his life.

Three to four hours after Verner entered the water, his core temperature had dropped to 32–33°C (90–93°F). The viscosity of his blood resembled that of motor oil, his thinking was sluggish, and amnesia stole over him. When he tried to speak—to the wind, his kayak, or loved ones ashore—his words were slow and slurred. As his mind sought solutions to the perils that assaulted him, hallucinations visited him.

Wayne Schueffley, an Alaskan fisherman whose boat went down, remembers his own hallucinations during severe hypothermia. He believed he had drifted 2,900 kilometers (1,800 miles) south through Alaska's inside passage and was floating next to Seattle's Ballard fishing terminal. "There were two doctors in white coats standing on the edge of the wooden dock, and they were holding out two steamy hot cups of coffee." In the grips of delirium, Schueffley concluded that it was senseless to stay in his life-raft with help so near. He had crawled halfway out of the raft in an attempt to swim to the waiting doctors when one of his crewmates saved his life by pulling him back inside (Walker 1991).

At this point, Verner's environment became an active threat to further survival. His major muscles moved only sluggishly and he was unable to use his hands. The only way he was able to hold onto his kayak was by keeping his arms hooked into the cockpit. When it was finally torn from him by a passing wave, he was unable to regain it, though initially it was only a foot away. He floated passively in the water, incapable of swimming, depressed and withdrawn.

Survival beyond this time depended on Verner's float suit and how it had positioned him in the water. If it had held his head above water, or caused him to float on his back, he could have lived for another hour or more. By now, his shivering had stopped and his face and hands were blue. Gradually his breathing and heartbeat slowed, his muscles became rigid, and he lapsed into semiconsciousness.

Although Verner's core temperature may have dropped to as low as 24°C (75°F), rescue could still have saved his life. At this core temperature, his body would have gone into a kind of hibernation, using oxygen at a much slower rate. Placed on the deck of a passing ship, he would have been stiff and blue, with no apparent pulse.

There is a saying in the search and rescue community that "No one is dead until they are warm and dead." Patients have completely recovered when left for dead in the morgue, and proper core-warming techniques have brought victims back from the depths of even severe hypothermia.

But for Verner, such a passing ship was not to be.

As Verner floated alone in the Strait of Georgia, Komogwa, the Indian god of the depths, watched from his underwater realm. Three of Komogwa's death shadows circled Verner like patient sharks, waiting to steal in and possess his defenseless body.

One shadow took the form of heart failure, which would swim in if the cold caused his heart to beat erratically.

If Verner's heart did manage to continue, eventually he would have been rolled over by a wave and begun to breathe in water. Then he would be taken by the second shadow—death by drowning.

Komogwa's third shadow was patient. It circled Verner slowly while the electrical activity in his brain became weaker and weaker, until finally it ceased altogether.

Whichever shadow it was, it swam in and gently collected Verner for the trip to Komogwa's underwater lair.

According to the Coast Guard's Search and Rescue Office, one to two people a month perish in the waters of the Strait of Georgia. Sometime on April 30, 2000, Verner Schyleko became one of them. He died as he had wished, cradled in the arms of the sea.

Verner was laid to rest in a coffin built by Ray and other friends. Inside were his kayak paddle, a length of rope, a sleeping bag to keep him warm, a crab shell found on a Lasqueti beach, a bag of the chocolate chips he craved, a painting by Eve, a lucky penny, and writings to him by several friends. They were placed there by those who loved him, provisioning him for his journey to the beyond.

Verner's ashes, requested by his parents, were dutifully sent off to them in California. But the rumor is, from one who knows, that his friends each held back a pinch to scatter on Lasqueti's waters.

Chapter 40
Island Spring

The air was fresh and clean and young, as if it had not before been breathed by any living thing, and came new-made from snowy mountains high beneath a dome of stars.
—J.R.R. Tolkien, *The Lord of The Rings*

May 6, 2000

An endless succession of small waves glided toward shore this morning from unseen wind and ships. Their fronts were hammered silver, their backs dappled gray.

A flock of terns worked seaweed at the water's edge, and behind them hopped an unruly murder of crows. Just offshore, a drift of sandpipers darted back and forth above the waves. The world belonged to the birds today, and their cries were the only sounds we heard.

Walking around the island, Theresa and I reveled in the wildflowers that were blooming everywhere—a fairyland of miniature blossoms.

As the day warmed, we dug clams, picked up some small oysters, and invited friends over to share our flowers and food. It's perhaps the area's remoteness that brings people together here, where we find ourselves spending more time with friends than we do in Gig Harbor.

May 7, 2000

Today dawned sunny, with just a little wind. I eased awake slowly as I read next to the floathouse stove, basking in its warmth.

Theresa and I took another walk around Olsen, enjoying its different rocks and glades. Opening our minds to what we saw, we realized the island had a hundred stories to tell.

Narrow paths of matted grass spoke of otters sliding their way back and forth. Ripped up patches of moss said that one of these otters made a nest for itself after finishing a meal. Piles of broken crab parts informed us of the otter's favorite food. An abundance of the same told us that otters came here often, suggesting that this was their chosen spot to lounge in the sun.

Down on the beach, cast high up among the oldest logs, was the graying end of a cedar boom-stick. It told us of a lone handlogger standing on a slope so steep that gravity alone pulled his fallen tree down to the inlet below. In the hundreds of meters that it slid, this tree born before Columbus gathered enough speed to shoot deep into the swirling tides. It stunned a surprised rockfish in its dive, which floated slowly to the surface with the venerable log.

Rowing out from shore, the handlogger lifted the rockfish aboard. Its delicate white flesh would make a delicious dinner after he had completed the exhausting work of boring holes at both ends of the log with his large hand-auger. The log was long and straight, and would be chained end to end with other such "boom-sticks" to corral the handlogger's collection of timber.

The boom-stick was a beautiful log, and it eventually caught the eye of the foreman at a voracious mill. Pulled from the water, its holed ends were sawed off and thrown back into the saltchuck. They separated on the first tide, then drifted for years through the archipelago, camping on different islands at different times. Finally, a storm lifted one high on Olsen's shore, where it watched generations of eagles with its patient eye.

On the island above where the boom-stick rested, a stone-lined well showed us where a fisherman had settled here generations ago. The remains of his shack in the woods let us know that the island looked different then, with clearings where trees now grow. An old apple tree announced that he'd hoped to spend years here, with dreams of future harvests. A nearby lilac bush and patch of iris revealed that a woman lived here too, determined to bring some beauty with her. In spring, she picked the flowers and put them in a treasured vase to brighten up the inside of their small cabin. Weathered juniper fence posts told us of the couple's battle with the deer and their vow to protect their small patch of flowers.

May 8, 2000

Theresa and I kayaked out to the Finnerties, which were covered with wildflowers: Indian paint brush, yellow daisies, chocolate lilies, snapdragons, and a host of other colorful blooms.

As we paddled out of the bay into this maze of small islands, we entered a passage almost too narrow to pass through, and too shallow for anything but a kayak.

The further we penetrated these labyrinthine clefts, the more we lost touch with the day and the year, and even the age in which we lived. Boats on the Strait disappeared, the sky became clearer, and the islands' scents more intoxicating. The noises of engines sputtering and dogs barking were replaced by the sounds of waves lapping and bird wings feathering.

Gliding between sheer cliffs, the sky was reduced to a slash overhead. Cast-off boulders squeezed us as we lifted our paddles in order to pass. Bonsaied junipers arched over us, twisting and spiraling in shapes impossible for any living thing. Reaching over the snug waterway, their outstretched hands cast spells on the currents, turning water to liquid magic.

Glimpsing waterside refuges of otters and deer, our eyes wandered up game trails tunneling through the brush. Small freshwater pools nestled in moss-covered rock, the drinking places of wild things.

These were ancient places, secret worlds in their own galaxy. We were so deep in the islands, so flooded with their scent and embraced by their beauty, that it seemed we were part of the islands themselves rather than kayaking through them.

Finally, gliding into a mirrored lagoon in the heart of the Finnerties, we knew that we had emerged into another world. Floating on the tide, we knew this was a place of enchantment. Surely the islands had slipped their moorings and ridden the currents to a different universe, the only land on a limitless sea. This was the heart that pumped hope through our lives and dreams.

CHAPTER 41
ARRIVAL OF THE ARK

God remembered Noah and all the wild animals ... that were with him in the ark, and he sent a wind over the earth, and the waters receded.

—Genesis 8:1, *New International Version*

June 29, 2000

This morning we caught the early ferry out of French Creek on our way to the island for our summer stay. In the middle of the Strait, we came upon a school of bottle-nosed porpoise that swam toward us and began surfing the ferry's wake, some within mere feet of the stern. Others leapt and cavorted in the air, working their tail vigorously as if trying to swim through the sky. The ferry captain considerately drove around in circles so everyone could enjoy the show.

When we arrived at Olsen the tide was out, preventing us from motoring to our favorite landing spot near the floathouse. We now faced two options: we could throw our anchor off the steep rocks in False Bay, or at the end of the sand-flats in the back pass. The former left our boat in jeopardy of banging against the rocks, and the latter left us with a long hike with our gear.

In past years on the island, we'd faced this frustrating situation many times. We'd also been island-bound at low tide when our boat went dry near the floathouse. So we decided to copy the "clothesline" mooring system used by friends on neighboring islands.

In False Bay, the rocks of Olsen drop off steeply. By anchoring a buoy and pulley offshore, and putting a set of pulleys on the rocks above high tide, we could pull a rope back and forth through the pulleys. This would function just like an old-fashioned clothesline, to which we could tie our boat and pull it out to a deep water anchorage. This promised the ultimate convenience, facilitating trips off the island during any tide.

We talked our plan over with Ray, whose clothesline we used each time we visited Higgins Island. Following his advice, I bought a couple of used sailboat pulleys and about eighty meters of line. Dick put the system together, and soon we were in business. This was a small step for mankind, but a huge one for us.

June 30, 2000

Theresa and I went out for an early morning walk around Olsen before breakfast. Along our way, we saw a mink among the beach logs, and found an eagle feather, a fish float, and a seal skeleton.

In the evening, we went to the Community Center to attend the poetry reading that was part of the annual Lasqueti Arts Festival. One gent in his 40s, who had never read before, got up and told us he was going to read his life's work. People laughed at what they thought was a joke, but this laughter died as he brought out poems he'd written all the way back to his teens.

When we got back to the dock in the dark, we were a bit disconcerted to see the fishing boats rocking back and forth and straining at their moorings, a sure sign of a rough ride home. Some of the rollers coming into the bay were breaking, which caused me more concern. But as we wove our way among them, we got just a little wet and didn't ship too much water.

Seeking shelter, we ran for the passage between Higgins and Wolf Islands. Notwithstanding our new clothesline, we moored our boat in floathouse cove, feeling it was too rough to attempt a landing on the rocks outside.

July 4, 2000

My first act of the day was to heat some water on the propane burner for a teapot shower. I took this out on the deck, pouring splashes of water into my hand and then rinsing off my "five hairs." It was invigorating in the cool wind, and nice to be at least a little clean.

For all my time on Olsen, I still find myself discovering something new on each jaunt around it. Today was no exception.

After breakfast, I fled the construction zone to explore the eel grass flats of the back pass. Walking near the rocks at low tide, I saw animal tracks and a scattering of freshly broken limpets near a series of trenches in the sand. From the paw prints and fastidious trenchworks, I knew a raccoon had visited us.

Sometime later, I came upon the coon as he was digging up a bright orange sandworm. He sat up on his hind legs and looked me over, then went back to eating and cleaning his paws. Only when I got much closer did he walk off, the big worm dangling from his mouth. Looking down the beach, I saw a buck crossing from Lasqueti to Olsen.

The odors of the undersea world are as wondrous as its creatures, and these were exposed in profusion by the low tide. As I walked the beach, I breathed in this fecund smell, rich with the mystery of undersea wonders.

The intertidal shallows I explored host possibly more life than any other habitat on our planet. This is a place so thickly populated that every square inch is occupied by some plant or animal. A place where plants grow on animals and animals on plants.

Here live snails whose radula are covered with rows of file-like teeth, hard enough to bore through clam and oyster shells. Rocks are covered with barnacles that brood their young within their shells, and inch-long limpets so strong that I can't dislodge them when they sucker down. Nearby flourish bisexual tube worms whose head segments are female and rear segments male, and hermaphroditic flatworms that alternatingly develop male and female gonads.

Some of the rocks bloom with anemones whose green color comes from photosynthetic algae living within their tissues. Like sun-following flowers, these anemones orient themselves toward light, expanding in moderate sun and closing in darkness. Nudibranchs glide upside down, suspended from the surface film of tide pools where starfish project their stomachs outside their bodies to envelope prey.

Reading up on the unique natural histories of islands, I came to understand that the keys to Olsen's and Lasqueti's flora and fauna were glaciation, deep water, and the islands' distance from Vancouver Island and the mainland.

Glaciation scraped our islands bare twenty thousand years ago. Though most coastal islands were connected to the mainland by land bridges that allowed anything that could walk or crawl to repopulate their barrens when the glaciers retreated, the depths of the Strait kept a kilometers-wide moat around Lasqueti and Olsen. Whatever plants and animals arrived here had to come by wind or water.

To visualize the repopulation of our isolated islands, we can look to what happened on the tropical island of Krakatau.

On August 27, 1883, a monstrous volcanic explosion blew most of Krakatau skyward. The blast was heard 1,600 kilometers (a thousand miles) away, and barographs around the world trembled. A resulting tidal wave killed thirty-six thousand people on the coast of Sumatra and Java, and the dust pumped into the atmosphere cooled the planet for years.

Nothing on Krakatau survived the eruption, not even a seed or spore. All that remained was a cauterized crescent of rock, which was renamed Rakata.

Though the first post-eruption expedition to Rakata found nothing but a solitary spider, life arrived relatively quickly. Within three years, a variety of mosses, flowering plants, and ferns had established themselves, and in another year, Rakata had dense fields of grass and a collection of young trees. Two years later, it hosted populations of spiders, butterflies, beetles, and flies, and at least one large monitor lizard.

A mere twenty-three years after Rakata's predecessor had been seared sterile by superheated rock and gases, the island's summit was carpeted with greenery and it's shores lined by groves of trees. Within fifty years of the eruption, over three hundred species of vascular plants were growing there.

Olsen and Lasqueti were probably repopulated more slowly. For while Rakata had neighboring islands and coasts that were teaming with life, Olsen and Lasqueti were surrounded by glacial barrens. All but the tallest peaks of Vancouver Island had been glaciated, as had the mainland coast and all of the islands to the north and south.

But as life spread out from unglaciated areas, it eventually arrived on Olsen and Lasqueti.

Birds were probably the islands' first visitors. Landing after searching for a place to rest in their flight over local waters, they brought with them the basis of an ecosystem.

Gulls, eagles, and sparrows all carried a host of hitchhikers. Mites and lice infested their skins, and propagules of moss were tangled in their feathers. Sticky eggs of insects clung to their legs, small worms hid in the mud on their feet, and all manner of seeds passed through their intestines. In their turn, each was deposited on our island.

As on Rakata, tiny spiders were other early arrivals. Paying a thread of silk out of their silk glands, they wafted aloft on rising columns of air, and then rode the breezes from distant shores.

Some early arriving plants were members of the dandelion family, whose seeds blew in from far away. Ferns settled here quickly as well, traveling as airborne spores.

Other life arrived by sea. Trees are their own small ecosystems, with all manner of burrowing things living in their rootballs, insects in their bark, lichen and mushrooms on their trunks, and animals within their branches. Undermined by some relentless river, such a tree may have toppled and been carried away to the salt and then to our island. A clutch of snake eggs could have survived among the roots above the waters, and a pregnant raccoon may have clung to a mast-like limb. Floating northward, the ancient tree could have brought an ark of settlers to Olsen's shores.

Though some large creatures are accomplished sea travelers, these would have been somewhat later visitors to postglacial Olsen. Deer are strong and eager swimmers, but would have been attracted to our shores only when there was sufficient vegetation to graze on.

When a new population begins on an isolated island, it usually starts from a tiny group. Perhaps a doe came first, followed some months or years later by a stag. Maybe it was a pregnant doe, or a doe and stag together. In either case, Lasqueti and Olsen's abundant deer population developed from just a few individuals. Such was the case with most animals that populated these islands.

Another visitor to Lasqueti and Olsen, oddly enough, could have been a mammoth. Along with deer, elephants are the terrestrial mammals most likely to swim to new territory. Fossil evidence places elephantid species on a variety of islands around the world. Many of these islands were not connected by land bridges to continental elephant homelands during periods of glacially-lowered sea levels. Long distance elephantine swimming may seem remarkable, but we don't have to look further than the Channel Islands off Santa Barbara to find evidence of it.

The deep water between the Channel Islands and the California coast was never less than four miles wide. There is no fossil evidence on the Channel Islands of any of the sabertooth cats, sloths, coyotes, bears, rabbits, or raccoons that inhabited Pleistocene southwestern California. Of thirty-eight extinct mammals found in the La Brea Tar Pits, only one was found on the Channel Islands, a pygmy species of elephant derived from North American mammoths.

Why the elephant alone? Arguably because it alone was able to swim there. In modern times, elephants have been observed swimming to and from various coastal islands in Kenya, India, Cambodia, Ceylon, and Bangladesh.

If a lone mammoth did happen upon postglacial Lasqueti, and it wasn't by chance pregnant with multiple, differently sexed young, it would have faced the same prospects as did any solitary mammalian visitor. Though food may have been plentiful, it would have eventually died a horny, species-lonely death, leaving no issue to follow.

Frogs and other amphibians were probably late arrivals. When the first Indians visited Lasqueti, it's possible that no chorus of frogs sang them to sleep near island lakes. For neither frogs, nor tadpoles, can tolerate even a splash of salt water. Though a founding population of frogs could have arrived on some large piece of flotsam, it's equally likely that they disembarked with human visitors. Hiding inconspicuously in the crevices of a canoe, or as young tadpoles in a gourd of water, the frogs may have used unwitting Indians as their means of crossing an otherwise impassable divide.

Lasqueti's swamps and lakes are now full of frogs. In contrast, there is not a single shred of evidence that a mammoth ever visited the island. But if we could have sat on the shore of postglacial Lasqueti, it would have been infinitely more likely for a mammoth to swim ashore than a frog.

CHAPTER 42
OUR ISLAND HOME

Nothing will content them but the extremest limit of the land ...
they must get just as nigh the water as they possibly can.
> —Herman Melville, *Moby Dick*

July 28, 2000
Moving Day!

We arrived in French Creek with our boat and Suburban packed full. Theresa and I had spent the prior month making lists and trips to the store, rounding up everything we needed to stock up our new home. We'd hoped to avoid those dreaded island words, "gosh, I guess I forgot that."

It took over an hour to empty the car and hand truck our goods down the ramp to the ferry float. Just getting down the ramp was a challenge in itself, as it was perilously steep from a very low tide. In front of me was a hand truck piled high with boxes that totally blocked my view. Underfoot was a metal grating made slick by the morning dew, splotched here and there with spilled oil and the curdled vomit of some seasick ferry passenger.

Gravity wanted to make a bobsled of my load. To slow my descent, I leaned precariously back under the hand truck, braking with my legs and grasping the ramp's railing with one hand. In response to my one-handed off-center grip, the hand truck wandered drunkenly down the incline. My load swayed back and forth, nearly tipping over the edge and falling into the water.

At the moment of greatest peril, when my sweaty palm was about to slide off the truck's metal handle, some young mother began to clap with joy as her toddler took his first steps up the ramp.

She saw a budding mountain climber. I saw roadkill.

After successfully humping a succession of loads down, I then reloaded everything into our boat and onto the ferry. Theresa was a great help, managing to run into several island friends that she had to gossip with while I portered boxes. Sweating copiously, I muttered repeated words of thanks to her under my breath.

While I enjoyed a break as I motored across the Strait in our boat, I knew my work had just started. For after I unloaded our boat on Olsen, I had to run over to Lasqueti to pack the rest of our gear *off* the ferry, and then reload what we could into the Grady for another trip to Olsen. Once there, we unloaded the boat as we fought to keep it from smashing against the rocks. Then we manhandled everything up over the uneven terrain to our house. After that, I returned to the Lasqueti dock for another boatload.

By day's end, I felt more mule than human. Theresa was all smiles.

***

One of the things I was excited to see was our fine new outhouse. No dark box in the woods, it has skylights woven into its shake roof, windows on the sides, and a Dutch door with a window in front.

The outhouse sits among sparse trees at the forest's edge. Its view is framed by bonsaied junipers and red arbutus. Just beyond is a small meadow of wild grasses which bursts with wildflowers in the spring, pushing its green fingers into the cracked rock of the shore.

This drops off into the waters below, which can be calm and blue, ruffled with sparkling silver, or a chaotic battlefield of gray and white. Seals and otters cruise by as gulls swoop down to land on the waves. Occasionally, an eagle flies majestically overhead or a deer grazes in the meadow. Crows caw in the surrounding trees and crickets chirp in the grass.

Fishing boats cruise into the bay, and sailboats unfurl their sails as they enter the wind of the Strait. To the right, I can see the distant peaks of Vancouver Island, and on the far side of False Bay, the rocky beaches of Lasqueti, where Prowse Point Lighthouse stands to guide boats in the dark.

I enjoy all of this from our padded outhouse seat.

In its devotion to the view, our outhouse is akin to those of our Lasqueti friends. Outhouses here are specially located to commune with nature. Though they have roofs and walls, most are left open to the view in front. To help users find their way in the moonlight, some have oyster shells along the paths leading to them.

Our outhouse has the unspeakable luxury of a light on its path and, as a gift to Theresa, a light inside. Guests are welcomed by an upturned horseshoe over the door that hopefully brings them luck.

My list of "Outhouse Rules" is posted inside:

1. Do not comment on other users' eating habits.
2. No peeing in the outhouse … use the woods.
3. Parking limit: 15 minutes.
4. In case of TP shortage, we cannot be responsible for books or magazines left here.
5. Please don't discuss your condition with others passing by.
6. Do not alarm the neighbors with "jake brakes" or other loud noises.
7. Waiting must be done outside.
8. After eating refried beans, sauerkraut, or pickled herring, use neighbor's outhouse.
9. Knock once to determine if occupied.
10. Knock twice if it's an emergency.
11. Get out quickly if you hear someone running up the path.

July 29, 2000

Our home was designed to survive the Strait's storms and stand for our children's children.

Plans started at bedrock, the huge plumes of basalt that form the island. Dick and his crew drilled this rock time after time, then sledge-hammered in thick pieces of epoxy-coated rebar that were cemented in place.

We wanted the island to be our anchor.

Onto the rock and rebar, we poured extra-wide footings, an incredible extravagance since every cubic foot of concrete had to be made and carried by hand. Cast into these footings were big galvanized bolts that held down oversized post holders. Massive posts were through–bolted to these saddles and ran all the way to our roof. Dick's team set huge floor beams into welded beam hangers that were bolted to these posts.

Metal cross-strapping was routed into extra-thick plywood atop the floor beams, the strapping screwed in place to prevent the house from twisting in the wind. Angle iron was screwed to our already-oversized rafters to further strengthen them. Windows were glazed with extra-thick tempered glass to resist shattering under storm-driven wind pressure.

When we built closer to the water, we took even more precautions.

Our boathouse, just above high tide, was built into a natural rock basement. Where the floor needed leveling, we did it with stone and mortar. As with the footings for our house, epoxy-coated dowels were sunk into the rock below. On top of these were hand-poured, thick concrete walls, which were faced with rock and mortar. Trunk-like cedar posts and beams supported the roof, all bolted in place. On top of this rested a deck of arm-thick cedar planks.

This use of massive cedar beams and planks satisfied something deep within our Northwestern psyches.

Cedar was the wood of myths. The magnificent voyaging canoes of coastal peoples had been hewn out of huge cedar logs. Moss-covered cedars lie forever in our forests, seemingly impervious to rot. Old-growth cedar stumps still stand proud among second- and third-growth trees, displaying the springboard notches cut by the coast's first loggers.

Cedar chests store family treasures and protect them from hungry moths.

Cedar, with its scent of incense and beautiful straight grain. Cedar that splits perfectly into fence posts and kindling. Cedar that is the wood of classic lapstrake rowboats, which glide perfectly over Northwest waters.

Cedar, the fire starter, whose natural oils are quick to flame. Cedar whose bark was woven into First Nations hats and baskets. Cedar that coastal lodges and generations of Northwest homes were built from.

Cedar that was carved into the god-masks of indigenous peoples. Cedar, the wood of myths.

***

We loved the island, and were protective of its every rock and plant. In building our house, our goal was to disturb nothing. When it was completed, we wanted Olsen's moss and wildflowers to reach right up to our porch. We wanted no roads, no landscaping, and no construction scars. We desired our home to be part of the island, not an incursion into it.

Dick succeeded in all of this through careful instructions to everyone working there and a series of scaffolded walkways surrounding the house. Deer graze right outside our windows, and yellow lichen brightens the nearby rocks. Other than the house itself, there are few reminders left of anyone being here. We didn't tame the island, just created a place for ourselves in its wilderness.

In the storms of the Strait, Olsen is a place of brutal assaults. Beach logs are snatched from the coast and batter the rocks. Trees in the forest are simply blown over, ripping their roots from the soil. False Bay is transformed into a cauldron filled with avalanching cliffs of water.

Our house sits on a rocky point, gripped in the teeth of these storms. The southeasterly winds of winter savage this point and sweep it clean. Except for some grasses and lichen and a few ancient junipers, nothing grows here.

We chose this spot so we could stand in the prow of the island ship as it plowed through whatever terror the wind and waves had to offer.

Our house was our audacious attempt to cheat nature. We hoped to live there and enjoy the spectacular fury of the elements at their wildest. Cut off from the outside world. Savoring the island's days and nights. And at times, simply surviving.

CHAPTER 43
OUR BOAT GOES MISSING

*The sun had fallen behind the tops of the jagged firs. Tired
and bedraggled, we hurried along a fir-needle path toward the
cove ...*

*Suddenly, "Dave! Dave!" Jeanne called from the beach. "Our
boat is gone."*

*Scrambling down the bank, I anxiously scanned the cove for the
cockleshell.*

"There it is—heading toward the gap," Jeanne pointed.

*Fanned by an offshore breeze, the boat was drifting toward the
narrow passageway. We had forgotten all about such a thing as a
rising tide.*

"What'll we do?" wailed Jeanne.

*"Swim for it." I was ripping off my shirt. "We haven't a second to
spare."*

—David Conover, *Once Upon an Island*

July 30, 2000

I lost several days in a blur of activity as we moved in and hosted the
troops of people who stopped by to visit our new home. We may be
remote, but you'd never know it from the number of visitors we've
had.

This morning, I was out fishing for some bait for our prawn traps
when I noticed a shift in the wind to the west. Looking out, I could see

the whitecaps of an approaching Qualicum. But fishing had just started to get good, and I tried to cheat fate by fishing a bit longer.

By the time I caught my bait and started lowering my traps, I was in twenty-five knots of wind and breaking seas. The wind and waves were pushing me away from the sinking traps faster than I could pull line off their reels, and I needed to get ahead of the streaming line to be able to tie their ends to my buoys. To slow this down, I tried backing into the onslaught, which sent waves over my transom and threatened to catch my line in the prop.

In a flurry I gave up that foolhardy maneuver and tried another. First I wedged myself between the seat and dashboard. Then, with one hand on the line and the other on the steering wheel, I tried to ease the boat forward and spin the wheel to take me into the waves. In the process I lost my balance and fell on the throttle, gunning the engine and almost throwing myself out of the boat.

And me without a float coat on. The day had been warm and calm when I went out, so I'd left my float coat at home.

I made little headway when I pointed the boat into the wind. Blasting spray over the bow and windshield, I almost ran over my line again as I attempted to maneuver forward.

Finally my temper shattered. Screaming obscenities at the wind and waves, I tried futilely to curse them into submission. But with the arrogance of gods, they ignored my invective and continued to throw me around.

When I finally swore my way into grudging silence, I resumed my work and eventually managed to get my traps down.

From his vantage point on Lasqueti, Ken had watched me set out in my boat. Since he hadn't seen me return when the wind blew up, he'd scanned the waters with his binoculars.

Finally, he got so worried that he called Theresa. His concern was in the spirit of all our False Bay neighbors, who always keep an eye out for one another.

Ken and Claire were going to come out for dinner, but cancelled due to wind and waves. I smiled at that, as it's a special treat to be cut off by the weather. Before dinner, I stood on the rocks and enjoyed the excitement of watching big rollers steam past Olsen and crash against Higgins' shore.

As the day slid into evening, the bay calmed and lured me out for some sunset fishing. Pulling our aluminum boat in from the clothesline, I headed out for the Finnerties and fished there until well after dark. Returning home relaxed and exhausted, I stumbled up the rocks to bed.

July 31, 2000

Dick came over this morning, and was surprised to find us home. He told me that since our aluminum skiff was gone, he'd concluded we were away. This perplexed me, as the previous evening I'd tied the boat to our clothesline in False Bay. A quick walk confirmed Dick's observation—no boat.

I knew I'd been tired last night when I tied up the boat. Now I wondered if I'd been so sleepy that I had forgotten some critical step in securing it.

Dick and I found the loop in the pulley system pulled all the way to shore. Had I simply stepped off my boat and neglected to tie it at all? Perhaps I'd made a feeble attempt to tether it and then forgotten to pull it out to the buoy. Then it could have worked loose and floated away. Or maybe I'd left it inshore, and it had hung up on the rocks during the night's low tide and was sunk out of sight right in front of us.

I couldn't bring myself to accept that I'd committed one of these feebleminded mistakes. I have a thick nylon bowline, which I change with the least bit of wear. I'm fanatical about each step in securing my boat, knowing that the knot I tie is all that keeps it from wandering. I always tie a bowline, a knot which absolutely will not pull loose, but which can always be untied no matter how tightly it has pulled.

Standing numbly on the rocks, I went over last night's landing again and again. I was sure I'd done the drill as I'd done it hundreds of times before. At least I hoped I was sure, as the possibility of letting my own boat drift away was too grim to contemplate. If I'd done that, I'd failed one of the most basic fitness tests for living on an island. Accordingly, I found myself more concerned about vindicating myself than finding my boat.

But our aluminum boat was a necessity, so Dick and I embarked on a two-hour search of local waters in the Grady. The trip along Lasqueti's coast and around local islands would have been a delight on any other day, but today it was a frustrating exercise of fruitlessly scanning beaches and bays with our binoculars. In the end, we had nothing to show for our efforts and returned to Olsen so Dick could gather the tools he had earlier come to collect.

Shortly after he went down to where his things were stored, Dick was back with a troubled look on his face. His tools were nowhere to be found. After I assured him that I had not moved them anywhere, the truth dawned on us at the same time. We'd been ripped off!

After the obligatory calls to the Coast Guard and insurance company, I lay down in the hammock to review my situation. It didn't take me long to realize that losing my boat to a thief was decidedly preferable to losing it to my own ineptitude.

The thief had to live with himself, and so did I.

August 1, 2000

Though our arms have been getting plenty of exercise pulling prawn pots, working fishing rods, and paddling our kayaks, Theresa and I felt our legs could use a long walk. So we set out for Lasqueti at low tide and picked our way over the sand flats of the back pass.

As we approached our neighboring island, great cedars brooded over their reflections in the tide pools we passed.

The green forest swallowed us, rich with the scent of sap and humus. Peering through the woods, we beheld an ancient tree scarred by lighting and generations of storms. It beheld the world silently, listening and watching, thinking its immense, slow thoughts. A thousand years of detritus lay at is feet, decayed remains of its own fingers and limbs.

This was a dark and primal place, smelling of moist earth and decay, untouched by roads or axes. Walking silently, we entered a forest as old as the island world itself, a conclave of stubborn sentinels crowded close together. Ancient trunks convened here, knitting their gnarted finger-branches together to block out the sky. At their feet, their tree-sized roots snaked over the forest floor, immense pythons that drank greedily from any rain that managed to drip through the umbrella of needles.

Peering through the gloaming, I shared John Valliant's observation in *The Golden Spruce* that "You have the feeling that if you stop for too long, you will simply be grown over and absorbed by the slow and ancient riot of growth going on all around you."

Lasqueti's woods shaded us from the hot afternoon sun. We followed old paths and game trails for hours, enchanted by wonders beneath the canopy of cedars. In an isolated valley, we found an abandoned homestead and its relics of forgotten dreams. Further on, we came upon a large swamp where we were serenaded by a chorus of frogs.

Deep humus cushioned our footsteps and absorbed the sounds of our walking. Forgetting ourselves in the quiet, we slipped into the contented silence of forest deer.

Awakening from the charms of maidenhair ferns and ancient trees, Theresa and I realized that the tide had been coming in through most of our walk. Quickening our pace over the uneven ground, we returned to the Lasqueti shore across from Olsen. On emerging from the trees, we found that the sand flats we had walked across were now under more than a meter and a half of water.

Laughing at our folly, we waded in fully dressed. Sharp rocks and oysters convinced us to leave our shoes on, and wearing our clothes was easier than carrying them. Thus weighted down, we hoped that the water had not deepened to where we'd have to swim.

As the water rose to my chest, I unconsciously began to tiptoe. Looking over at Theresa, I saw small waves lapping at her shoulders. To push our way through the bay and make progress toward Olsen, we had to lean forward slightly, which wetted us further toward our chins. The tide still came in rapidly, steadily deepening our route home.

At last, our passage began to shallow as Olsen's beach steepened beneath our feet. Emerging soaked and shivering, we stripped off our clothes and headed for our outdoor shower to warm up.

CHAPTER 44
MOSQUITOES

This sceptered isle, ... this other Eden, demi – paradise, This fortress built by Nature for herself... this little world, this precious stone set in the Silver Sea, which serves ... as a moat defensive to a house ...

—William Shakespeare, *King Richard*

August 2, 2000

We had been planning a "thank you" party for everyone who'd worked on our house, so this morning I kayaked over to the dock to talk with Aurel Girard to see if he'd ferry our guests from Lasqueti to Olsen.

Aurel is the captain of the *Argent,* an old fishing boat that's usually moored at the Lasqueti dock. Everyone here knows both captain and craft, as once met, they are impossible to forget.

With his false teeth out and a corncob pipe clenched tight in his mouth, Aurel is a dead ringer for Popeye, though a crazier character than in the cartoons. One minute he'll reach into his freezer with a smile and give away a popsicle to a little girl who doesn't have the money to buy one. The next he'll melt the tar off the dock's pilings with profanity when someone offends him. Though Aurel recently won Lasqueti's "Citizen of the Year" award for hauling freight and people when the ferry wasn't running, a case of beer occasionally has priority over his service. When our boat was stolen, he offered to patrol our island and shoot off his shotgun now and then to deter potential thieves.

The *Argent* is a bright green fishing boat with a two-meter-high skull and crossbones adorning the cabin and several potted marijuana plants growing on the fly bridge. Aurel's dog, Buck, patrols and craps on the back deck, barking at and occasionally biting passersby. At a recent soccer tournament, when Aurel was sitting on the ground enjoying his lunch, I saw Buck lift his leg and pee all over Aurel's back.

On my way home from talking with Aurel, I stopped to admire a beautifully restored tug that was anchored in the bay. It was owned by a dentist who'd sold his Seattle practice and started a floating dental service.

Lasqueti had previously been served by another dentist who would arrive in his sailboat, drop anchor, and stay as long as the patients kept coming. He had a dental chair in one of the boat's cabins and kept busy serving the remote communities on British Columbia's coast and islands. The work was nothing fancy, but as it was done locally and with plenty of Novocain, it was much appreciated.

***

While we sat on our porch this evening being swarmed by mosquitoes, our arms flailed the air as we sought to intercept the incoming attackers. So many penetrated our defenses and landed on me that I was able to kill three in one swat. Theresa, however, had it even worse than I. Like other dark-skinned friends, Theresa is a mosquito magnet.

After our numerous bites began to itch, we tried to tame them with a battery powered "bite-zapper." Apparently the "itch" in mosquito bites is thermosensitive, for when we pressed the zapper's heated tip on our bites, their itch actually disappeared. We've heard of other islanders soothing their bites in a similar manner with a hot washrag.

Last winter I'd dived into my library to study up on mosquitoes and learned that females are the only ones that seek our blood, doing so to nourish their eggs. When their blood–thirst strikes, these hungry females may travel miles to feed.

Approaching at speeds of up to three miles per hour, with wings beating as furiously as 500 times per second, mosquitoes find us in several ways. Sensors on their antenna are attuned to the carbon dioxide and lactic acid we exhale, as well as other chemicals coming from our bodies. When a mosquito flies into our scent plume, she uses her antenna to orient herself and stay within it. Any movement we make catches her eyes, and when she finally gets close, the radiant heat of our body guides her to the hottest spots, flesh not covered by clothes or hair.

In her landing, the mosquito alights so gently that she often avoids our notice. In search of a supply of blood, she'll poke our skin up to twenty times.

Her sampling and eventual feeding is done with an apparatus far more complex than a simple straw. The mosquito's proboscis is composed of two tubes surrounded by two pairs of cutting stylets. As the mosquito puts pressure on this bundle of tools, the sharp edges of the stylets slide against one another and slice through the skin. She then slips her bundle of mouth parts into this opening, bends them at a sharp angle, and begins searching for blood.

The mosquito's goal is to nick a blood vessel and create a puddle of blood under our skin. If she doesn't accomplish this on the first try, she withdraws slightly and then angles in again in a different direction. With each probing, her fine salivary tube injects a chemical that keeps our blood from clotting. The contents of this saliva are what irritate the "bite" after she has gone.

Once our little vampire tastes blood, she holds very still. Within ninety seconds she will suck two to three times her body weight into her expandable stomach.

After finishing her meal, her majesty withdraws her mouth parts and flies aloft to the nearest vertical surface, where she lands to digest the water out of her cache of blood. Within forty-five minutes of feeding she completes this fete, excreting pinkish droplets of urine.

When we sense a mosquito feeding, we are surprisingly unsuccessful in our attempts to swat her. Mosquitoes can detect our movements and the shadows of approaching doom, and Spielman and D'Antonio (2001) suggest that "they may also sense the change in air pressure as a hand approaches." As only the most alert escape, natural selection has operated to make mosquitoes that live in close proximity to humans especially careful feeders. Astonishingly, the ones that escape our swat may live as long as six months.

Different varieties of mosquitoes feed at different times, some at dawn or dusk, others after dark, and still others during the day.

These unique varieties also have other special behaviors. Some lay their eggs in clear fresh water, while others prefer brackish saltwater pools. Some are human-feeders, while others focus on horses or birds. Some fly in low and bite on the ankles or calves, while others come in high and prefer the neck and hands. Some bite only after a person has been still for a few minutes, while others actually chase in an attempt to feed.

Our first local mosquitoes no doubt arrived here from the south, blown in on the wind after the glaciers retreated. They came with the birds and animals on which they fed, hosts that had developed resistance to mosquito-born diseases.

To our local fauna, mosquitoes are only a nuisance. On other islands, however, mosquitoes have had deadly effects on the ecosystem.

There were no mosquitoes on the Hawaiian island of Maui when the first Europeans arrived, and the native birds had never been exposed to avian malaria or birdpox. Having developed no resistance to these diseases, the endemic birds were at great risk when the British ship *Wellington* anchored off Lahaina in 1826.

The *Wellington* had previously watered in tropical Mexico and the dregs in her water casks were swarming with mosquito larvae. Prior to filling these casks from a stream behind Lahaina, the sailors dumped the old cask-water into the stream, which by coincidence was a perfect habitat for the Mexican mosquitoes. Within ten years, mosquitoes were well-established on Maui, Kauai, and Oahu.

Though the night-flying *Culex pipiens fatigans* were merely annoying to Hawaiian people, they were far more dangerous to native birds. This particular mosquito is the principal carrier of avian malaria.

Like human malaria, avian malaria is caused by a parasite carried from host to host in mosquito saliva. Though it may have been previously and intermittently present in shorebirds and ducks migrating through Hawaii from the Americas, without a mosquito to spread it to Hawaiian birds, the native birds were safe—until that nasty cask-water was poured into the Lahaina stream.

Birdpox probably came ashore in colonists' poultry, but it too was benign until the mosquito arrived to spread it.

All counted, over seventeen types of Hawaiian birds were sickened to extinction by diseases carried via descendants of the *Wellington's* mosquitoes. Many surviving native birds have retreated to live above 600 meters (2,000 feet), the ceiling of the *Culex* mosquito's habitat.

But not only birds disappeared as a result of the mosquito's arrival in Hawaii.

As fauna and flora co-evolved on the Hawaiian Islands, an exclusive pollinating relationship apparently developed between the Hawaiian honeycreeper and the Hawaiian plant *Hibiscadelphus*. The long curved bills of the honeycreepers matched the curve of the *Hibiscadelphus'* narrow tubular flowers, which could not be pollinated by bees, moths, or bats. When the honeycreepers were driven over the precipice of extinction by the parasite-carrying mosquito, *Hibiscadelphus* could no longer be pollinated. As older plants died, no new ones germinated. The result was the extinction, or near extinction, of all five species of *Hibiscadelphus*.

Sitting on our porch in the dark after most of the mosquitoes winged elsewhere, we were entertained by bats fluttering around us. Picking the remaining mosquitoes out of the air, they allowed us a pleasant evening watching the bay drift off to sleep.

CHAPTER 45
COMMERCE ON LASQUETI TIME

An unhurried sense of time is in itself a form of wealth.
—Bonnie Friedman in *The New York Times*

August 3, 2000

When our boys went off cliff jumping, Theresa and I kayaked out to the Finnerties and climbed to a rocky summit with fine views of the surrounding islands and channels.

After lounging in the sun for a while, we decided to try some clamming. We found that our secret Finnerty lagoon was full of small manillas just under the sand, which we easily dug with our fingers.

After we had leisurely pawed out our fill of clams, we gathered some mussels and oysters and then headed for home. We then cooked our collection of shellfish into a delicious dinner.

The boys tried sleeping in the hammocks, but got chased inside by mosquitoes.

August 4, 2000

Today was hot and calm and windless—a classic summer day in the islands. After a leisurely morning, we boated over to the Lasqueti dock and walked up the dirt road to the bakery for lunch.

On the way back, we stopped by a Lasqueti gift shop that a friend opens a couple of days a week, and then only if she's in the mood.

If you think this is an odd way to run a business, then check out the island's schedule of commerce:

Ferry: No service Tuesdays or Wednesdays.

Gas: Sold only at the Blue Roof (the derogatory name given to Lasqueti's small waterfront hotel, whose bright blue roof offends many islanders). Gas pump is open from 2:00 PM to an indeterminate time on "Ferry Days" only. Tanks of gas must be hand-carried from the pump behind the Blue Roof down to the boat dock.

Bakery: Open three days a week. Pizza available on Friday night, exclusively by pre-order.

Joy's Shop: Open on different days and hours, depending on how busy she is with the rest of her life.

Dump: Open on the third Saturday of the month. When you attempt to unload your trash, the attendant picks through it and tells you who on the island could use different things, and what you should take to the free store or recycling center. He very clearly discourages you from leaving these items at the dump.

Propane Service: Takes several calls and, perhaps, a wait of several weeks. Delivery to the small islands and roadless homes on Lasqueti's coast takes even longer, as barge service and tides must be coordinated. When the tides are right and the barge isn't busy, the Lasqueti propane truck is driven onto the barge and boated to isolated island homes. As the barge noses against the rocks and is kept in place by keeping it idling in forward gear, the propane line is run to the hidden tank ashore and propane is pumped from floating truck to island tank. Eventual delivery depends on the propane man's estimation of how close you are to being bone dry. Until he believes you are at a critically low level, he simply won't come.

Free Store: Recycles items through the island's residents until not even the most ingenuous mechanic can repair them. Open odd hours when volunteer staff are present.

Whole Foods Store: Last winter the owners closed its doors, tired of feeding the business money. So for months there were no groceries available on the island.

Lasqueti Hotel Restaurant: Has been shuttered, who knows why. Even with the closing of the whole foods store, the hotel store hasn't expanded its meager offering of ice cream, videos, and motor oil.

*Propane Update: The fellow running the propane service has quit. Bob Dunlop (our electrician) has been hired to replace the departed operator, but no one knows when he's going to start. Of note is the fact that Bob hates the water and being in boats, which raises eyebrows on all of us who rely on the propane barge.

August 5, 2000

Ted Salmon cruised into the void left by last winter's closing of Lasqueti's whole foods store. Operating out of the same small building, whose two sections are about as big as the average home's living and dining rooms, Ted's enterprise is run even more casually than the past one. There are no posted hours and, initially, no electricity or lights. Ted lives aboard the *Seal*, his old wooden troller moored at the Lasqueti dock. Islanders know the "store" is open when they see Ted walking up the dock in the morning or holding court outside with his buddies.

When I want something from Ted's store, I walk up to this group and wait for a lull in the conversation. After politely chewing the fat with Ted for a few minutes, I ask him if he has what I want. His offering and outages are as unpredictable as the hours.

If my luck is good, Ted will heave his magnificent bulk out of his chair and unlock the storeroom. Dry goods are stocked on plywood shelves, and perishables kept in large white ice chests. If he has just returned from a supply run, my quarry might be stacked on the fan tail of his boat. Some boxes are marked with the nickname a waggish supplier gave him: "Tedoski Salmonella."

Nothing in Ted's collection of provender is priced, and Ted figures on the spot what to charge. This can vary depending on his mood, the amount of stock he has left, how fresh it is, and his keen eye for how badly someone wants it. My personal prices are not helped by the fact that my boat is relatively new and I have my own island.

Ted also sells gas, which he insists is much purer than the gas they sell at the Blue Roof. For me, the advantage is that Ted sells gas off his boat, saving me the arduous task of lugging tanks of gas from the Blue Roof to the float. Ted is too savvy to mention this, but his slitted eyes betray that he knows it. I watch him silently calculating how much he feels this convenience is worth.

I am here today for a loaf of bread and some gas, and getting the bread has already taken half an hour. Reluctant to wait for the hallowed time when the Blue Roof turns on its gas pumps, I mention in resignation that I'd like some gas. In response, Ted smiles broadly and invites me to his boat.

First we move around several ice chests so we can position my gas tank lower than the large rusting reservoir mounted on the *Seal's* stern. Seeing this tank's crusting of salt, I wonder about the premium I'll be paying for the purity of Ted's gas.

After eyeballing my container to judge how much it will hold, Ted opens the valve to the garden hose that gravity-fills my tank. There is no meter, and Ted rounds the charges to the nearest dollar. As he stuffs my wad of bills into his pocket, I vainly try to figure how many gallons I got and how much per gallon I paid.

Total elapsed "store" time: an hour for a loaf of bread and a few gallons of gas.

CHAPTER 46
THERESA BATTLES THE DEER

*For, lo! The winter is past, the rain is over and gone; the flowers
appear on the earth; the time of the singing birds is come …*
—*Song of Solomon, 2:11-12, The Holy Bible – King James Version.*
2000

August 6, 2000

This spring Theresa had planted a carefully selected collection of flowers
in some big pots she'd lugged to the island. We'd placed these pots at
the edge of the small meadow directly below our front porch. Having
heard tale after tale of the depredations of island deer, and having seen
the tall deer-fences our friends built to protect their gardens, I shrouded
Theresa's pots in a protective cocoon of chicken wire. But when she
discovered this crude cage, it was hate at first sight.

Though Theresa's flowers had grown into a riot of blooms, she
remained steadfast in her conviction that their beauty was unnecessarily
compromised by their chicken wire prison. Whenever we sat on our
porch above the flowers, Theresa snorted her disapproval and pestered
me with suggested improvements. As her frustration mounted, she
became convinced that *any* protective measures were superfluous. Our
deer were *nice* deer, and her flowers too beautiful to eat.

As we breakfasted outside this morning, Theresa's anxiety reached
a crescendo. Twitching out curt rejoinders to my polite defense of the
chicken wire, she made it clear that my solicitous concern for her flowers

was no longer welcome. Marching down from the porch in mid-meal, she tore apart my enclosure and left it in a heap in the meadow.

Returning to her breakfast on the porch, Theresa gazed at her blossoms and smiled. Sighing contentedly, she remarked on how delicious her coffee tasted.

Overwhelmed by the joyous liberation of her imprisoned friends, Theresa refused to recage them when we left for the day. Scoffing at my suggested precautions, she skipped light- heartedly down to our kayaks and paddled happily away.

Upon our return to Olsen, Theresa pranced up the rocks to say hello to her flowers. Arriving there short minutes later, I saw her standing dejectedly by her denuded pots. As she turned to me with tears in her eyes, I saw that everything in the pots had been eaten down to the dirt by our deer.

I was thus surprised by Theresa's magnanimity when we ran into the doe and fawns on our nightly island walk. Theresa lectured them sternly about staying away from her potted garden, and with a shake of her finger told them how naughty they'd been. They politely faced her until she finished, then contentedly returned to their grazing.

August 7, 2000

A calm, clear morning with little wind. The doe and her two fawns are feeding next to the pile of chicken wire in the meadow just off our porch.

Until this morning Theresa had always enjoyed our island deer. They seemed especially contented in Olsen's refuge from guns and fences, and their visits to our house had always brought a smile to her face.

But with this morning's arrival of replacement flowers for Theresa's pots, things changed dramatically.

Put simply, Theresa *loves* flowers. And notwithstanding our mutual commitment not to duplicate our Minter Creek garden on the island, Theresa couldn't restrain herself. In an orgy of abandonment after the deer ate what few flowers she had, Theresa got on the cell phone to a Vancouver Island nursery and ordered up a storm. Flats of blossoms and a bevy of ornamental pots arrived this morning on the ferry.

Theresa's solution to the deer problem was to move her planting containers onto the billowing rock above the meadow. As she was planting her new arrivals, I asked her off-handedly about her plans to protect them from the deer. Without looking up, she dismissed my concerns with a wave of her hand. "My pots are on the *rocks*," she mumbled as she caressed her lovelies.

Needing to stretch her legs after hours bent over her pots, Theresa proposed a walk around the island. Biting my tongue against the desire to editorialize on the lack of security measures for her newly planted flowers, I politely accepted.

After lounging in the sun on Olsen's west end, we finally made our way home. Cresting a rise, Theresa swore as she saw that deer had visited in her absence. Though the stems and leaves were left intact on her new plants, all the blossoms had been neatly trimmed off. And with that, trimming the deer-loving Dr. Jekyll metamorphosed into the cantankerous Ms. Hyde.

Periodically through the rest of the day, I heard Theresa yelling, growling, or barking like a dog. She placed small piles of throwing-rocks strategically around our house and left our front door open with the radio turned up loud. Regularly prowling the perimeter of the woods, she allowed that she'd like a pellet gun for her birthday. When not making her rounds, she lay in the hammock above her pots performing guard duty.

But now Theresa faced a quandary. Our good friends, the Nichols, were arriving this afternoon, and we'd planned to take them to the Lasqueti Fireman's Picnic. This is held at Lasqueti's historic Teapot House, and is *the* event on Lasqueti's social calendar. And as Theresa's friends know, her love of flowers is matched only by her passion for socializing.

Theresa chose to abandon her newly adopted children, but wanted them to survive the separation. Her solution was to put the pots on our porch. Upon obsequious inquiry, I was informed that "Deer won't come on the *porch*."

After breaking our backs lifting up the pots, we set off for the picnic, which as usual lived up to our fondest expectations.

Ice cream, burgers, hot dogs, beer, hard cider, and shots of tequila were for sale. The aroma of marijuana occasionally drifted by. Pans of homemade brownies sat on a table, free to all takers. Some of those brownies were laced with a special ingredient, as Ryan inadvertently discovered.

The firemen were shooting the kids with the fire hose to cool them off from the heat. Elizabeth Nichols ran back to us laughing, drenched from head to toe. Local talent sang and performed on a makeshift stage that was rigged on a rockery platform above the grass. Folks sat in groups in the shade of the old apple trees, talking and enjoying picnic lunches. A classic, old-fashioned community picnic, for the benefit of the all-volunteer Lasqueti Fire Department.

Unfortunately, while we were on Lasqueti the deer had their own picnic. Upon our return, we found that Theresa's flowers had been clear-cut to the dirt.

August 8, 2000

Walking outside this morning when still half-asleep, I beheld a scene of carnage. Our deck was stained red, as if some animal had been slaughtered there while we slept. I wondered momentarily if Theresa had gone on a midnight rampage to revenge her beloved flowers. As my head cleared, however, I realized that the deer were culprits rather than victims. We'd left a big bunch of beets outside last night, and the deer had patiently eaten them all. Unable to swallow the beets whole, they'd pushed each one around the deck as they gnawed it to nothingness. Saliva had mixed with beet juice and painted the cedar blood-red.

When Theresa came out to inspect the mess, she no doubt wished it *was* deer blood.

Chapter 47
Hand-Catching a Salmon

... Robin captured a rarely seen moment in the life of the [whales] we were studying – a salmon kill.

"As the bottom loomed up from the depths [while I was diving with my underwater camera] I caught a flash of silver erratically ascending towards me. Halting with unbelieving eyes, I gaped as a large salmon writhed vertically past me in the water column. I have viewed salmon underwater only on the rarest occasions and had never before been approached by these skittish animals. This fish was obviously disoriented and, although it did not display any physical injuries, I felt the whales (which had just exited the bay) were responsible."
—Alexandra Morton, quoting her deceased husband Robin Morton, *Listening to Whales,*

August 9, 2000

I emerged slowly from sleep this morning, still wrapped in dreams. Listening carefully to the bay, I felt it was whispering secrets that I was on the verge of comprehending.

Theresa's offer of fresh-baked scones roused me from my lethargy, and in short order I was devouring these wonders with raspberry jam she'd made from our Minter Creek berries.

After breakfast, John Nichols and I did some fishing from the rocks in front of our house, where I caught eight rockfish and John caught zero. As with all types of fishing, this differential was ascribed either to luck or technique, depending on who was talking.

Theresa and Laure paddled the double kayak over to visit Allen on the *China Cloud*. Afterward, when they passed by Olsen on their way to the Finnerties, John and I grabbed our kayaks and joined them.

On our return, John and I got up to the house first while the women were still securing their kayaks. I was dismayed by immediately receiving two cell-phone calls inviting us to off-island social gatherings: dinner at John Cantrell's and a porch party at Ken and Claire's. Both invites were from good friends, but I deflected them with the excuse that the ladies were still gone in the kayaks and that I had no idea if they'd made other plans. This was only marginally true, but I was determined to have a full day on the island and its waters.

August 10, 2000

This morning dawned hot and calm, a day of floating dragonflies and humming crickets. The Strait was a perfect sphinx, revealing nothing of the mysteries that swam within her.

After a few morning chores, John, Ryan, and I went out to do some bottom-fishing. Close to the Sisters Islands, we teased up a variety of fish. We started fishing in shallows right next to the rocks where we could see the bottom, then drifted out to hundred-foot depths. On these drifts we caught several varieties of rockfish, lingcod, cabezon, and many greenling.

Fishing offshore from a seal rookery, my pole suddenly bent to the water in a *big* hit. I could feel something strong lunging about down below as it fought to free itself. After thrashing for a moment, it headed away at full speed, singing line off my reel.

Adrenaline pumped and our imaginations jumped into high gear. Was it a big halibut? Or perhaps a monster lingcod?

Ryan fired up the engine and began to follow the denizen to keep it from stripping all my line.

When the monster headed for the shore, my fantasies came to an end as I was forced to conclude that I'd hooked a seal. Whereupon I tightened the drag and broke it off.

Mixed with my shattered dreams of a monster fish was a small dash of obligatory concern for the seal. But not enough to delay me tying another jig on and getting it down again. For as all fisherman know, catching *anything* increases your certainty that the hook-up of a lifetime is only moments away.

The toughest part of fishing is reeling up my line for the last time, and after more futile hunting for the shadowy catches of our dreams, we resigned ourselves to one last try. As this brought nothing aboard but fantasies of future trophy fish, we stowed our gear and headed back to pull the prawn traps. Our efforts rewarded us with a nice load of big prawns which snapped around in the bottom of the cages.

When we finally reached home, we were just in time to clean up and depart for dinner at Dick and Terry's. Having spent all day in the motor boat, we opted for kayaks for the trip. We were joined around the table by Allen Farrell, Ray, and Eve, which added pleasant company to our meal.

Kayaking home in the light of a half moon, I narrowly missed several rocks. And on occasion had to paddle furiously to avoid being rammed by Theresa and Laure, who laughingly pursued the rest of us in the double kayak.

When not playing boat tag, we sought island shadows to see the phosphorus better. This was exceptionally bright in the shaded confines of floathouse cove. Trails of winking lights glowed around everything that swam or glided or scuttled, rippling in the shallows where unseen creatures dwelt.

After enjoying this display, John and I kayaked around Olsen, still not ready to get off the water.

***

I was awakened by a midnight call from Ken. Another boat had been stolen from local shores, towed away as the helpless owners watched in fury. A phone tree was alerting everybody who could help. It would be a slow trip to wherever the thieves were headed, as the wind had blown up considerably since we went to bed.

I was to man a listening post on Olsen, lest the culprits attempt to return to False Bay. John Cantrell ran out through the waves to the Finnerties, then cut his engine to wait in ambush.

No trace of the pirates. Lucky for them.

August 11, 2000

I awoke late to another sunny day. The wind had mellowed down from the gusts of the night, but it was still a good day for sailors.

Allen Farrell came by in the *China Cloud* with Ray and Eve, and as they passed close by the rocks, invited us out for a sail. Dick, who was on Olsen for a spot of business, ferried us out in his rowboat as Allen held *China Cloud* motionless offshore.

The shores of the local islands drop precipitously into the deep, and Allen is a master at using every inch of water around him. As we tacked back and forth upwind to the Finnerties, Allen sailed head-on to within touching distance of the rocks. Then he calmly swung over the tiller, gliding *China Cloud* around within a hair's breadth of collision. At first my jaw dropped open in anxious disbelief. But Allen showed neither alarm nor concern, and even had a ghost of a grin on his face, as if he were baiting us to react.

I believed I was observing a master sailor showing off his skill. When I mentioned this to Ray, he was adamant that Allen was simply inattentive, cheating disaster only by drawing on an incredible storehouse of luck. While Ray was able to clench his mouth shut, his eyes got wider and wider each time we approached the shore.

After we anchored in the Finnerties the ladies made a delicious lunch and then joined Allen in the stern and showered him with attention. As usual, this brought a grin to his face and a twinkle to his eyes.

***

Today's sun had heated up our island's rocks to where they were almost uncomfortable to walk on. Removing some steaks from our freezer when we returned from our sail, I put them on the warm rocks to thaw. Glancing back at the steaks as I was climbing into the hammock, I saw an eagle circling suspiciously low. Disentangling myself from the hammock, I sprinted back and retrieved the steaks. In minutes they would have become eagle food.

August 12, 2000

As we were walking in on the Lasqueti dock this afternoon, Ray suddenly exclaimed, "Look at that fish!" In front of the Blue Roof swam an obviously disoriented salmon. One bystander lobbed a couple of rocks near it, which did nothing to scare it away. As everyone gaped, I gleefully announced that I knew exactly what to do.

Doffing my shirt and hat, I waded out to chest deep water where the salmon was swimming.

Someone shouted, "But it's sick—"

I yelled back, "Makes no difference to the barbecue!"

First I tried to grab the salmon by the tail, but it proved too slippery for that. After a second such attack, the fish decided that perhaps a trip to deeper water was in order, and attempted to swim past me.

Spreading my arms out under water, I did my best to direct the salmon back toward shore. Though it wanted to escape, the salmon moved sluggishly in its attempts to do so, displaying nothing of a salmon's typical speed and agility. After slowly herding it to a cleft in the rocks, I grabbed it by the gills and then held it aloft for everyone to see.

The mug-huggers on the pub's deck, who had been watching my antics with amusement, broke out in applause.

One obviously dimwitted woman asked, "Are you going to kill it?"

In reply, I waded from the water proudly displaying my catch, a beautiful king salmon shimmering in the sun.

Some years ago, I'd made a similar catch in Lasqueti waters. Sailing near the Fagan Islands, we'd spied a salmon finning lazily on the surface. Seemingly oblivious of our looming hull, it wandered distractedly as we tacked in close and netted it.

But both of these incidents perplexed me.

Salmon are skitterish fish. Seldom seen even by divers, they'll approach a boat or fisherman only when brought in forcibly on the end of a line, and only then when totally exhausted.

I've caught salmon with large wounds from seal attacks and scale scars from gill nets. These fought as aggressively as any other salmon I've landed. I've brought in others on remote Alaskan rivers, hundreds of kilometers from the salt water, weakened from weeks of starvation and swimming up rapids and falls. Even these salmon battled gamely, and on the occasions when I released them, recovered quickly and darted fearfully away.

Today's fish, and the one I netted from our sailboat, had no such blemishes or reasons for exhaustion. Yet both acted as if they'd been knocked senseless, which they probably had.

The likely culprits were killer whales.

A big question for toothed-cetacean scientists has always been how such ponderous beasts catch their prey. In terms of agility and speed, a fifty-ton sperm whale is no match for the giant squid that are its favorite food. Neither can an eight-ton killer whale outmaneuver a reluctant salmon. Yet sperm whale stomachs have been found to contain up to 7,000 squid beaks, and resident orcas feed primarily on salmon.

Researchers now believe that killer and sperm whales sometimes stun their prey with sonar, literally buzzing them senseless with sound.

Whalesong is a wondrous thing, a complex language in which each pod of killer whales has its own dialect. But orcas use sound for more than keeping in touch with their brethren. In the dark of their undersea world, killer whales broadcast directional sounds that bounce off everything around them: boat hulls, islands, sea lions, and salmon. By reading the returning echoes, the whales see all of this.

Killer whales can radiate their voices up to ten miles, filling a hundred square miles of water with their song. But these whales can also concentrate their sound in a beam. Beneath a killer whale's blowhole are air sacs that change in size and shape to direct intense echolocation sounds forward. Entering the acoustic lens of the killer whale's face, the sound passes through fatty tissue that amplifies it, and a spiral structure of differing densities that steps its transmission down from the high-density whale to the lower-density seawater.

The intensity of whale sounds can be staggering. Blue whales, the earth's loudest animals, can call from the mid-Atlantic and a quarter-hour later, hear echoes from 900-mile distant Bermuda.

After echolocating their prey, killer and sperm whales focus their sound on the intended targets. This concentrated sound creates a blast of pressure that stuns, paralyzes, or even kills the salmon or squid they are pursuing. Both of the drunken salmon I found may have been stunned in this manner and still disoriented when I happened upon them.

August 13, 2000

This morning, Ryan and I ran over to French Creek to pick up his twin brother Chris. It was great to have Chris home after his two-month stay in Bolivia playing soccer. Notwithstanding that he and twin brother Ryan were very glad to see each other, they immediately launched into their usual bickering about who had whose clothes and CDs, and who'd snitched the other's candy.

Our Gig Harbor friends, the Nichols, were still visiting us, and in early afternoon John and I went out bottom-fishing at the Sisters. Our catch included three seals, which put up quite a fight before shaking the hook or breaking our lines.

These seals swam in close to satisfy their curiosity, surfacing within a few meters of our boat and eyeing us over. Oftentimes, they bobbed around in a pack of ten or so. We were sure they were all adolescent boys, as they appeared to be up to some kind of mischief.

The Sisters were alive with oyster catchers, cormorants, gulls, and sandpipers. Occasionally we were pestered by biting flies, attracted by the seal scat and bird guano that covers the rocks of these isolated isles. We could always tell by the smell when we were downwind.

After fishing, John and I pulled the prawn traps and then barbecued our catch with salmon for dinner. Our last chore was to toast marshmallows over the coals to make s'mores for dessert.

As we were eating these tasty treats, a doe and her two fawns grazed to within feet of where we sat on the porch. Numb to Theresa's flower protection antics, they have continued to make this evening visit, coming in close when our day's activities are done.

CHAPTER 48
OUR "THANK YOU" FEAST

The ornament of a house is the friends who frequent it.
—Ralph Waldo Emerson

August 14, 2000

On the morning low tide, the boys and I dug clams for tomorrow's party to honor the crew that built our house. We used oyster and clam shells to do most of our digging, finding them easier to work than shovels.

After spending the rest of the day preparing for the party, I caught the late ferry to French Creek to take delivery of our new welded-aluminum boat.

Aluminum is the material of choice for island skiffs. Rocky landings quickly wear through fiberglass or wood, and in rough water, when we bang against the rocks, anything but aluminum would be holed.

Aluminum's toughness allows me the docking method I use to get our passengers safely between boat and island when conditions deteriorate. I shove our boat's bow against the rocks under power as the waves grind it up and down, holding us firmly against the shore.

I ran back across the Strait in our new craft and got only a mild soaking from the moderate swells. I wore my float coat and attached the motor kill lanyard to it, fully aware that the wrong pitch of a wave could throw me overboard.

Still paranoid about boat theft, Theresa woke me up in the middle of the night when she thought she heard a noise out at our buoy. We saw no one, but did discover an incredible display of Northern Lights.

The sky was strewn with pulsating clouds and curtains of brilliance. Phantasms of liquid music throbbed and swirled, dream shapes of gods that rarely reveal themselves. Some were white and others green, and occasionally they were pierced by shooting stars, one of which exploded at the end of its comet-like run across the sky.

Theresa roused Laure and John so they could watch this show, and then she called Ken and Claire. We could hear Ken howling all the way across the bay as he accompanied the light show on his conga drum.

August 15, 2000

A quiet, sunny morning, pleasantly cooled by a light breeze. The boys dozed in the hammocks as Theresa and Laure baked apple crisp for tonight's party, while watching deer graze on Little Olsen.

I picked up Sylvain the rock wizard at the Lasqueti dock, where we loaded the Community Center's monster barbecue aboard Aurel's skiff. After towing this to Olsen and setting up the barbecue on the floathouse porch, we made a buffet table on our back deck out of plywood and saw horses, and then launched into a full day of cooking.

About 5:30 PM, Aurel arrived in the *Argent*, which he brought right up to Olsen's rocks. We rigged a plank from his bow to the shore, and all forty passengers balanced across the plank from boat to island. Shortly thereafter, John and Morgan arrived by kayak, Sailor Johnson's family by oyster barge, Alan Farrell and one other couple by rowboat, and several other groups by their aluminum skiffs. And with perfect timing, two Gig Harbor friends stopped by on their way home from Desolation Sound. As everyone made landfall at about the same time, the party began in earnest.

We started the feast with smoked salmon and mussels, then brought out buckets of steamed clams smothered with pesto sauce.

Next came barbecued lamb kabobs. Sylvain had killed and butchered two wild Lasqueti lambs and marinated the meat for several days. After all this was consumed, we brought out trays of apple crisp and chocolate mousse for dessert.

When everyone was sated, Ken, Merrick, and Noel started playing on accordion, guitar, and fiddle. Ronan joined in on a drum improvised out of an upturned five-gallon bucket, and finally Ronan's wife Shari brought out her trumpet.

Aurel danced a jig, much to the delight of all, and then led several toasts. Sylvain produced hula hoops, and soon the adults and kids alike were showing off their stuff in the hoops. Everybody had a different technique, and some were hilariously unsuccessful.

Earlier in the evening, Aurel had pulled me aside and mentioned that since he had the responsibility of hauling everyone back and forth on his boat, he wouldn't be drinking much, and accordingly would appreciate a half-gallon of wine so he could indulge himself afterward.

I agreed to this out of concern for our guests, and then grinned through the rest of the party as I watched Aurel down copious quantities of beer and wine and smoke a few joints for good measure. The only thing he didn't do was eat the magic mushrooms that he said he was responsibly saving till later.

At the end of the evening, I ferried people out to the *Argent*, which we had tied alongside the Grady at its buoy. A great time was had by all.

August 16, 2000

I took Laure and John to the early ferry, then spent the rest of the day in post-party clean up.

Our always adventurous boys figured out a new way to get out of work, and at the same time amuse themselves on the island's rocky shores.

First they located a cliff with a tree on top. Next, they rifled my island stores and made off with a big pulley and 150 feet of rope. Their plan was to rig a tight-line from the tree to the beach. The pulley hung from the line, and they were going to hang from a loop tied to the pulley. The goal, achievable only at high tide, was a high-speed ride from cliff top to water.

They anchored the line to the tree and then ran it down to a metal cylinder they buried in the sand. Then came several engineering failures, followed by a search for Ray to get his advice. Predictably, this led to a successfully stabilized tight-line.

From the whoops of laughter that I heard when the water got deep enough, I could tell that their thrill ride worked perfectly, replete with hair-raising defects that put the rider at significant peril.

***

Theresa and I were early to bed, where we started a game of backgammon that I interrupted repeatedly to chase down mosquitoes with our battery-powered mosquito zapper. This is shaped like a badminton racket, with parallel wires where the strings would be. When I press two buttons on the handle, a charge is sent through the wires that zap, with a satisfying spark, any insect that happens to come in contact with them.

I get my best results hunting mosquitoes on our ceiling when its dark and I turn on our bedside lights, allowing me to distinguish mosquito shadows from small dark spots in the wood.

By now I know all of the mosquito look-alikes on our ceiling and no longer waste my time crawling out from under the covers to chase down a knothole.

CHAPTER 49
A TALE OF TWO HERMITS

*How I spurned that turnpike earth!—that common highway
all over dented with the marks of slavish hoofs; and turned
to admire the magnanimity of the sea, which will permit no
records.*

—Herman Melville, *Moby Dick*

House guests are like fish. They begin to stink after 3 days.

—Unknown

August 17, 2000

Today dawned clear, calm, and warm. Lounging in bed, Theresa and I
watched reflected light from the water dance on our ceiling.

After rising, we sat on the rocks overlooking False Bay and enjoyed
the island's myriad entertainments.

Sailboats motored away from last night's anchorage in Cocktail
Cove, seeking wind elsewhere. Small waves slapped hollowly against
the aluminum boat at our mooring. A seal popped its head up in the
waters out front.

A few adventurous mosquitoes tried to dive-bomb us, not realizing
who they were dealing with.

Bait fish broke the surface, some jumping clear of the water. What
predator was chasing them?

Another mosquito landed, lifting its hind legs as it probed my thumb with is proboscis. A few small clouds clustered around the peaks on Vancouver Island.

Small chickadees chirped in the junipers and a gull cried overhead. A distant murder of crows discussed something vigorously. Tall grass stems began to waver in the first hint of a breeze. Ripples on the bay sent the sun's path into a riot of silent sparks.

Moving to the hammock, I spent some pleasant time reading, ignoring Theresa's reminders that there were chores to be done. Her attempt to enlist the boys met with similar failure, albeit with a bit more backtalk.

Theresa finally kayaked off in a huff, feeling mistreated by all the men in her life. Her pique had been a challenge to our collective manhood, and we winked conspiratorially at one another as we watched her paddle away. Her anger only made our victory more sweet. The hammock became softer still, my book more enticing.

The boys and I went out to the Finnerties to do some cliff jumping, and afterwards visited the island where Verner used to live. The foot of the trail to his cabin was marked by parallel logs set in the rocks, over which he'd pulled his kayak when coming ashore.

Stooping low under the brush, we followed something more akin to a game trail than a path to someone's home. Following the track on hands and knees through a thicket, we realized how much Verner valued his privacy.

Emerging into a small clearing, we quieted as we beheld Verner's cabin. It resembled the detritus of an old forest more than a house, dissolving into a pile of weathered boards and junk at the base of its walls. Moss and lichen camouflaged its sagging roof, which was a nest for fallen branches. The door hung open, silently inviting for us to enter.

The cabin's one room had a dirt floor, and in one corner was a woodstove with one of Verner's cruising suits hanging next to it. Fetishes of crab claws and animal skulls adorned a wall nearby. The bed's mosquito net was the hovel's one touch of self-indulgence.

Walking outside, we found crossed jawbones nailed to an old mailbox. The mailbox attested to Verner's sense of humor, as this remote island had never seen mail service and surely never would. Snail and mussel shells hung above it, and various small bones lay scattered inside. This voodoo chest mimicked the fetish we'd seen inside the cabin, making me wonder if they were just Verner's small treasures or a shaman's collection of spirit callers.

Taking our leave of Verner's private world, we motored home to switch boats so we could pull the prawn traps. To our consternation, the rising wind turned our traps into sea anchors, tripling the amount of effort needed to lift them from the depths.

For all our effort, we only harvested a moderate load. If our dinner guests could see what sweat and risk went into the capture of these prawns, they'd worship rather than eat them.

We returned home for a quick swim, an outdoor shower, and some last minute prep for the arrival of our third set of house guests in two weeks. Julie Shipley and Bill Mitchell live in a log cabin on Filucy Bay, and we'd had a lot of fun with them through the years. But by the luck of the draw, they were the last in a succession of people we'd entertained this summer. As their arrival approached, I found myself wishing I lived alone in Verner's shack

August 18, 2000

Once I cast off the lines that moor me to the outside world, the gulf I cross is immeasurably wider than the miles I travel. The rituals of my daily life change inexorably.

Though a sense of schedule is deeply ingrained in me, I do my best to lock it in the car in the marina parking lot. What sneaks across the Strait with me is soon absorbed by the wild waters or lost on our island's rugged shores.

On the island, I spend hours lazing in a hammock, alternating between reading and staring at the bay. Languor and a harmless type of selfishness pervade my days.

The edge of my world is close at hand, defined by the line where the island plunges into the sea. A sea which serves like a castle's moat.

But this year's stream of guests had breached our island's insularity. A sense of schedule intruded. Obligations arose. Languor dissolved as if it was morning mist submitting to the sun.

This languor is highly narcotic. When it is destroyed by others, I experience withdrawal symptoms and engage in an addict's destructive behavior. Enter the sociopath, an embarrassment to himself and all.

***

I picked up Julie and Bill at the Lasqueti dock, ferried them to Olsen, and then ran the boys across the Strait to French Creek. After hugging Chris and Ryan goodbye on the dock, I sat back down in my boat. While chewing the inside of my cheek, I decided not to return to the island for a while. My sanctuary had been violated and I needed time to think.

Or, perhaps, to avoid thinking.

Fishing, no doubt, was the answer.

When I walked up to chat with the old salt at the marina store, he told me that a twenty-kilo (forty-pound) salmon had been weighed in last night, and that he'd seen daily catches of many other nice fish. Though this crusty fellow has a reputation for spinning yarns in order to sell fishing tackle, his story still hooked me. Within minutes I was clutching a fresh selection of lures in my hands and walking excitedly back to my boat.

I fished off French Creek for an hour or so at the precise depth where the old man told me all the lunkers had been caught. Trolling back and forth in his magic spot, I tended my gear with rapt attention. Had another boat crossed my path, I would have looked up only after ramming it.

Finally tiring of my folly, I peered across the water toward the store. Seeing a small flash from the bench where the salty dog had been sitting, I imagined it was his gold tooth. No doubt I'd kept him entertained all the while, grinning in the midday sun.

Pulling my gear, I ran across the Strait to try the northwest shore of Jenkins Island. After lifting my spirits with some successful rockfish jigging, I did some more trolling for salmon, again without luck. In the boredom of my failure, I fantasized about catching a huge salmon, speeding back across the Strait, then casually strolling up to the store with my catch and lying brazenly about the larger ones I had on ice in my boat.

Rising wind and waves rocked me out of my reverie, helping me realize that Theresa would be worrying over my extended absence. Accordingly, I headed back to Olsen.

My welcome home was a bit frosty, as befitting someone who abandoned his spouse and newly arrived guests. Thankfully, their icy glances were warmed by our dinner of clams smothered in garlic butter.

For some reason, however, jaws began to clench when I shared my observations of "Good Guests" and "Bad Guests."

Bad Guests
1. Pee in the outhouse.
2. Expect to be fed without bringing any food.
3. "Hey, I'm on vacation! Do the dishes yourself."
4. Can't figure out our system for separating garbage, forcing me to dig through the trash each day.
5. Repeatedly leave doors open, letting in big-feeder mosquitoes.
6. Seem to have an allergy to brooms and dust pans.
7. Down a pack of cookies at a sitting.
8. Believe the island is one big sandbox for their kids to rearrange at will.
9. Take away our clothes, books, headlamps, and other carefully collected items, and forget to return them.
10. Bring their dog.
11. Bring the worries of the outside world.

Good Guests
1. Don't pee at all.
2. Come laden with exotic foods and fine wines.
3. Wash dishes, chop wood, and clean out the outhouse.
4. Take our accumulated trash with them when they leave.
5. Go without mosquito repellant, thereby drawing all the bugs in the area to themselves.
6. Smile when I plop in the hammock.
7. Smile more broadly when I go fishing.

8. Treat our treasured stashes of cookies and MacKintosh Toffee with reverence, refusing to eat any.

In comment on these lists and my behavior, Julie Shipley came up with her own lists:

Good Hosts

1. Are polite or, at a minimum, speak when spoken to, without lips quivering in a canine snarl, teeth bared and saliva running down chin.
2. Don't spend all day in the hammock, out fishing, or in other antisocial behavior.
3. Don't threaten in feigned humor to drown, keelhaul, starve, trip, torture, poison, or otherwise dispose of guests.
4. Don't hover around those trying to eat, closing lids on jam jars, putting cookies away, or otherwise engaging in thinly veiled "don't eat so much" conduct.

Bad Hosts

1. Charlie Walters
2. Charlie Walters
3. Charlie Walters

August 19, 2000

Theresa and I got into quite an argument last night. For some reason, she objected to my monosyllabic interchanges with our guests and the disappearing acts which followed. She's made her own list—a short list of finalists for the "Jerk of the Year" award. My name appears to be the only one on it, scrawled angrily in heavy black pencil.

In atonement for yesterday's sins, I got up early this morning to do the dishes and sweep the floor.

With an obsequious smile, I was the perfect host when Julie and Bill arose, replete with sufficient bowing and scraping to communicate my apology. This was my last opportunity to be civil, as they were catching the first ferry off Lasqueti to start their journey home. After serving them breakfast and portering their bags to the boat, I made sure they had dry cushions to sit on for the ride to the Lasqueti dock.

With a sunny smile I waved goodbye as the ferry pulled out, and with a Cheshire Cat grin cruised slowly back to the island.

CHAPTER 50
GLASS SPONGES

British Columbia's Glass Sponge Reefs are a seafloor Jurassic Park.

—Natural Resources Canada

August 20, 2000

The morning was quiet, the water lightly rippled by the slightest breath of wind. A dragonfly hovered outside our window, eyeing the plump mosquitoes on our ceiling who were fat from gorging themselves as we slept.

I padded to the window to confirm that both boats were secure at their moorings, true to the discipline I follow whenever I get up from bed.

I take simple pleasure from such routines of island life: walking into the woods to take a pee; going everywhere by boat; clambering over rocks; checking out passing vessels through binoculars; seeing our friends coming from a distance; being island-bound by weather; watching small crabs devour prawn heads; leaving shoes outside.

After two island weeks, my calf muscles are still sore from the stretching they get as I navigate Olsen's uneven terrain. My hands are swollen and sore from the work they do, covered with slow-healing cuts from prawn and rockfish spines.

Theresa's feet are cracked and dry from repeated dunking in salt water. Last night she rubbed them with bag-balm before she climbed into bed, then put socks on to moisturize them as she slept.

I pulled the prawn traps today and harvested sixty crustaceans and a small octopus. On other days, my 400-foot-deep traps have rewarded me with tantalizing glimpses of the fantastic creatures that inhabit these depths: diminutive plated starfish whose compact bodies are specially suited to 400 feet of water pressing on their backs; a huge octopus that entirely filled one trap; incredible crabs covered with a fuzz of spines, able to fold claws and legs together in a seamless puzzle of camouflage that resembles a coral-covered rock; and delicate sponges covered with glass hairs, unlike anything growing in our familiar world.

Where I prawn near Olsen, these glass sponges are isolated specimens. But in four places in British Columbia's Queen Charlotte Basin, and another two locations in the Strait of Georgia, glass sponges have grown together into reefs of astounding size.

In the mid-1980s, scientists were engaged in a project to map the seafloor of Queen Charlotte Sound and Hecate Strait. As they bent over their sonar survey, they were puzzled by unusual shapes rising above the seabed, mysterious images that ranged over huge areas of bottom. While their extent was geologic in magnitude, the structures were acoustically distinct from the rock below, presenting a total conundrum to the researchers.

Returning the following year to investigate this benthic mystery, the scientists were stunned speechless. The puzzling seafloor anomalies turned out to be towering glass sponge reefs believed to have gone extinct in the time of dinosaurs. When a few lucky researchers descended into the dark in a small submarine that illuminated the reef with its light, they were the first humans to study a sponge reef other than by examining fossils.

In Jurassic times, when much of modern Europe was beneath the sea, the depths of the Atlantic held a 7,000-kilometer-long (4,200-mile) glass sponge reef that stretched from Europe to North America. Considered the largest biologic structure on the face of the earth, it was over three times as long as Australia's Great Barrier Reef.

Growing on the sea floor for over 9,000 years, British Columbia's glass sponge reefs are globally unique, except for a small glass sponge reef recently discovered thirty miles off the Washington coast. Described as "living fossils," the reefs have been noted to be "very similar to those of the late Jurassic" (Sponge Reef Project, www.porifera.org). Surviving since prehistoric times, they have been nominated for World Heritage status by the United Nations Educational, Scientific and Cultural Organization (UNESCO).

Though the reefs have been compared to the Amazon rainforest because of their size and biodiversity, we should remember that a glass sponge is a *creature*, or more accurately a community of creatures. The silica-rich hard parts of the reef are skeletons, within which are the bodies of the sponges.

Glass sponges need a hard bottom to settle on, and in the Queen Charlotte depths they found ideal conditions. Near the end of our last ice age, when the sea level was lower and the glaciers calved to pieces, icebergs grounded and ploughed the seafloor. Berms of cobbles piled up on both sides of these scours, and when the fine sediments washed out, they left a perfect home for glass sponges. Along these iceberg furrows glass sponges began to grow.

This area of British Columbia is near the edge of the continental shelf where the upwelling waters are full of nutrients. Filtering out the abundant feed, individual sponges grew into magnificent structures resembling warm-water corals, up to two meters wide and tall.

In the dark, they glowed red and yellow and a host of other brilliant colors. Hiding in the depths, the sponges formed cups and funnels and fantastic branching structures of fingers and tubes. And when a colony finally died after a century or two, it raised the foundation of the reef higher and its descendants anchored their own colonies to its branches.

Spreading laterally and sprouting up from the skeletons of their ancestors, these sponges grew into reef complexes individually covering as much as 300 square kilometers (186 square miles). These animals are filter-feeders, and the amount of seawater processed by the reefs is staggering—over 1.75 *trillion* liters (460 billion gallons) per day.

In waters that are 165 to 240 meters deep (540 to 780 feet), together these northern reefs cover over 1,000 square kilometers of seafloor (620 square miles). Their towers are up to twenty-one meters high (68 feet), and their meadows are many kilometers wide. Individual mounds the size of small office buildings rise out of huge sponge fields, "sprawling over the seabed like underwater cities" (Vancouver Aquarium website).

Spurred by the discovery of these northern reefs, Canadian scientists began an extensive search of other waters that might hold glass sponge populations. And in 2001 they hit pay dirt. Two reefs were discovered on McCall Bank, east of Bowen Island off the sunshine coast. Another was found off Gabriola Island. Though these Strait of Georgia reefs are considerably smaller than the northern systems, covering only four square kilometers, their individual mounds reach almost as high—up to fourteen meters. Here, too, the reefs lie on remnants of glacial till.

CHAPTER 51
THE SECRET LIFE OF PRAWNS

That head upon which the upper sun now gleams has moved amid this world's foundations. Where unrecorded names and navies rust, and untold hopes and anchors rot; where in her murderous hold this frigate earth is ballasted with bones of millions of the drowned.

—Herman Melville, *Moby Dick*

August 20, 2000, continued

When I was back on shore heading today's prawns, I noticed a group of starfish following the rising tide up the rocks. They crept slowly toward the prawn heads I threw near them, patiently reaching out bright purple arms to draw the tasty morsels to their mouths.

Gazing out over the Strait, I spotted the three-kilometer-distant Sisters Islands. On the waters in between, several commercial prawn buoys bobbed in the waves, for the depths below were some of the best prawn neighborhoods around.

There the bottom slopes down to a 250-meter-deep trench. Resting on that incline, typically about a hundred meters deep, sat hundreds of commercial prawn traps.

I'd been amateurishly prawning here since the first year we arrived, having outfitted myself with a set of recreational traps. The canned cat food and butchered dogfish I stuffed into my bait tubes did attract prawns, but since the poor design allowed prawns to feed on my bait without entering the trap, only the unluckiest of prawns actually got caught.

I had tied my traps to a spool of the cheapest rope I could find: thin, slick, yellow polypropylene. Lubricated by seawater and weighted down by the rocks I put in my traps, it was almost impossible to pull up. To my repeated dismay, I found that temper tantrums and profanity offered only marginal assistance.

My luck changed on a recent trip to French Creek. At the dock, a commercial prawn fisherman was offering his old gear for sale. I emptied my wallet on the spot, purchasing thousands of feet of thick prawn line and a pile of commercial prawn traps. As we loaded this bounty into my Grady, we talked of pot depths and soak times and feed. As a bonus, though perhaps out of pity, he added a gratuitous bag of commercial bait pellets to my haul.

After roaring back across the Strait to my favorite prawning grounds, I examined my new gear carefully as I deployed it. My new traps were significantly different from my old ones in the design of the entrance funnels and bait containers, making escape and freeloading more difficult.

Loading my bait tubs with bait pellets, I smiled with relief that I was done slaughtering dogfish in the back of my boat.

Now it was time to apply the knowledge I'd gleaned from the professional prawn trapper. After locating an area of prime prawn depth, I used my depth finder to search the surrounding waters and get a feel for the bottom's topography. The seafloor had bumps and hollows in its slope to the trench before the Sisters, and at one point dropped off an abyssal cliff. I had neglected the depth finder once and drifted over this drop-off while setting my traps, losing all my gear in the process. That was a several hundred dollar mistake, and even worse, had left us prawnless until I was able to secure new gear.

I'd spent years trying to get to know the unseen bottom here, using my depth finder to locate promising prawn real estate. Relying on charts and electronics, triangulating my position between nearby islands, and recalling where I'd had my most successful hauls, I tried to find that featureless patch of water that hid the best prawn habitat below.

Once I located the spot where I wanted my traps to land, I ran back up-current and dropped them like a bombardier. My hope was that as they descended into the gloom, the current would deposit them at my targeted spot. To the extent that I misjudged the lateral distance the current would carry my traps, I would either land them on less productive shallows or in trap-swallowing deeps.

Throwing my buoy in after my sinking line, I hoped for a record catch of spot prawns, the largest shrimps in the north Pacific.

***

If we were like the prawns I was hunting, all our children would be born male. After maturing to about one year of age, we'd function as breeding males for about two years, then transition into females for our final year of life and spawn at about age four.

As the human equivalent of prawns, we'd be encased in a shell of armor that we'd repeatedly shed as we grew. Five pairs of wrist-thin legs would sprout from our chest, each with two knees. A segmented tail would extend from the rear of our torso, strong enough to pull us backward far faster than we could run.

Hanging from our tail would be five pairs of swimmerets, small paddle-like appendages that allowed us to swim slowly forward.

Reaching out from the front of our face, our whiplike antennae would stretch forward four times farther than human arms could reach. Probing the dark like flexible white canes, they'd allow us to feel what lay unseen ahead. If we encountered a predator there, we'd fend it off with the four-foot-long serrated sword that lanced forward from the top of our head.

Our lidless prawn eyes would be fist-sized orbs projecting on stalks from the front of our face. Instead of our one little human nose, near the front of our tapering head we'd sport two articulated antennules. Covered with sensory hairs connected to a brain half-dedicated to the sense of smell, these antennules would be critical to our feeding.

When we fed in the near-black depths, our eyes might as well be covered with seaweed. The odor of food would come from up-current, and like the other hairs on our body, those on our antennules would help us judge the direction of flow. Facing into it, we'd hold our antennules upright and apart, allowing the water to wash over their sensory-hair array. If the current was confused, in the prawn equivalent of sniffing, we'd repeatedly flick our antennules up and down, seeking to further sample its eddies.

At the first scent of attractive molecules, we'd flick our antennules and begin to move. Within seconds we'd be crawling toward the odor's origin, using our antennules to orient us in the current. As one or the other antennule detected a stronger concentration of smell, we'd adjust our course in that direction.

Another scent that could draw us forward would be that of a prawn of the opposite sex. But because we lived deep, much about our sex life would be unstudied. If we stretched our human-prawn analogy a bit further, however and assumed that our sex lives resembled those of American lobsters, prawns' much-studied crustacean cousins, we'd engage in some pretty unusual behavior.

Lobsters use chemical communication to differentiate between sexes, signal readiness to mate, turn off aggressive behavior, and select the most desirable partner. American lobsters urinate from the front of their faces, and their pheromone-laced urine plays a key role in their mating rituals.

If we were a female lobster, we'd be able to mate only after molting. Since our new shell wouldn't harden until days after shedding the old one, we'd spend our first post-molt days in hiding, mushy and vulnerable. But at the scent of mature males, as soon as we could walk, we'd crawl up-current to investigate. After identifying the most dominant male by the scent of his urine, we'd seduce him with ours. As a lobster female, we'd be the one doing the choosing.

Once proper rapport was established, the lobster male would roll us onto our back and mount us in the missionary position. With a few quick thrusts of his tail, his forward swimmerets would deposit capsules of sperm into the seminal receptacles in our thorax, where we'd store the sperm until we were ready to extrude our eggs.

Pushing our eggs out from within our body cavity, we'd glue them to the underside of our tail with cement from glands on our swimmerets. When our eggs were in place, we'd open the sperm pouch and fertilize them ourselves.

During the time we carried our eggs, the maturing embryos within them would shed their diminutive shells some thirty-five times. When our eggs were on the verge of hatching, we'd send them floating with a few flicks of our tail.

As a spot prawn, this batch of eggs would probably be our only one. We'd carry our eggs for up to five and a half months before flicking them free.

Upon hatching in March or April, our prawn larvae would swim up toward the light, and then rely on coastal upwelling, currents, and windblown surface water to get to inshore shallows. In this journey, our young would be widely dispersed, and we'd never see them again.

During their first months of life, our larval young would molt though a series of different swimming body forms. But in the warming waters of mid-June, they'd leave their planktonic form behind, molting and settling to the bottom as small prawns. Here they'd seek out shallow-water nurseries that provided daytime hiding places: kelp beds and eel grass flats.

Our forgotten young would remain in these nursery areas through autumn and part of winter. At about eighteen months of age, when they matured as males, they'd begin their down-hill march to deep-water adult habitat. There they'd join the hoards of prawns covering the bottom where I set my traps.

CHAPTER 52
NEW NEIGHBORS

After leaving the sea, after all those millions of years living inside the sea, we took the ocean with us ... The water inside our bodies is almost exactly the same as the water of the sea. It is salty by just the same amount ... Our blood and our sweat are both salty almost exactly like the water from the sea is salty ... We carry oceans inside us, in our blood and in our sweat. And we are crying the oceans in our tears.

—Gregory David Roberts, *Shantaram*

August 21, 2000

One of our biggest surprises in these remote islands, which became one of the biggest joys of living there, was the people we met.

I'd been lured to Lasqueti by my best friend Ken, a dreamer whose passion for the coast had lured him to one of its most wondrous places. As we got to know other folks living on the small islands and bays near Olsen—Ray and Eve on Higgins Island, Don and Deb on Wolf, Dick and Terry on Lasqueti's "Cocktail Cove," Allen Farrel and *China Cloud* in Mud Bay, and Dag and Maria on the entrance to Johnson's Lagoon—we realized that other dreamers had come here for similar reasons.

Living in the islands gave all of us the ability to retreat from the outside world. We were self-sufficient in a wild place, where our most frequent visitors were otters and eagles and seals. If we didn't stray from our isolated homesteads, the closest contact we'd have with other people was seeing a boat go by.

This made socializing a special treat, and accordingly our group of False Bay friends sought out each other's company. We had dinner parties and music fests, kayak adventures and sailing trips. Clam expeditions and fishing derbies, movie nights and tea ceremonies. There were basket weaving socials and bocce ball tournaments, scrabble games and forest hikes. The women got together for group pedicures and the men to pull prawn traps. We went swimming in the Finnerties and cruised around Lasqueti, made boat trips to Blackfish Sound and paddling jaunts to the Fagan Islands.

Though some of these get-togethers were planned, many were spontaneous. We'd kayak over to Ray and Eve's to say hello, and end up staying for most of the day. Allen would sail by and we'd join him for a sunset cruise. When one of us boated out to pull our prawn traps, we usually stopped by to pick up a friend. Anyone coming for dinner was always welcome to bring other unannounced guests, and frequently did.

When Peter Steinbergen and Christine Hosford moved onto Wolf Island last summer, their love of adventure greased this already well-oiled social machine. With their ready smiles and passion for life afloat, they fit in perfectly.

Peter had lived on Lasqueti for years, then sailed away to the South Seas. He spent years cruising their remote islands, diving in crystalline waters, and holing up in mangrove swamps to ride out typhoons.

In Fiji, Peter learned the local lesson that "you haven't been around until you've been aground." After sailing the wood-hulled *Kapduva* onto an unseen reef in a falling tide, he escaped disaster only by scrounging planks from a nearby island and wedging them between his hull and the coral. When the tide rose some hours later, he was able to float *Kapduva* off without damage.

On another Fijian island, Peter ran into an entanglement that he made no effort to escape. Christine Hosford was sailing there on another boat, and soon enough Peter was admiring more than the cut of her jib. Now the two sailors spend half the year living aboard Christine's *Lulia* in New Zealand, and the rest of the time a stone's throw away from Olsen on Wolf Island, with *Kapduva* anchored just offshore.

The four of us had deepened our friendship on a sailing trip out of Auckland last winter, and this summer I smiled in anticipation whenever I saw Peter heading out to pull his prawn traps. He often picked me up on the way, and I looked forward to both the pleasure of his company and the entertainment his prawning provided. For while Peter was a master of most everything having to do with the sea, he was humorously inept at catching prawns.

To my disappointment, however, out of embarrassment over his puny catches, Peter had recently begun pulling his traps alone. While I was harvesting a half-bucket of prawns a pull, Peter was managing only a handful. I could tell how poorly he did by the distance he kept from Olsen on his return trips—the farther offshore, the smaller the catch.

Peter and Christine motored up late this afternoon in *Kapduva* and invited us aboard for an evening cruise. In light of his recent penchant for privacy in all things related to prawning, I was pleasantly surprised when we set out to pull his traps.

As we neared his buoy, Peter and I discussed the merits of pulling our pots with some type of power assistance. Though we had both waxed philosophical at our friends' incredulity when they heard we hand-pulled multiple traps from 130 meters (400 feet), both of us were tired of breaking our backs in the Strait's wind and waves. We were committed to finding a better way.

Peter's solution was to use *Kapduva's* power windlass, which in theory sounded like a good idea. In practice, I was going to learn otherwise.

Even in calm waters, *Kapduva* didn't maneuver well under power. Simply getting to Peter's prawn buoy, which was swinging back and forth in the current, required several approaches. When we finally managed to get the buoy close by our port side (where it had to be to use the windlass), the fun began.

Leaning out over *Kapduva's* life lines with a three-meter-long boat hook, I reached under the curve of the bow and tried to snag the line below his buoy. After managing this on my third try, I braced myself on the bow sprit and struggled to retrieve my catch through the maze of shrouds and stays and lines that cobweb Peter's classic wood sailboat. With Christine at the tiller and Peter pulling in the rope beneath the buoy to give me some slack, I then ran the line outside the cat's cradle of rigging, over the roller on the port bow, and back around the windlass.

Meanwhile the line was streaming down under *Kapduva's* substantial keel, en route to snagging there or feeding the hungry prop. Though we managed to avoid those calamities, Peter had to monkey-climb out over the bow to free the line from the bow-sprit stays, where it had gotten stubbornly tangled.

Then, as Christine held the boat in place in the current, Peter came back on deck and started the windlass. As I kept the line on the roller and away from tangling elsewhere, Peter guided it into his stowage tubs.

Though the windlass did save us the muscle work of hauling Peter's traps, we were both annoyed by the complex process of getting them to the surface.

We weren't finished with our challenges, however, for when the knots tied onto Peter's traps reached the windlass, the traps still hung down in the water. This meant that we had to muscle his three pots up through the tangle of rigging and onto *Kapduva's* high deck.

As we heaved the pots aboard, I was dismayed to find them nearly empty. Peter was happy with his twenty prawns, and Christine all smiles as she disappeared into the galley to fry them up in garlic butter and sweet-chili sauce. Though our catch was meager, it provided an excellent dinner.

Before making further comment, I must state that I hold Peter in high regard as an islander and boatman. He's spent much of his life afloat, and his sails are always perfectly tuned, his rigging well-organized and his boats meticulously maintained.

Rigging prawn traps, however, was not his forte. When I took a close look at them, I found there was good reason for his consistent failure to bring in a meaningful catch. What he'd been deploying were closer to feeding stations than traps.

A well-rigged trap is bottom-weighted, has its netting stretched tightly over its frame, and the bait container suspended in the middle. This setup requires prawns to find their way inside to feed, and makes subsequent escape difficult.

Peter's netting sagged like the breasts of an eighty-year-old crone, and his bait containers were set where the prawns could eat at will from them without entering the traps. His trap-weights were attached to the top side of the traps, which positioned them upside-down on the sea bottom. Any prawn that happened to crawl inside could thus just as easily walk right out again. Since his main trap anchor was attached to his bottom trap, any current would have lifted the top two traps off the seafloor and out of reach of all bottom-feeding prawns (which is *all* prawns).

After politely drawing these deficits to Peter's attention, he began digging through his boat's stores for materials to set things right. And in this I knew he would succeed. In the following weeks he did, and was soon harvesting full loads of prawns.

For as a veteran islander and sailor, Peter is an expert in the skill required of all who dare to live in such places—improvisation. For on an island or afloat, you never have enough, or the right tool, or the correct supplies. You learn to make do, and the limits of your imagination set the limits of how well you cope with life's stream of breakdowns and projects.

I'd seen Peter at work on Wolf Island, and aboard *Kapduva* and *Lulia*, and knew him to be a master improviser. Unfortunately, though he had improvised well in refitting a collection of broke-backed prawn traps, he had no idea of what he was trying to create, and had thus inadvertently built cafeterias rather than traps.

Earlier this summer, however, on several occasions I'd seen the master at the height of his craft. Peter had been fighting bronchial congestion, and mentioned this to friend Karl Darwin. Karl suggested that some oxygen might help, and loaned Peter a meter-and-a-half tall welding cylinder full of it, replete with lines, gauges, and cutting torch. Peter strapped the cylinder to *Kapduva's* deck and ran the lines inside through a hatch. Then he attached an oxygen mask to the torch tip and was soon self-medicating while relaxing at anchor.

A week or so later, Peter had his beautiful wood runabout, *Little Wren*, delivered by barge to Wolf Island. Though *Little Wren* arrived on its trailer, there were only footpaths between the island's two sides. The barge had landed on the south side of Wolf, and Peter wanted to store his treasured boat next to his cabin on the island's north flank. So Peter strapped the trailer tight to the boat, let the boat and trailer roll down into the water, and then towed the boat, with the trailer hanging underneath it, around to the other side of the island.

There he confronted another challenge.

His landing area, where he planned to build a boathouse for *Little Wren,* had a Volkswagen-sized boulder resting in its middle. An insurmountable problem on a remote island? Not for Peter. He used a house-jack to pry up one side of the boulder, put some smaller rocks under to hold it up, then reinserted the jack and raised the boulder some more. By repeating this time after time, he single-handedly rolled the several-ton rock out of the way.

Recently Peter had wanted to set out a new mooring for *Kapduva.* He'd scavenged line from neighbor Ray, found a buoy while beachcombing, and discovered an abandoned anchor in False Bay. After retrieving the anchor's old mooring rope with a long boat hook, he tied it to *Kapduva's* stern and used the rising tide to lift the block. Then he sailed it to his favored spot in front of his cabin, cut the line, and dropped it into place.

But improvisers are by necessity cannibalizers, and when a project challenges them, they will gnaw off their own fingers to feed their project's hunger.

Peter needed a rust-free thimble to attach the anchor line to the buoy, and told me how he'd used "a piece of hose" to make one. While visiting Peter yesterday on Wolf, I noticed that the "hose" he'd cannibalized was the suction hose of his new fire pump. Such pumps rely on these hoses to draw water from the bay, and without them are useless. Hopefully fire would wait until Peter was able to improvise a replacement.

CHAPTER 53
LASQUETI CARS: THE DEAD
AND THE NEAR-DEAD

*"The flower stickers were the only things that held the car
together."*
*"There was no heat—unless, that is, the auxiliary gas tank
caught fire."*
*"After the floor boards rusted out in the rear, they would fill up
with water and freeze. I ended up putting soda crates on the floor
in the back to keep people from falling through and under the
car."*
*"My Chevy Vega actually broke in half ... the whole rear end
came around slightly to the front, sort of like a dog wagging its
tail."*
*"At least it had heated rear windows—so your hands would stay
warm while you pushed."*
—Anonymous, from respondents to *Car Talk's* "Worst Car of the
Millennium" survey, (www.NPR.org)

August 22, 2000

Morning skies hosted gray clouds, and the waters of False Bay were
silver with blue waves. Out on the Strait, the water was all dark, telling
of rougher conditions. With a steady wind blowing, it looked like a
morning to lounge in bed and do a bit of reading.

Reaching for my book, I beheld the telling clutter on my island nightstand:

1. My reading light
2. A flashlight
3. Several novels
4. Our VHF radio for weather forecasts
5. Mosquito repellant
6. Our battery-powered mosquito-killing racquet (the "Wand of Death")
7. Cortisone for itchy mosquito bites
8. My journal
9. An empty hot chocolate mug
10. The operating manual for our outboard motor, which I'm trying to fix
11. A research book on local marine life, so that I can identify what I've found during my fishing, prawning, and beachcombing
12. A special shell I found during a recent low tide

After lunch I went salmon fishing at the Finnerties. The skies to the north were a fluid mosaic of whites, blues, and grays, melting into the green-black of distant hills and the silver of slack water. I caught a beautiful orange rockfish that disgorged its swim bladder and died on the way up, as they often do when pulled from the deep.

Seals and their pups lazed on the rocks, the pups cooing and adults gargling. All raised their heads and tails out of the water as the tide came in, scooting this way and that to avoid getting wet.

Back on Olsen's rocky shore I looked over the bay and marveled at the lives of the seals I'd seen and the rockfish I caught. As a surface dweller, I lived in a world of fixed places and three dimensions. I moved through predictable places, knowing at all times where my house was and what it would look like when I walked in the door. Food was in the refrigerator and I ate it off our table.

Living on a surface, I naturally focused on places and surfaces. Snorkeling off Olsen, I dove for the bottom. Kayaking, I headed for another island. And gazing out across the Strait as I was doing now, I beheld the waves that sparkled on the water's skin.

From where I stood, the water proclaimed itself but another surface.

As a rockfish or seal, I would know these waters as boundless playgrounds where gravity lost its importance. Except near the shore or distant bottom, the only other surfaces would be the sides of other swimming things. Other than the glow overhead and the darkness below, my world would be one of utter randomness, a place of no fixed places. My most distant vista might be fifteen meters away if I were near the surface, or mere centimeters in the depths. Swimming through life, I would never pass through the same water twice.

Unpredictability would be all that was predictable, everything constantly new. I would take advantage of a meal when it came along, never knowing what I was going to find. Accordingly, my memory would be small, while my sense of smell and sensitivity to movement would be keenly developed.

August 23, 2000

We spent most of the day getting things in order for our departure, carrying kayaks and crab pots to the boathouse and stashing sleeping bags in the attic. I tarped the woodpile, lugged deck chairs to the boathouse, and took the hammocks down and stored them in the closet.

Claire thoughtfully spared us from cooking by inviting us over for a birthday dinner for Theresa. We feasted on fresh king salmon, island veggies, apple tart, and double-chocolate cake.

After dinner, I drove Ken's old pickup down to the Arts Center to pick up our Allen Farrell painting from an exhibit of his work. Ken's aging rattle-trap is a classic "island beater." Unlicensed, dented, missing a door handle, and covered in dust, it is the perfect Lasqueti vehicle. It even runs most of the time.

Island beaters exist at the extreme fringes of the automobile world, consisting mainly of the dying and near-dead. Many look like they could not possibly run, the victims of multiple accidents and near-death experiences. It is thus difficult to know whether the cluster of vehicles near the Lasqueti dock is a parking lot or an auto graveyard.

Most of these beaters have been repeatedly resurrected from the dead. Lurching along as mechanical Frankensteins, they make it clear that those who coax them back to life are more sorcerers with wild senses of humor than auto mechanics. The closer the vehicle is to death, the higher the owner's stature in the island community.

The patched wounds on these relics display humorously creative repairs: plywood window replacements, doors sealed with expanded foam, galvanized hardware latches holding things closed, and plenty of duct tape and plastic sheets to keep the rain out. Several have been hand-painted with wild designs, but more out of necessity than artistic fancy. Peering at their thick layers of wild color, it's clear that there's more paint than metal holding their bodies together.

The measures employed to deal with breakdowns occasionally set new standards of imagination. One islander had an emergency brake that slipped, but needed to park on the hill near the ferry for a quick departure. Borrowing a length of rope, he tied his bumper to a nearby tree and ran to catch the ferry. The car hung there for several weeks, its rope taut as a bowstring.

Just as tree rings proclaim the age of our forest patriarchs, so do wheel wells betray how long a car has been on-island. Salt solutions have been sprayed on island roads to keep the dust down, and the same salt that has attracted dust-dampening moisture to the roads has mercilessly chewed away at the metal fenders of the vehicles driving over them. Some of Lasqueti's long-term vehicles have magnificent arches where their wheel wells used to be, fringed by a lacework of rust.

None of these derelicts is ever washed, and all are of indeterminate color, some shade of island dust. In the winter they host colonies of algae and moss, and the most treasured have small seedlings spouting from their accumulated dirt. One recently sported a message scrawled in the grime covering its rear window: "My girlfriend is dirtier than this car!" Another was so littered inside that it looked more like a giant bird's nest than the interior of an automobile.

These beaters are often billboards for the passions of the owners. Some are adorned classically with provocative bumper stickers, while others have their politics painted in big sloppy letters. Still others are rolling displays of whatever the owner would like to show to the rest of the island. This summer a whale skeleton was dug out of the gravel at Spring Bay, and for months an immense whale rib was paraded around the island atop a diminutive subcompact beater.

For-sale ads in the monthly island paper are careful to note whether the beater actually runs, and if so, whether reliably or sporadically. Such vehicles are occasionally sold in pairs of the same model: one that is alive and driven, and one that is dead and cannibalized for parts.

Ken's truck had no backup lights, and I was largely unfamiliar with the island's meandering tracks. With huckleberry and salal scraping its sides, I bounced over rutted paths through pitch-black woods. No doubt I put a few more scratches on its fenders, further enhancing its character.

August 24, 2000

I was up early in a frenzy of packing and closing up the house. As we started to load the Grady, which I had anchored in the shallow lagoon by the floathouse, we found we were in a race with the ebbing tide. The boat sank deeper with each load we added, and I had to continually move it farther out to keep it from going aground, which would have stranded us for another twelve hours.

***

Remnants from the night's gale kept the Strait in intimidating turmoil. When we peeked out of the pass behind Olsen, a wave crested over our bow and broke inside our boat. Our cats got soaked in their carriers and yowled in fright as Theresa and I stared at each other wide-eyed. Knowing that we shouldn't risk another near-swamping, I gunned us quickly onto a plane. This gave us too much speed and shot us off swells to collide with oncoming breakers, forcing us to hold on with both hands to keep from being thrown from our seats. I tried several courses to smooth things out, and thought I'd finally succeeded when I turned downwind after slamming directly into the waves. But the discomfort of the crossing had brought tears to Theresa's eyes. When she cried out after one vicious pounding, her fear lit the tinder of my own anxiety and I yelled at her to keep quiet. This earned me a mid-crossing tongue lashing, where in tearful screams I was informed of my insensitivity and poor seamanship.

CHAPTER 54
THE LASQUETI DOCK

*It has always been easier here, where only the fundamentals
count, to learn what every man must learn in this world.*
— Margaret Craven, *I Heard the Owl Call My Name*

October 5, 2000

Heading North in a quieter time of year, Theresa and I ran into several
friends on the Lasqueti ferry, which made for pleasant conversation
on the ride across. Vancouver Island's mountains stood in brilliant
silhouette against the clear fall sky.

Ray, our always-obliging island friend, met us when the ferry pulled
in, and together we chatted up various friends on the Lasqueti dock.

Almost everyone and everything going to and from Lasqueti passes
over the dock. We all keep up with what's happening on the island by
mingling in the anthill of activity there.

Our friend John Cantrell is leaving for a short afternoon in Parksville.
What's the latest on his relationship with Morgan? Discuss it on the
dock, and the whole island will know.

Hubert, the kind man who painted our house, bemoans problems
with his wife. Lawrence Fisher bends over some new machine for the
button factory, exploring its intricacies with several onlookers. Judy
Dempster arrives with several other ladies for a "women's weekend"
on Wolf Island, piling all their gear into a small aluminum boat for a
questionably safe ride across False Bay.

I, and all others on the dock, know all of this. Within hours, so will everyone else on the island.

Pickup trucks drive down onto the dock to collect or drop off loads for the ferry. Other vehicles wait their turn on the dirt road above. Hand trucks are loaded with blue plastic bins full of groceries and are pulled up the ramp from the float.

New hair styles arrive from off-island and new tattoos peek out from bare midriffs. "Jack seemed a little more frail than usual." "Hey Charlie, did you hear they found your stolen boat?"

Tender touches and deep smiles are exchanged between couples who are glad to be together again, looking forward to private time. A newborn baby is presented for everyone to see, the most precious thing in the world to its radiant mother.

October 6, 2000

After a morning of fog rolling in off the Strait, the day turned clear and warm. Fishing off Olsen's rocks with a light rod, I caught eighteen small cod in less than an hour: six on six casts, one miss, then twelve on the next twelve casts.

I fought each fish to the surface, and then watched it swim around in the clear, glass-calm water. The rockfish came up with their dorsal spines bristling up and lateral fins flaring out to the sides. They took any opportunity to swim for a crevice in the rocks, where they attempted to wedge themselves in with their fins. Only with constant pressure and quick reeling could I get them to the surface. As usual, when I fished off our shore, I released everything I caught.

After finally satisfying my passion for fishing, I explored some Lasqueti woods hunting wild mushrooms. Today, my only reward was the pleasure of my walk.

October 7, 2000

I surfaced with infinite languor from the depths of my dreams, savoring the warmth of our down comforter. Coming slowly awake with my eyes closed, I was filled with the bounty of my senses.

A breath of air wafted through the open window near my head, washing my arms clean of sleep's heat. Detecting the elusive odor of juniper trees at dawn, I flared my nostrils in an attempt to savor it more deeply.

When I finally decided to open one eye, I found the pink light of sunrise dancing on our ceiling, shimmering from its reflection off the water.

An immobility born of ecstasy stole over me. I half closed my eyes to concentrate on the fullness of my sensory harvest, keeping at bay anything that was not pure sensation.

Aroused by suspicious movements below the water's edge, I rose on an elbow. Squinting through narrowed eyes, I imagined I saw salmon slowly awakening from the sleep of the exhausted reveler. Big king salmon that had slept rocking in the shallows, humming their songs and joining me in the swim through my dreams.

Closing my eyes, I saw them dancing in the waning starlight, weaving rhythmically beneath the waves. With a twist they disappeared into the depths, diving into their own private dream world.

Diving after them, I was gently massaged as small whirlpools eddied around me. I found myself slowly moving my fingers through the water, reveling in its coolness.

Surrendering myself to the sea, I glided down into the depths. To escape being whisked from the water by feathery barnacle tongues, I transformed myself into a school of herring and swam through a cloud of plankton.

Tiring from my exertions, I drifted to the bottom. Lying perfectly still, I felt a moon-snail burrow beneath my skin and deposit her eggs. My skin prickled as hundreds of small starfish feet marched over my back. As I finally looked upward, I saw a cormorant paddle across the huge lens of my eye, diving deep to chase a flitting fish.

October 8, 2000

Morning dawned clear blue, its waters caressing the rocks with an unhurried touch. Birdsong gently wiped away my dreams, transporting me from the island of sleep to the sea of wakefulness.

I went casting off the rocks again and caught a dozen rockfish in a short while. In the waters below me was a huge orange sun-star, its twenty legs radiating outward, welcoming me to gaze upon it.

After fishing, Theresa and I sat on the front porch in our shorts, playing cards in the sun as if it were summer. Feeling that it was a perfect day to do some exploring, we lowered ourselves into our kayaks for a leisurely paddle to the Finnerties. On the way, I caught a small salmon on a rod held between my knees.

CHAPTER 55
A WINTER PARTY

Whenever I find myself growing grim about the mouth; whenever it is a damp, drizzly November in my soul; whenever I find myself involuntarily pausing before coffin warehouses, and bringing up the rear of every funeral I meet ... then I get to sea as soon as I can.

—Herman Melville, *Moby Dick*

December 27, 2000

Returning to the island two months further into winter, we were happy to be back on the rock.

Our house was toasty when we got there, thanks to the fire Dick had started in our woodstove. After stowing our gear, we went down to meet Larry Manahan, the caretaker we'd invited to live in the floathouse. In return for a place to stay, he'd agreed to keep an eye on our home while we were away.

Larry's first island stay had been on the Finnerties, where he'd moved last February to live in a tent. When he told me of his living arrangements, I rocked backward in amazement. While we'd been riding out winter storms in a house of massive timbers anchored to the rock, Larry was braving them on an even wilder island, with nothing but tent cloth between him and the fury of the elements.

I was further astonished by his Finnerty stay when Larry told me that he couldn't stand being cold. His discomfort was no doubt aggravated by his rigid diet of raw vegetables and nuts, which left his lean frame particularly susceptible to getting chilled. He told me that though he had no heat in his tent, he did have a sleeping bag. My unspoken question was, "Did you stay in your bag twenty-four hours a day?"

Larry's transportation to and from the islands is an old, blunt-nosed dinghy, which is heavy and difficult to row. He'd holed this several times when landing in rough conditions, then amateurishly patched the growing sieve. Since it is too heavy to pull out of or into the water, Larry leaves it "floating" at anchor. "Sinking" might be more accurate, for the half-hearted patches let in a steady flow of water. As a result, the humble wreck bobs half-sunk at the end of its tether.

Theresa had to bite her tongue when Larry confessed to never wearing a life jacket. His rationale was that the chilly winter waters would slow his swimming, and if he couldn't swim to shore quickly, he'd die of the cold. "So why bother staying afloat?"

While Larry has the tenacity of the area's early settlers, he harkens from the prairie and hasn't yet got saltwater in his veins. He is all elbows and knees, clumsily banging about in an alien world.

As a caretaker he'll be fine—honest and diligent. My concern is that he'll drown himself.

December 28, 2000

As I was out fishing this morning, a juvenile sea lion began to circle my boat, juvenile in that he probably weighed only 300 kilos (660 pounds).

I thought about my own juvenile sons, prone to impulsiveness, extremes of behavior, and generally driven by hormones. Looking again at the sea lion, I realized that one thrust of his tail could put him in my boat, capsizing it in the process.

Wondering what mischief a juvenile sea lion might be capable of, I retrieved an oar from where it was wedged next to my seat. I put the oar within easy reach lest my "friend" try to get really friendly. Yelling at him only had the effect of him tightening his circles around me.

Eventually he concluded that I was neither food nor a potential mate, and began to swim away. This didn't stop me from checking my back periodically as I continued jigging along the rocks.

Cruising back to Olsen, I noticed small trickles of water running off the islands I passed, even though it's been days since the last rain.

Rainwater saturates these islands' thin layer of soil, and then gradually drains down over the underlying rock.

Such wet conditions are the reason for Islanders' love of gum boots. These calf-high rubber wonders are the winter footwear of choice for all who live here. Getting in and out of a boat, slogging up the muddy path to a friend's house, or just going for a walk through the sopping-wet woods, all are accomplished with dry feet thanks to our gum-boots.

Coastal Indians had their own ways of coping with muddy trails and the challenge of disembarking from their boats. In Stephen Ambrose's book on Lewis and Clark (1996), *Undaunted Courage*, Ambrose describes the winter their expedition spent among the Clatsop Indians near the mouth of the Columbia River. Speaking of the Clatsops, Ambrose says, "They were always barefoot, and women as well as men covered themselves only from the waist up, for the good reason—as Lewis took care to note—that they lived in a damp but mild climate and were in and out of their canoes in waist-deep water much of the time. Lewis remarked he could do a visual examination for venereal disease on every man who came to the fort."

***

Theresa and I later boated over to Higgins Island to wish Eve a happy birthday. Unfortunately, she was just emerging from a bad cold, and her spirits were obviously ebbing. But the delight of being pampered and worshipped brought a gleam to her eyes, and our unannounced visit ended up extending into a wonderful dinner of prawns and scallops, with Grand Marnier and a chocolate orange for dessert.

We headed home in the dark, with a clear patch of sky giving us just enough starlight to steer by. Though the slight glow of the clouds allowed us to pick out Olsen's silhouette in the distance, the bay was mined with logs that had floated off beaches during recent high tides and I almost hit a big one. Luckily I was putting along slowly, mindful of the hazards. When not looking out for logs or Olsen's shores, we were entertained by the fireflies of phosphorous flickering in our wake.

December 29, 2000

Today I got up in the dark, and after stoking the fire, went back to bed with my book. Theresa and I had both slept fitfully, too hot for comfort. Our woodstove had done too good a job keeping the house warm.

I went for a morning stroll down island with Theresa, where she showed me a deer skeleton she discovered yesterday. From its size, we knew it was a youngster, and Dick confirmed that of late he had seen only one of the summer's twins.

Theresa took this stroll in her pink flannel pajamas, whose top hung down below her yellow rain coat and bottoms were tucked into her black gum boots. On her head was a camouflage-patterned hat of greens and browns. In response to my laughter at her crazy appearance, she proclaimed that "This is my 'I don't care if I look ridiculous' look." I knew I was being treated to a fashion show that I'd see only on a remote island with no chance of anyone else catching the slightest of glimpses.

December 30, 2000

A quiet, misty morning—bay calm. Today's predicted heavy weather hasn't materialized. Gazing at the bay's smooth waters, I wondered if the storm was going to visit us later or pass us by. But the wind and sea guarded their mysteries and gave no hint of what was to come. Like Egyptian women behind their veils, they looked at me through hooded eyes, revealing nothing of their thoughts.

December 31, 2000 through January 1, 2001

We've been pinned down on the island through forty-eight hours of very strong winds, and haven't seen a single boat brave the cauldron in False Bay.

January 2, 2001

Another gale was blowing when we awoke this morning, or perhaps the same gale that has lashed us through the past two days and nights. Cold winds reddened my hands when I went outside to the wood pile, where I watched wave spray blacken rocks far above the shore.

Winter is the chanciest season to plan a dinner party, as winter storms ring our cell phone with last-minute cancellations. But winter is also the season when friends living on small islands most treasure an evening together.

In summer, our False Bay friends see each other frequently: meeting the ferry, paddling our kayaks, motoring across the bay, or dancing at the community center. We drop in on each other for unannounced "tea" visits that often take up half a day. In between these encounters, we're busy with guests that migrate here in the heat.

In winter we retreat deep into our burrows, isolated by wind and waves. Huddling separately in our island homes, we stoke our fires and stare out mutely into the rain. Our pulses slow as we begin to hibernate.

But the chance to do some winter socializing stirs our thickened blood and snaps us out of our solitary pursuits. Putting away our dominoes, we pull out our fancy clothes.

The need to escape our isolation boosts our tolerance for wind and waves. Through the last two days we'd been marooned by fifty-knot winds, but when the winds finally dropped to thirty-five knots, Theresa was off the island like a shot. Though immense breakers still scoured the rocks, and while we never ventured forth in such conditions in summer, Theresa absolutely *had* to visit a Lasqueti friend. Covered head to toe in foul-weather gear, she set out alone in our skiff to sneak through semi-protected passages between nearby islands. Though I tried to deter her with words of caution, the dream of winter tea with a friend possessed hypnotic power.

A dinner party Theresa and I had planned for tonight had a similar draw on our False Bay friends, island-bound through the days of the persistent gale. Out of necessity they'd hunched against the horizontal rain when they visited their outhouses, then gladly retreated to the cozy warmth indoors. Though all had watched over their boats on their moorings, no one had braved a trip through the waves.

Our dinner invitation changed all that. Our friends were delighted by the prospect of escape and accepted gladly. Though dark was falling and the storm still howled, our phone remained silent. Tonight there would be no last minute cancellations. All these friends had spent too much time pondering the knots on their ceilings and working diligently on winter projects.

Peering through the gloaming when I expected our guests to arrive, I scanned the bay for a sign of them. Finally, I saw spray arch skyward from behind a low point on Higgins Island. As these geysers moved slowly closer, I caught glimpses of a skiff of people in exposure suits, hanging on to their bucking boat with both hands. As each wall of water shot skyward, it was immediately blown back over the huddled figures. Only the one at the tiller dared face forward.

Donning full rain gear and gum boots, I hurried down to the rocks to help with the landing. After catching the Rubbermaid totes that were thrown to me, I grabbed for hands covered in commercial fishing gloves. As I helped each person jump from the boat to the rocks, I could only distinguish sexes by peering into their tightly cinched hoods. Scarves betrayed the women, and apostles' beards, the men.

Dripping wet, we methodically trudged to the house. As we stomped and shook off the rain outside our door, our eyes gave away our delight at seeing one another. Exchanging smiles through these tiny orbs, we hugged each other clumsily.

Inside our home, a magical transformation took place.

When a fishman's mitt shed to the floor, I realized I stood before the crysalis of Eve. Her fingers were bejeweled with rings of her own making, sparkling light off gold and diamonds and sapphires and pearls.

Stepping out of her worn exposure suit, Eve emerged in elegant yards of golden silk. Shaking out her magnificent head of curls, she reached into her waterproof tote and pulled out a stylish pair of heels.

While the men looked on, Terry tore open the Velcro of her own well-used suit, and out stepped a siren in black velvet. Then Dick emerged in jaunty red trousers, and Ray in the white muslin of a Brahmin priest.

After the cruising suits were hung to dry and purses and fancy footware retrieved from plastic totes, we reached reverently into the sealed food containers. Ray produced an ancient hunk of cave cheese, and Terry a plate of grape-leave-wrapped dolmas. Dick brought forth bottles of home-brewed wine and beer, and Eve an elegant cake topped with tropical flowers from her sun room.

So began our winter evening, all of us butterflies warmed by each other's smiles.

Chapter 56
A Risky Crossing

Only by being guilty of Folly does mortal man arrive at the perception of Sense.

—Herman Melville, *Moby Dick*

February 27, 2001

Boarding the *Queen of Alberni* in Tsawassen, Theresa and I were on our way to a midwinter stay on Olsen. As the 400-car ferry pulled out of its slip, a monstrous gust slammed it into the pilings beside us. This miles-long river of air momentarily pinned us in place as complaints squealed from the hull's battle with the dock. An announcement came over the loudspeakers, informing us of the location of the ship's life preservers. Only when the ferry won its battle with the gale could the boat pull away.

As the 11,000 horsepower engines shoved into a howling northerly wind, the front of the ferry shuddered from the battering it took.

In front of us, cars and trucks bounced around on their springs. Aerials bent backwards and cold air shot through our car's air vents as the storm moaned over the ferry's superstructure.

This was a 140-meter (460-foot) super-ferry, and the forecast called for building winds in the night. All I could think of was next morning, when I was supposed to pick up my four-meter (fourteen-foot) boat in French Creek and run it across the Strait.

When the ferry pushed to full cruising speed, we were jerked around roughly as it fought its way through the blow. In moments, the captain reduced speed and changed to a course oblique to the gusts. Though he had massive power at his command, discretion was the measure of his seamanship.

I wondered what discretion I would exercise in the morning with my planned crossing of the Strait. How much wind could I handle? Was there enough weight in my bow to hold it down on the water? Should I sneak behind the Lasqueti Ferry and follow it across? Would the mechanic deliver the boat on time to allow me this option? And how would we get from Lasqueti to Olsen if conditions forced me to leave our boat in French Creek and ride the ferry instead?

February 28, 2001

Though the morning wind had eased, Small Craft Warnings were in effect for the Strait, and I could see plenty of whitecaps from the French Creek Marina. My boat was delivered on time, and by 9:15 AM, I had loaded most of our gear and Theresa on the ferry and kissed her goodbye.

Then I had a choice to make. I could either wait thirty minutes and humbly follow the ferry across, or I could strike out on my own.

Swathed in full rain gear and my float coat, I felt impervious to the elements. Though there were sizeable seas running, I wanted to believe the wind wasn't more than I could handle.

Idling my motor just off the gas float, I looked back and forth between the ferry and the Strait. Anxious to get underway, I chose the Strait.

As soon as I passed beyond the breakwater, I was into the swells. The ponderousness in the gusts assured me that I was doing something foolish, and as I beheld the Strait's carpet of white, I shuddered in my seat.

Speeding my boat onto a plane was out of the question. The swells were rolling downwind at perhaps ten knots, and even motoring slowly, I soared off the wave tops. Then one of several things happened, depending on the strength of the gust that hit me.

Sometimes the boat dropped straight down, smashing hard on the water. This jarred my back, sent spray flying into my face, and made me worry the boat would break apart. Hammered in other waves, some of its welds had already cracked.

Other times I settled down gently, held aloft by the wind's giant hands. I then proceeded with extra care, all too conscious of how the wind was toying with me.

In moments of respite from the stronger gusts, I sped my engine and made better progress over the next few swells. But my speed was inevitably choked back when a particularly steep comber headed my way. I shot skyward off such swells, leaving only my engine in the water. Then the wind caught the boat's bottom and thrust its bow toward the clouds. The ferry captain, cruising up behind me, was convinced I was going to be blown over backward.

Midway across, I ran into an especially nasty set of swells with steep flanks and curling tops. On the first one, I twisted the throttle back to idle, fearing a huge launch. Without my motor's thrust, however, the wave began to shove me backward down its face, threatening to submerge my transom. Instinctively I sped up, choosing flight over a boatful of water. This shot me off the crest, and when I crashed down on the wave's backside, the landing smashed my motor out of the water.

The spray I repeatedly took in the face complicated matters as it forced me to shut my eyes. Each time I opened them again, I was on an unexpected course, surprised by new waves and chop.

My mouth grew salty from all the seawater hitting me. This water collected in the bilge, and periodically I heard the bilge pump working to send it overboard. This set me to worrying that my battery might smash into the float switch and disable the pump. Usually the battery was strapped to the floorboards, but Dick had removed these to paint them. Now the battery was sliding around in the back of the boat, restrained only by its wiring harness.

In front of the boat's middle seat I had three full gas cans and a storage tote stuffed with gear. The tote's lid, just higher than the seat it banged against, periodically popped off and floated in the wind as it prepared to fly overboard. This obliged me to make emergency stops and climb into the bow to smash the lid down again.

I had tightened the drawstring of my rainhood around my face, but the wind and constant motion eventually had their way with it. Soon the wind blew the hood off my head and spray began running down my neck.

Trying to rearrange my hood with one hand, I found that my fingers had gone numb from the February cold. Gripping the tiller and gunwale tightly, I hadn't even noticed my hands go through painful cold to where I couldn't feel them. I eventually had to stop and use both hands to set things right.

Underway again, I spied a log off my starboard bow. As its bark had been recently peeled from banging against some rocky shore, the log stood out brightly against the waves. But in moments I lost it among the chop and swells. Searching the waves, I was fully aware that such a log could disable me. I hoped I could maintain my course and make it safely past.

More ominous were the fully barked logs I occasionally glimpsed. Dark against dark, they were difficult to see and snuck into the surfeit of hiding places among the waves. With my eyes periodically closed against the spray, I relied on luck to keep me clear.

Spotting drift and sizing up the waves occupied me the entire time. Wallowing slowly with my bow up, I was able to see ahead only when going down a wave or when I swung my bow sideways. I learned the danger of this latter maneuver when I found myself beam to a rushing wave that rolled me heavily on my side.

When the ferry finally passed me I was tempted to swing in behind, but by then I was most of the way across and so I pushed on alone.

Finally turning into False Bay, I was able to run with the swells and surf down their faces. My only danger came from burying my bow in the wave ahead. By the time the ferry reached the Lasqueti dock, I had almost caught up with it.

Theresa was wide-eyed when she met me. She and the rest of the passengers had worried about me the whole way across. For most of the trip, all they could see was the spray shooting skyward from where I crashed through the waves.

The captain, a member of the local search and rescue team, expressed displeasure with my judgment. Matter of factly he told Theresa, "That's how people die out there." He'd slowed the ferry down on the last leg of its run to make sure I made port safely.

Thanking him on the dock, I was embarrassed as the passengers eyed me over. No doubt the island grapevine would soon be buzzing about the idiot from Olsen Island.

Arching her eyebrows and shaking her head, Theresa sarcastically observed, "You made history today."

True enough, but not the kind I wanted to make.

CHAPTER 57
FISHING WITH JACK

There's a fine line between fishing and just standing on the shore like an idiot.

—Steven Wright

A fishing rod is a stick with a hook on one end and a fool at the other.

—Samuel Johnson

Fishing is a delusion entirely surrounded by liars in old clothes.

—Don Marquis

April 19, 2001

Jack Thomas is a passionate fisherman. He's had a summer cabin on Lasqueti for many of his eighty years, and is still as enthralled with the island as Theresa and I are as relative newcomers. Jack and I talk fishing whenever our paths cross on Lasqueti, and always promise each other we'll soon get together on the water.

Planning to head up to Olsen for a long spring weekend, Theresa and I knew that Jack's sense of humor would make him a fun traveling companion. I also wanted to wet a line with him. So we gave Jack a call and made a date for a trip up to the island together. I was told by John Cantrell, who speaks with Jack often, that Jack had his bags packed a week in advance in excited anticipation.

These bags, typical of those of all islanders, were stuffed with much more than a few shirts. He had gallons of paint, a journeyman's supply of tools, and—I suspected—a couple of concrete blocks inside, all necessary for the island projects he'd planned.

As soon as we picked Jack up at his Seattle home, he and I launched into enthusiastic yarns about the great fishing adventures of our lives. But we were soon both humbled when Theresa dozed off in the middle of our tales.

Dick had our skiff waiting at the Lasqueti dock when we arrived. After dropping Jack off on the rocks below his home in the inner reaches of False Bay, T and I headed out for Olsen. Climbing up to our house, we were delighted by the Blue Eyed Marys blooming all around it.

April 21, 2001

As often happens when a fisherman attempts to humbly recount his past exploits, Jack had regaled me with tales of incredible catches. He spoke of monster lingcod he'd boated at secret holes within spitting distance of Olsen, and recounted the many salmon he'd hauled in while gazing at our shores. Today he was going to make good on his promise of guiding me to the exact locations of these conquests, places that when plumbed with his special gear were certain to produce prodigious results.

Several hours later, I had a number of fish to show for my efforts. Jack had only the tattered remnants of his pride.

Following our fishing trip, Jack and I began sending each other emails about our fishing experiences.

Charlie,

Any news of fishing on the rock? Haven't been there for a while. My son and I are yarding in lots of silvers just outside the Ballard locks. Maybe the next time we're together I can give you a few fishing lessons, in hopes that you might someday catch a salmon.

Regards,
Jack

Jack,

Last week I went down to fish Gray's Harbor with a friend. We launched at Westport, and ran up the harbor for a couple of miles. I caught two nice kings—a fifteen and a thirty-eight. The thirty-eight was chrome, and a real fighter. Just finished smoking it last night.

When did you want to give me those fishing lessons?
Charlie

Dear Charlie,
After your latest news we may need to cut back on the lessons. The last time I played a fish that size on eight-pound test leader it took quite a while.

Jack

Jack,
The eight-pound test I use is for heavyweight backing. I have found that a single strand of horse hair works best for a leader, though unfortunately it is too light to register any resistance on the test gauge used to verify line weights for record catches.

Charlie

Charlie,
Your latest has me believe you think your fish was a record catch, if it weren't for the inefficient test gauge.

Right now I am tying up some cobweb leaders to go after some sea runs.

Jack

Jack,

I think you'll find that cobwebs are a bit heavy for sea runs. There is a miniature cave spider that lives only in the mountains of Borneo, and its silk threads are so fine that they are invisible to the naked eye. I have my lures tied on under a microscope. Next time we get together, I'll share a few with you.

Charlie

Charlie,

You left one of your Borneo (spider-wire) leaders in my boat last summer. Later, when I put it in service, I foul-hooked an orca. Several hours later, near Campbell River, I decided to break him off. Failing at this, I threw the rod over and motored home. Can you spare one more? The Makah tribe at Neah Bay wants one.

Regards,
Jack

Jack,

I know that as one enters the "golden years," one's eyesight begins to fail. No doubt you were reaching for one of my leaders, hoping to improve your fishing. Seeing something gray, and recognizing by feel that it was approximately the same weight as your own leader, you understandably mistook your anchor chain for a fishing line and tossed it over the side. I am encouraged, however, to see that you are having better luck catching orcas than you are catching salmon.

Cheers,

Charlie

Charlie,

Your reference to the golden years did not pass without notice. It seems a little premature to attack my angling abilities, since we have only fished together at the same time and place one time, and then you wanted to call the media over your six-inch rock cod taken on a two-pound jig. In my advanced years, I am catching trout, salmon, and steelhead and I am often approached by beautiful women at the Safeway store. Should you reach my age in your checkered life, you might be lucky to catch a flue bug, but I wish you the best.

Jack

Dear Jack,

Regarding beautiful women approaching you in the supermarket—you didn't tell me that you had taken a job manning one of those free sample booths! What fun! Tell me, what works best for luring them in, the mini pizzas or the krab dip? If you have the same luck at hooking these young beauties as you did when we were out fishing, I'll assume that they are quite safe. I will assume that your "salmon, steelhead, and trout" are caught at the same Safeway where you angle for your beauties. You might also try picking up some of the stuffed sole and crab cakes, which I believe are stocked at the same fish counter where you are "landing" your other catches.

Enviously,
Charlie

Chapter 58
A Rough Night on False Bay

The water that supports a boat can also sink it.
—Chinese Proverb

The night Pacific is little at all like the day's. With the demarking line of horizon unseeable the ocean draws up dimension from its deeps ... And all the while every hazard, rock, shoal, reef, shelf, and snag is being whetted against the solid dark.
—Ivan Doig, *The Sea Runners*

April 21, 2001, continued

After my fishing trip with Jack, Theresa and I headed off to attend Dick's fiftieth birthday party at the Lasqueti Community Center.

As we motored to Higgins Island to pick up friends Ray and Eve, we rode some large swells coming in from the Strait. I thought nothing of it, presuming we were catching the waves of a big freighter that had passed out of sight.

After tying our boat to the Lasqueti dock, the four of us laughed as we jammed together with ten people into Sylvain's compact pickup truck. With carefree abandon we headed off to the mid-isle Community Center. Though we knew we'd boat home after dark, the journey didn't give us much concern. We'd made similar trips many times before, enchanted by phosphorus and skies full of stars.

Tonight we had a party to attend, and the bay seemed asleep under waters of silk.

As we danced in the hall in the woods, a new arrival made hushed mention of a big blow coming into False Bay. And in that moment revealed how Qualicums weighed heavily on our collective unconscious.

The whisper of big wind seemed heard simultaneously by everyone in the hall. Like the first note of some distant siren, it sparked off an instant uneasiness in us all, a straightening of backs and straining of ears. Those needing to cross False Bay displayed small facial tics. We craned our necks as we looked past those we were speaking to, seeking to catch a glimpse of the trees outside. Trees that were telltale signs of the wind.

Our night of fun was over when we heard word of strong winds. In clipped conversations, those of us living on the bay worked through our options. Within minutes, Theresa and I and Ray and Eve had said our good-byes and bummed a ride in a car full of people Noel was taking to the dock.

Noel drove a battered, old, monster station wagon, too large to turn around easily within the confines of the pier. Thoughtful as ever, however, Noel drove us to the far end so we wouldn't have far to walk. Then she started maneuvering her bus around so she could drive back up the dock after letting us out. Since the beast's motor died whenever it idled, Noel did her jockeying with one foot mashed on the accelerator and the other pumping the brake.

I was hunched in the rear luggage compartment, which could only be opened from the outside. The rear hatch was held shut by large galvanized latches screwed to the car's frame, which I knew I couldn't kick out. Listening to the racing engine and bracing myself as we lurched back and forth, I figured we'd plunge through the rail at any instant.

When the motor finally quit, Ray released me from my cage. Peering through the dark, my stomach knotted as I glimpsed what was happening around us.

The ferry and fishing boats moored at the dock were rolling through huge arcs as the swells passed under them. These twenty meter (sixty-foot) boats were being heaved about like toys in a tub.

With us were several friends who'd boated to the dock from their homes on Lasqueti's shores, which they could otherwise reach only by forest trails. When they confronted the cauldron in the bay, they left their boats tied tight to the float, choosing to hike home through miles of wind-whipped woods with limbs crashing down around them.

Unfortunately, Ray and Eve and Theresa and I didn't have that option.

I was grimly aware that for all the turmoil at the dock, it stood in a relatively protected place. Olsen lay in the jaws of the bay, where its rocks bit down on all the wind and waves had to offer. To reach home we would negotiate much larger seas than those tossing around the ferry and fishing boats, and have to pass through a stormy spot off Higgins Island we especially dreaded. Past experience had taught us that the waves were particularly angry there.

Following the beams of our headlamps, the four of us picked our way out on the bucking floats. Shouting to be heard above the wind, Ray warned us to watch out for the opening and closing gap between the rafts in front of us. Thankful for his help, the rest of us jumped to the seaplane float, which thudded powerfully against the shoreward section.

We found our fourteen-foot boat bobbing like a cork, and were sobered by how puny it looked in the waves.

Casting off from where we'd tied between two larger craft, we found that leaving was a tricky maneuver in itself. We were hemmed in on three sides by other boats and the float, each of which was thrown about in its own chaos of motion. When we tried to maneuver, the wind and waves constantly pushed us backward and rolled us on our beams.

When we finally cleared the buffer of float and boats, we found walls of black rushing at us. While we were able to push obliquely over some swells, their brethren that were breaking caused me real concern. Without warning, these breakers came upon us out of the dark, and I knew I had to point my bow straight into them to avoid swamping.

At the top of the swells, the pirate wind boarded our boat and fought me for control. It threw our bow sideways, forcing me to jerk hard on the tiller to avoid being pushed broadside to the waves.

A piece of the darkness disengaged itself from the bay and attacked our boat, then disappeared silently behind us. My confidence teetered on this wave's crest as the quiver of its power touched me through the night. With each succeeding pounding, I became more certain that instead of clawing our way home, we were forcing ourselves deeper into disaster's black mouth. For the night multiplies a storm's power, and once fear begins in the dark, there is no cure.

In a night storm, special laws of gravity take hold, lateral and violent. Wind and waves rule, battering the islands with such relentless power that they seem to hunch low to keep from swinging on their moorings. Though offshore breakers seethe with fury, it seems that small islands excite them into fiercer anger, enraging the sea at their insolence. Our forested dabs of rock are hostages, paraded among the waves and spray in punishment for having presumed to trespass too closely.

After a few swells, I managed to get a feel for their direction and rhythm. As Higgins lay diagonally across their line of travel, I steered a zigzag course, running directly out over the crests and covering sideways distance toward Higgins through the intervening troughs.

This worked well enough and we were finally able to drop off Ray and Eve on the rocks at the base of their trail. Thankfully, this lay in the lee of their island.

Motoring out into False Bay again, Theresa and I hugged the shore of Higgins for as long as we could, seeking to prolong its shelter.

Dark clouds boiled in a black sky, and soon we were in wind thrashing everything around us. Sneaking out from Higgins' protection, we approached the part of the bay where the waves were typically at their worst.

Tonight this place of tough water wasn't going to disappoint us. Sometimes we dropped off a crest into a hole, smashing into the water below. Shooting off of waves into the empty spaces beyond, we hung on with both hands as we bucked our way toward distant Olsen. Luckily we'd left a light on, so at least I had a beacon to steer for.

When we finally neared our island, its wind shadow gave us some relief. In its lee the swells no longer broke around us.

Now, however, we had new challenges to face. First we had to locate our landing area among the rocks, for since the tide was low and the landing slick, we needed to use our "clothesline" ropes to help us disembark. After locating them in the dim beam of our headlamp, we headed in.

Surging toward the rocks, I knew that another problem was at hand. A lazy eye left Theresa with only limited depth perception, and landing on Olsen's outer rocks was typically a drawn out affair even on calm days. Though physically fit and confident, Theresa had to probe cautiously with her feet to find safe spots to step.

Tonight's landing was going to be difficult. It was pitch dark, and the feeble beam of our one headlamp was lost in the shore's tangled mass of black. Returning at low tide, we confronted seaweed-covered, near-vertical walls. These were repeatedly wetted by swells that bore us up and down and strove to smash us against the rocks.

Our timing proved perfect, however, and in a few deft motions we were ashore. Quickly tying the boat to the clothesline and pulling frantically to keep it off the unforgiving boulders, we managed to avoid slipping into the water. To our mutual surprise, we made it to the top of the rocks without falling. Thereupon, I repeated the exhortations I'd been making about never going anywhere in the dark again.

CHAPTER 59
PIRATES PAY US A VISIT

In the case of pirates ... that profession ends only at the gallows.
—Herman Melville, *Moby Dick*

May, 2001

How remote Olsen was, and the unique dangers its isolation brought, was underscored one calm May morning.

While strumming his guitar in the floathouse, caretaker Larry was surprised to see three men picking their way along Olsen's shore. Going outside to greet them, he was told a story of shipwreck and woe.

Cruising the islands in a drunken all-night joy ride, they had run aground when attempting to navigate the waters off Olsen. Their boat was perched on a rock, left high and dry by the receding tide, and they claimed to be marooned with no way of escape. The men spoke to Larry of their plan to wait for the rising tide to float their boat and then paddle to Lasqueti for repairs.

As the day wore on, Larry became increasingly suspicious of the men's intentions. He occasionally caught them peering in the windows of our home and boathouse, and wondered at their apparent lack of interest in their grounded boat. Breaking glass jerked the pieces of this puzzle into place, and Larry began to worry for his safety. He had no phone or radio, and here were three drunken men apparently forcing their way into our home.

As he snuck up to get a look at what was happening, Larry inadvertently surprised one of the criminals as he was breaking into our boathouse. Reaching inside his coat, the thief told Larry that dire consequences would follow if he tried to intervene.

Fearing that the man had a gun and meant to use it, Larry raced for the rocks facing False Bay. Leaping from the low cliff top, he dove for the bay and swam frantically for Higgins Island.

Unfortunately for Larry, Higgins laid a half-kilometer away through frigid spring waters. Larry was not a strong swimmer, and when the endocrine of his flight wore off, his lean frame became quickly chilled.

Watching from the rocks above, the intruders realized that Larry's escape would have one of two endings. Either he would reach Higgins and bring others back, or he would drown. Thankfully for Larry, neither alternative was acceptable to them.

Grabbing a kayak from our boathouse, one of the men paddled out to where Larry was floundering, pulled him over the kayak's deck, and carried him back to shore. "We're thieves, not murderers!" he informed Larry indignantly.

Thankfully murder wasn't on their minds, but thievery still was. After getting Larry into some dry clothes, one of the crooks tied him up and stole his valuables. By this time, the others had launched our new boat and filled it with bounty from our house. Having untied his bonds, Larry came outside and interrupted their departure. Threatening Larry with bodily harm, they chased him into the woods and then made their getaway. Larry hid in the woods through the night, until the next day's low tide allowed him to escape to Lasqueti and seek help.

We kept little of value on the island through the winter except our boat. What they stole from us was insignificant. What they took from Larry, however, was far more precious. Never again could he be at peace on the island.

We'd never expected pirates, but we met them like any other challenge the island threw at us. Fortified with flare guns, a cell phone and a new security system, we put this incident behind us and were ready to thwart another try.

If we could survive the wind and sea, we could certainly prevail against the hand of man.

CHAPTER 60
EAGLES

The eagle, he was lord above ...

—William Wordsworth

July 4, 2001

After failing in its first attempt at flight, an immature eagle has taken up residence in the small meadow just below our eagles' nest. It stands in the shade, occasionally crying out to its parents. They answer back from their perches in nearby trees, where they keep constant watch over their offspring.

After climbing up the bank below the meadow, Theresa and I crept in close to check on the youngster's health. It was obviously recovering from some injury, as its feathers were untidy and its head drooped. Notwithstanding this lethargy, however, the young eagle was ready to defend itself. When I came too close, it spread its wings and pushed its head forward menacingly.

July 5, 2001

Concerned for the immature eagle, I went out fishing to catch it some food. After climbing close to where it stood, I tossed in the rockfish I'd caught. The eagle jumped back when they landed, then cocked its head and warily eyed the offerings. It made no move in their direction, though we assumed it was hungry. Later, Theresa brought a large bowl of water in case the bird needed something to drink.

From its size we suspected this eagle should have been flying, as it was nearly as big as an adult bird. We hoped that our efforts would help it through its infirmity, though we were reluctant to intervene too aggressively. This was, after all, a wild creature in a wild place. Death happens here to those unfit to survive.

July 8, 2001

We continued to feed the young eagle for several days, but today had to return to Gig Harbor for a spell. We suspected we'd been keeping the bird alive, and knew that our departure might be its death sentence. If it was going to live through the next weeks, it would have to do so on its own or through the succor of its parents.

The crew of the ferry recently went on strike, taking out of commission the only "official" transportation to Lasqueti. Though we had avoided using the ferry during our first few years on the island, in recent times we had come to rely on its convenience.

Aurel Girard cruised into the empty sea of the strike, providing a semblance of regular service between Lasqueti and French Creek aboard the *Argent*. Though his passengers rode across the Strait sitting on piles of rope, and on rough days were assured of getting wet, Aurel's service was appreciated by all. Riding in Aurel's old fishing boat was more fun than the ferry anyway.

Today was hot and glass-calm, and the rear deck of the *Argent* was a perfect place to enjoy the trip through the Strait. Lounging in the sun, we passed the crossing in relaxed conversation with friends.

Disembarking in French Creek, we ran into our friend Jack Thomas. He had quite a load with him, including a new motor for his boat. On his last trip up he had gone fishing alone near the Finnerties, where in building seas his motor died. He was miles from the cove where he lived, in an area of strong current flow. So as anyone else would do, eighty-year-old Jack got out his oars and rowed home. Today he proudly displayed his new engine and couldn't wait to get out fishing again.

July 26, 2001

I arrived on Lasqueti today via one of the ferry's "essential service" runs. Though the crew were still officially on strike, they were running the boat a couple of days a week to make sure that their neighbors didn't go without necessary transportation.

Theresa had departed Gig Harbor a week earlier with our friends Cheri and Sue on their boat. Their plan was to make a leisurely trip aboard *Mabel* through the San Juan and Gulf Islands, and arrive at Lasqueti in time for the Firemen's Picnic. Shortly after I tied up our boat at Olsen, I spied *Mabel* entering False Bay. There was no way the women were going to miss this highlight of the Lasqueti social season.

As we were eating lunch we heard a racket coming from Little Olsen. Across the cove from us, an adult eagle was perched in a tree, ripping up a fish held tight in its talons. In a tree nearby, an immature eagle squawked like a small child, impatient to be fed.

Finally the adult flew off to the rocks above the floathouse, followed immediately by the younger bird. After dropping the proffered meal, the adult bird flew back to perch on a snag, where it cleaned its beak by rubbing it on the hard, dry wood.

Though the youngster could fly, it had not yet learned to hunt. We were confident this was the same young bird we'd fed, which had finally escaped its prison on the ground. To confirm this, I climbed up to the meadow where we'd thrown fish to the bird. There I found plenty of fish skeletons, but no dead eagle.

Our adolescent eagle was one of the lucky ones. Forty percent of young eagles do not survive their first attempt at flight.

Yet this peril is not the first test of survival an eagle must pass. Though there may be up to three eggs in a nest, most often only one chick will live to get the chance at flight. While multiple chicks may survive the hatch, it's not uncommon for the older chick to kill the younger ones. This is especially true when the older eaglet is female, since they are consistently bigger than males. Observing such fratricide, neither parent makes the slightest move to intervene.

After hatching, a young eaglet adds a kilo of weight every ten days. By six weeks, it is nearly adult size.

At eight weeks, the parents are hunting almost continuously to feed the voracious youngster. Waiting in the nest, it stretches its wings in response to gusts of wind. At times it lifts off its feet for brief moments, using its wings as air foils.

As the young eagle approaches ten weeks of age, it cries eagerly for food whenever an adult flies toward the nest. But now the parents begin to come in with empty talons. As days pass, the young eagle loses its body fat. It becomes quicker in its movements and lighter on its feet. When the wind blows, it becomes airborne from time to time, paddling less and less with its wings and barely touching the edge of the nest.

The parents now fly by, just out of reach, with a meal hanging tantalizingly from their talons. Screaming for food, the young eagle teeters on the edge of the nest, furiously beating its wings. At night, the parents no longer return to comfort the young bird.

As days pass, the nest's store of old bones has been picked clean. Though once a warm place of abundant food, the nest is now a prison. By now, however, the prisoner has shed its baby fat and firmed its muscles. Finally, one day when a parent flies close by displaying another meal, the young bird lifts off the nest. Half-starved and eager for food, it is drawn into the sky and its first real flight.

Juvenile birds like ours are distinguished by their mottled appearance. It's not until four to five years of age that they reach sexual maturity and develop adult plumage.

At maturity, bald eagles weight from five to seven kilograms (ten to fourteen pounds). A bird's 7,000 feathers weigh less than half a kilo, and its hollow-boned skeleton only half that. Mature females are slightly larger than the males, developing wingspans of over two and a half meters (seven feet).

Though bald eagles mate for life, if one dies, the survivor will readily accept a new mate. Their average life span is fifteen to twenty years, and some birds live as long as thirty.

CHAPTER 61
LESSONS IN TACT AND HUMILITY

When dealing with people, let us remember that we are not dealing with creatures of logic.

—Dale Carnegie

Temper gets you into trouble. Pride keeps you there.

—Anonymous

July 27, 2001

Today, Theresa and I went out to recover our prawn traps in rising wind and waves.

Pulling the pots was backbreaking work, for when the wind blew our boat away from them, it greatly increased their effective weight. I was working hard at a frustrating task and kept getting tangled in the rat's nest of rope that was piling up around my feet. Unable to manage the task alone, I persuaded Theresa to tail the line and wind it on a spool.

Though Theresa was a big help, I couldn't keep from blaming her for the continued problems I was having. It soon became clear that my repeated comments on the quality of her work were not well received. Crossing her arms and announcing she was going on strike, Theresa left me to do the two-person job by myself. She insisted she wouldn't lift a finger until I apologized, which I adamantly refused to do.

Standing in our small boat as I was thrown off balance by the waves, I alternately heaved on the line and tried to wind it on the spool, just to show her that I could manage these tasks without her.

Failing miserably and crumbling in my resolve, I offered up her demanded apology. Though my wounded pride caused me to bark it insincerely, Theresa had her victory. My lack of sincerity mattered not. She even smiled as she resumed her work.

For all our efforts, we only got a dozen prawns, poetic justice from the mother sea in conspiracy with Theresa.

July 28, 2001

Our fast was broken with an omelet with fresh prawns, delicious enough to wipe away the foul taste of their capture.

Later I went over to pick up Dick for an afternoon of fishing. Theresa and I had been invited to Dick and Terry's for dinner, and Dick and I were to catch the main course. On our way out of their house, Terry asked politely if she should plan a backup meal. Indignantly, Dick and I puffed out our chests and assured her that the men would provide.

We had a great afternoon together on the water, and managed a couple of beautiful fish, a striped rockfish from the Finnerty Islands, and a kelp greenling from the Sisters. Both were brightly colored and would delight any fisherman, but their combined weight was short of what we needed for dinner. So when we should have been heading in, we tried fishing one more spot off Lasqueti.

As soon as Dick's jig reached the bottom, something big attacked it. After a hard fight he boated a sizeable lingcod, which led to "high-fives" and nods of approval. Stowing our gear, we ran for the Lasqueti cove where Dick lived.

Proud providers, returning from sea.

July 29, 2001

Gordon Ashacker is a frequent sight in the waters off Olsen. Launching his small rowboat in False Bay, he rows out past us to troll for salmon near the Finnerties. By oar power, he catches more fish than anyone on the island.

Gordon recently told Ken about a maze of underwater pinnacles on the back side of Lasqueti. It was prime lingcod habitat, and Gordon had been catching some nice fish there. Ever since we heard this, Ken and I had been planning a trip to fish Gordon's lucky pinnacles, and today was the day.

Ken cruised up to the deep water just off Olson, where I stepped from our rocks to his bow pulpit. Motoring out of False Bay and north through the Finnerty and Fagan Islands, we rounded the end of Lasqueti and picked our way down its east flank. After consulting our charts a number of times, we stopped at what looked like Gordon's secret spot.

Jigging the rocky underwater slopes, we repeatedly hooked into big, strong fish. Some we got to the boat, others spit the hook during a hard fight and further inflamed our imaginations. Like blind men, we groped the distant bottom to find the pinnacles where the lingcod lurked.

After seven hours of productive fishing, we decided we needed a break. So we pulled up our gear and headed to the west side of Lasqueti to fish for salmon.

Mooching deep with herring, I hooked into something that bent my pole to the water. It stayed down near the bottom, running this way and that, peeling line off my reel. At different times I thought I had a big king salmon or a frenzied shark.

When I finally managed to pull the fish to the surface, I was excited to see a lingcod a meter and a half long, the biggest I had ever caught. Knowing this to be a rare fish in these waters, and surely a female with unborn generations inside her, I eased out my hooks and let her swim away. I must admit, however, that this act of self-denial was made possible by the state of our fish box, which already held all we could eat.

When we got home, I added some fillets to the pot of clams, oysters, and prawns that Theresa was cooking. This concoction simmered into a delicious seafood stew that fed us for days.

CHAPTER 62
AN UNUSUAL SUMMER STORM

The calm is but the envelope and wrapper of the storm.
—Henry Melville, *Moby Dick*

July 30, 2001

Today was a hot one, and early afternoon found me lazing in my favorite hammock.

Swaying gently among the junipers above False Bay, I thought things that were not properly thoughts. A great quietness ruled and the sun lay heavily on me. Simple truths ordered all I saw.

My plans for the day melted into shimmering surface slicks and finally evaporated in the heat.

Beyond my cocoon, the sea and sky gestured to me silently, inviting me into their world. In a deep relaxation just before dozing, I dilated and accepted the dream powers that drive these things.

July 31, 2001

Looking to stretch our legs, Theresa and I kayaked over to Lasqueti's Mud Bay. Opening the umbrellas we'd brought along and resting their canopies on our front decks, we held tight to the handles as a strong breeze pushed our kayaks smartly along. We didn't have to use our paddles until we were deep in the wind shadow of Mud Bay. After carrying our kayaks up the beach and tying them to an overhanging tree, we proceeded on our island stroll.

When we began our paddle home, Theresa and I were pleased to find that the sea has calmed to glass. We had anticipated a workout against wind and waves.

While we were captivated by the small waterways we paddled through, we were disturbed by the stillness that had flowed over our world, an eerie quiet that didn't belong. In search of answers, we stroked into False Bay to get a better look around us.

What we saw was both stunning and disquieting. Some huge gravity had pulled the sky down, concentrating its blue. In doing so, it burst small veins in the fabric of the air, bleeding purple into it.

Unease pricked across our skin. Though we were surrounded by the colors of a brilliant sunset, sunset was hours away. As we watched, the sky gradually shrouded the shores around us. Vancouver Island, and even the nearby points of Lasqueti, shimmered and then disappeared.

When I looked at Theresa, I saw that her face was an eerie blue. The enveloping bruise seeped up her nostrils and dyed the islands behind her an unnatural hue.

Suspending our paddles over the water, we realized all sound had ceased. There were no seal splashes on the bay, no seabird cries. Theresa's mouth hung open as she hovered, ready to speak. But she said nothing, held in thrall by the cloying colors that engulfed us.

As I finally saw the sky for what it was, I shuddered in my seat. In that flash of awareness, what had been hypnotic became deeply unsettling.

With a thief's creep, storm gods had stolen the sky. After consuming the horizon, they turned our pleasant afternoon into something as moist and thick as an exhaled breath.

When Theresa finally found her voice, she whispered that the colors were strangely tropical. And with that utterance, both of us comprehended that what we beheld was anything but benign. Bobbing in our kayaks, we realized we were looking at the underbelly of a storm.

Knowing that the gloom was the fuse of a coming explosion, we thrust our paddles into the water, straining to quickly get off the bay.

Digging towards Olsen, we saw the shrouding mist begin to strain at is outer edges. As huge forces stretched the sky, splits in the gloom signaled bad things ahead. We realized that when the purple was finally pulled apart on the sky's torture rack, when bone and sinew snapped and the muscles of the atmosphere tore, the Strait would descend into a hell where we didn't want to be.

Paddling determinedly for home, we were relieved when our bows finally scraped shore. But we had barely made it. As we climbed up on the rocks, the sky caved in and the storm crashed upon us. Lightning exploded down and thunder shook the rocks.

That night, the dark hummed with electric tension. Time after time our bedroom shot to impossible brilliance as lightning pitchforked into the water. Though I worried constantly that a bolt might strike our island, the pouring rain quenched my concerns of fire. Nightmares blossomed in the rare moments that sleep came, as even unconsciousness failed to shelter me from the violence.

Exhausted from these insomniac hours, I felt no pleasure when the sky gradually calmed. Dawn found me weary, thick with the need for sleep.

CHAPTER 63
EARTHQUAKE PERILS

When the inevitable happens ... the earth shall quake ... and the mountains shall crumble ...

—Mecca Suras, *Koran*

August 1, 2001

Yesterday's storm lashed the Strait into a seething cauldron. But as the wind often prowls our island abode, we were able to read the signs of its approach and escape without incident.

Much more perilous are demons that attack so infrequently that we forget they exist. When they pounce without warning, there can be deadly consequences for local islanders.

On June 23, 1946, deep in the geologic basement under central Vancouver Island, something massive faulted. In moments, Canada was jolted by its largest historic onshore earthquake, measuring 7.3 on the Richter scale.

When the quake hit the waters of the Strait, it heaved up waves that raced toward a Lasqueti fisherman trolling off the island's western shore. Taking him by surprise, they capsized his boat and pitched him overboard. As the chilly waters filled his lungs, he slipped into the blackness of death, puzzling over his rogue attacker.

What happened that day in the dark rock under Vancouver Island has been recurring around the world since the earth was formed. The plates of the earth's crust are almost always in motion, though their noses creep forward in a series of staccato jumps rather than a continuous slide.

Each such slip produces an earthquake, though most are so small that they are undetectable without the help of a seismograph. As the Juan de Fuca plate stutters forward in its dive beneath the North American plate, it produces thousands of such small quakes a year.

But if the junction between two plates becomes locked, almost unimaginable stresses accumulate as the plates behind them keep moving. When the fault finally releases, the size of the leap can be staggering. In the 1906 San Francisco quake, the two sides of the San Andreas Fault slid six meters (nineteen feet) along each other. And in an 1872 quake, the Sierra Nevada Mountains jumped up a meter as they lunged seven meters north.

When such quakes occur beneath the sea, they can be especially perilous to coast dwellers. For when they produce abrupt movements of the sea floor, the resulting tsunamis can be much larger than the waves that claimed the lone Lasqueti fisherman.

On November 18, 1929, a magnitude 7.2 temblor, two hundred and fifty kilometers south of Newfoundland, triggered a submarine slump of an estimated two hundred cubic kilometers (124 cubic miles). This slump shoved up a tsunami which raised sea levels between two and seven meters (up to twenty-three feet) when it humped up on Newfoundland's shores. At the heads of several long and narrow bays, the tsunami's momentum pushed waves as high as twenty-seven meters (eighty-eight feet). The devastation ashore was captured in the words of Hon. Dr. Mosdell, who arrived aboard the rescue ship *Meigle*.

"Houses were reduced to a condition reminiscent of wartime description of the effects of heavy shell fire. Former sites of gardens and meadows now thickly strewn with boulders ... thrown upon the shore by the devastating force of the tidal wave. Motorboats, stages, wharfs and piers lifted bodily and thrown far inland in heaps of ruins" (*The Daily News of St. John*).

In the tsunami that wreaked this havoc, twenty-seven people perished.

Our house on Olsen Island might survive such a tsunami, if the depths off our steep shores allowed it to pass without cresting. But other locals wouldn't be so lucky.

The head of False Bay, which shallows as it narrows toward the Lasqueti dock and a number of houses, would be devastated. Lasquetians would face a wall of water like that which rushed down Newfoundland's narrow inlets.

And given the lacework of faults under Vancouver Island and the Strait—as geologists say, the question is when, not *if.*

Vancouver Island has seen a lot of development since its remote quake of 1946. The destruction that such a quake would cause in British Columbia's more urban areas is grimly suggested by the devastation wreaked in 1989 by California's 7.1 magnitude Loma Prieta quake.

Spreading from this quake's hypocenter at 5.6 kilometers (three and a half miles) per second, three distinct types of shock waves combined to set the earth in motion. Houses built to California's strict earthquake codes bucked and twisted as the shock waves shattered their windows and splintered their framing. One man's house lurched thirty meters (ninety-eight feet) away from its foundation and settled in ruins on top of him.

Near Santa Cruz, bicyclists were thrown to the pavement as cars bounced up and down around them. At the trendy Pacific Garden Mall, where old brick structures had been transformed into boutique shops, buildings of different heights shook with different periods of vibration and knocked each other down. Twenty-one stores collapsed, burying ten people beneath them.

As the shock waves sped outward in all directions from the quake's hypocenter, screaming car alarms traced their journey. Above them, redwoods swayed side to side like windshield wipers, some snapping like pieces of chalk. Landslides were set off at the same time as the car alarms, shooting dust clouds into the sky. One slide alone covered eighty-five acres, and took dozens of houses with it.

When the shaking reached Stanford University, sixty uninsured buildings sustained 165 million dollars worth of damage.

In San Francisco, chimneys toppled onto cars and elevators clattered in their shafts. The pilot of a blimp overhead felt the shaking, and the officers of a naval ship off Point Reyes believed their ship was running aground as it shuddered violently.

Rapid transit passengers in the BART under-bay tube wondered if the train had jumped its rails and was bouncing over rocks, and drivers in the Interstate-80 bore under Yerba Buena Island watched the tunnel writhe like a hose.

The entire superstructure of the Bay Bridge came alive, sending monstrous ripples out from its swaying towers. This violent motion sheared wrist–thick bolts that had attached a five-hundred-ton section of roadway to its supporting towers, allowing it to hinge downward and smash open the deck below. Hurtling toward the breach, a bus driver wrestled his skidding bus under control, stopping just short of plummeting into the waters beneath him.

One section of the double-decked Nimitz Freeway vibrated at an identical frequency to the muddy landfill it rested on. This resonance amplified the shaking over 700 percent, causing support columns to fail. For over 2,200 meters (7,200 feet), the 600-ton upper roadway slabs crashed down, one after the other, on the road below. Cars and trucks were flattened and many people in them died.

***

These Vancouver Island, Grand Banks, and Loma Prieta quakes all measured between 7.1 and 7.3 on the Richter scale.

An M9 "megathrust" earthquake would bring almost unimaginable devastation. Measuring 9.0 on the Richter scale, the amplitude of its ground motion would be twenty times that found in the magnitude 7 quakes described above. In terms of TNT explosive force, a magnitude 7 quake produces the equivalent force as about 31 megatons of TNT (megaton is one million tons. Thirty-one megatons equals 62 billion pounds). A magnitude 9 quake produces the approximate energy of about 31 *gigatons* of TNT, 1000 times more explosive force than the 31 megatons of a magnitude 7 temblor. That's the equivalent of approximately 62 *trillion* pounds of TNT.

Geologic evidence suggests that our coast has been devastated by thirteen such megathrust quakes in the past 6,000 years. These monster quakes are the world's largest, and they occur when there is a sudden slip along the boundary between a subducting and overriding tectonic plate.

To the west of where we sit on our island, the western edge of the continental plate projects out under the Pacific. Over the millennia, the subducting oceanic plate has slid down beneath it.

But for some time, these plates have been locked. The ongoing convergence has compressed the continental plate's forward edge and pushed up a spring-like bulge behind it, storing almost unimaginable energies in the tortured rock.

This bulging and compression is starkly chronicled in GPS studies of our coast, which show Victoria moving toward the mainland seven millimeters per year and Vancouver Island's southwest coast rising four millimeters in the same time.

Prior to the 8.8 magnitude quake that hit Chile in 2010, the same thing was happening there. The oceanic plate was locked with the continental one, shoving Chile's coast (and even the whole of Southern South America) eastward. When the plates broke apart, the area around Concepcion, Chile leaped westward by about ten feet. Buenos Aires, Argentina, on the other side of the continent, moved westward about an inch.

***

At 9:00 PM on January 26, 1700, when the Pacific Northwest's plates were locked as they are now, the stored energy caused a megathrust quake along 1,000 kilometers (600 miles) of the offshore Cascadia Thrust Fault, extending from mid-Vancouver Island to northern California.

The oral traditions of British Columbia's coastal First Nations Peoples chronicle the devastation wrought by this quake, whose shockwaves collapsed houses of Vancouver Island's Cowichan clan. The ground shook so violently that people found it impossible to stand, and continued for so long that it sickened them as they lay helpless on the ground.

This quake's tsunami destroyed the Pachena People's winter village, leaving no survivors, and along the coast giant waves picked up canoes and threw them into the tops of inland trees.

After crossing the Pacific, as recounted in precise Japanese records, hours later this tsunami reached Japan.

The footprints of this quake give grim testimony to the devastation that such an event can bring to our coast. Buried tidal marshes and coastal forest soils show a sudden coastal subsidence from northern California to Vancouver Island, and changes in the tree rings of coastal old growths suggests a drowning of their roots from widespread flooding. Sand layers on top of forest soils and marine organisms preserved in the mud of coastal lakes indicate a large tsunami rushed over the subsided coast. "The earthquakes reshaped the intertidal zones, moved bays, blocked estuaries, destroyed marshes and drowned [Indian] village locations" (Ames and Maschner 1999).

Offshore landslide layers on top of the ocean bottom were likely caused by strong seismic shaking that carried sediment from the continental slope to the deep seafloor.

All our senses tell us that continents don't move. We consider oral histories "myths," and believe freeways only collapse in California and Japan. Sediment records are arcane science and cataclysms from 300 years ago too remote to worry about. But according to Natural Resources Canada, "from measurements of present elastic strain building up in the continent near the coast, [there is] … observed deformation [that] corresponds to that expected for a locked thrust fault … The subduction fault is probably locked along the whole coast from southern British Columbia to Northern California."

Speaking of the 1700 megathrust quake that occurred off our coast, considered to have been an M9, they conclude that "a similar offshore event will happen sometime in the future and that it represents a considerable hazard to those who live in southwest B.C. … The new evidence … results in hazard estimates that are similar to those for regions well-known for very large earthquakes such as California and Japan."

Chapter 64
Wind and Eagles

Poseidon loves this time of year, when he can rage and stir up mountains of water and waves ...
—Margaret George, *Helen of Troy*

August 1, 2001

In today's wind, I watched our boat the way an animal watches its young when it smells a predator nearby. In between my trips to the window, I sought the comfort of familiar rituals: tending the fire in our woodstove, cooking a pot of oatmeal, playing a game of Scrabble with Theresa. Their soothing familiarity was almost strong enough to convince me that my concerns for our boat were groundless. When an unusually powerful gust slapped the house, however, I strode to the front window to check on it once again.

Though Theresa and I had planned to visit some friends today, the elements persuaded us to stay home. It's an easy choice to be island-bound in the wind, when the waves crashing against the rocks make leaving an ordeal. We were not disappointed in the least, as the island's solitude was its own reward.

August 2, 2001

More wind today, accompanied by rain. My brother Marc and his friend Dick Walker arrived on Aurel's first run across and were delighted by our island home.

I wanted to get some fresh prawns for dinner, but the day's foul weather had kept me off the water. When the wind finally dropped a bit, Marc and I seized the opportunity to go out and pull the pots.

Marc had no idea how to use the swell to help him raise the traps, and kept losing his balance as he tried to pull them standing up. Marc is extremely fit, however, and his strength overcame his lack of finesse. In short order, he had the pot-lines streaming into the boat. For his exertion he was rewarded with a fine load of prawns.

August 3, 2001

Still a lot of wind and waves attacking us.

I made a run to the Lasqueti dock to drop Theresa off for her yoga class, and had difficulty landing when I got back to Olsen. My challenge was to keep our boat and motor from smashing against the rocks.

Marc was with me when I went to retrieve Theresa, and I was looking forward to his help executing our return landing on Olsen. As we neared the rocks, I coached Marc to use the same technique he had used on yesterday's prawn traps. His job was to hop ashore and pull quickly on the clothesline after I leapt out of the boat.

Unfortunately, I lost my balance as I jumped out on the rocks. Grabbing the outgoing side of the clothesline, I pulled furiously in an effort to bring myself upright.

Per my prior request, however, Marc was hard at work on the other side of the clothesline. With his back turned, he was feeding me more slack than I could possibly take up. Toppling slowly backward, I yelled at Marc to stop. He turned just in time to see me fall into the waves.

At least the boat was safe, and my pride and clothes would dry out.

That afternoon, we joined Ken to revisit our lingcod hot spot on the back side of Lasqueti. But we were foiled by nasty wind-blown chop, and instead put down in the lee of Lasqueti's north end.

After catching a variety of bottom fish, we reeled in a cod that had disgorged its swim bladder. We left this fish floating on the surface, hoping it would equalize and swim away.

A nearby eagle had other plans, however. Spying the fish immediately, the eagle began circling our boat.

Eagles have eyes that are nearly human size, but eyesight that is more than four times sharper than that of a person with perfect vision. With two centers of focus, allowing them to see both forward and sideways at the same time, they can spot prey over three square miles of sea.

Like other raptors, eagles also see infrared light that lies beyond the limits of human vision. With eyes that function like night-vision goggles, they can see their prey's heat. This allows them to spot prey hidden in foliage or swimming beneath the waves, and enables them to track a potential meal by its heat trail.

As soon as the fish drifted a few feet away from our boat, the majestic hunter swooped down with extended talons. The small cod was within the eagle's two-kilo (four-pound) lifting power and would make a tasty meal after the eagle killed it by driving talons into its flesh.

Eagles seldom drop their catch, thanks to a unique locking mechanism in their feet. When their open talons hit prey, they close instantly and will not open until the eagle lands and pushes down on something solid. This can create problems if the eagle closes on a fish too heavy to lift or plunges too deep after their prey. For in the water they have no ability to release their grip, and cannot take off if even temporarily submerged. Instead, they use their large wings to paddle to shore. Though eagles are strong swimmers, they may succumb to hypothermia if the water is cold and they are a long way from land.

This eagle, however, had no chance to use its talons or display its swimming ability. Apparently spooked by our boat, it flared off to the side just before grabbing the fish.

Winging powerfully skyward, the eagle wheeled and dove again. Flaring as it neared the water, it shot its open talons forward, then once more banked away just before hitting the fish. Repeating these acrobatics time after time, the eagle held us spellbound in the boat. This gave the cod time to equalize and finally swim away.

Lucky fish, hungry eagle, and delighted fishermen.

***

Son Chas arrived on the last ferry, his belongings wrapped in garbage bags to protect them from the rain. This is Theresa's and my usual procedure in bad weather, and I was glad to see Chas had figured it out on his own.

Ken, Claire, and Aaron later joined our expanding family for dinner. Marc cooked up linguini with fresh prawns and clams, which was followed by music and dancing. A great night was had by all.

August 4, 2001

I awoke to broken clouds and hoped for enough sun to recharge our solar power system's batteries. Days of poor weather and a house full of people had drained most of our stored electricity.

After breakfast we gathered around the weather radio, which promised "unseasonably strong gales." This, in turn, led me to insist that we were going to spend the day on-island.

My numerous boat trips in the past days of harsh weather had pushed me over an unseen edge. Landing and leaving, both potentially perilous maneuvers, demanded both luck and skill. Wind and waves combined to pin our boat to the shore, and spray doused me as each wave broke against the island's wall. At low tide I had to jam my feet in jagged cracks to keep from slipping on the seaweed-slick rocks.

Experience taught me that, once in the boat, I had to start the motor quickly and reverse into the waves, sending water over my transom and into the boat. In seconds I had to jam the tiller over hard, reversing back toward the rocks in order to swing my bow into the wind. As I did so, I always came perilously close to smashing my prop on underwater ledges.

Hence my determination to stay put. The last thing I wanted was to go through the drama of another landing on the rocks.

To escape the tension the forecast had brought, I took a hike to the top of the island. There I found that our water tanks were completely full, despite nine people drawing them down. For this I could thank our surfeit of rain, which Theresa had observed "looks like October!"

Foul weather kept everyone inside most of the day, busying themselves at games and chores to pass the time. At one point we divided up our supply of wooden matches for a protracted poker game.

During one sunny period around noon, the fabulous Uncle Marc grabbed some lemons and Tabasco sauce. Like the Pied Piper, he led the boys to the beach out past the floathouse. There they feasted on raw oysters, seasoned with a bit of fresh seaweed. Chris even managed to swallow a few small crabs, still wriggling as he popped them into his mouth. No doubt this performance was meant to entertain the girls visiting our sons. Suitably impressed, they gagged at the sight.

August 5, 2001

When we listened to the morning forecast on our weather radio, we were glad we'd stayed put on the island yesterday. After calling for local gales, the Coast Guard broadcast a sobering plea. "This station is requesting mariners to forward any information known about the sailing vessel *KW*, last seen one week ago. Report any sightings or information immediately to the Coast Guard. The *KW* was last seen in Oak Bay and was headed for the North Coast."

This was the second such announcement we'd heard in this week of strong winds, and both dealt with vessels passing through the Strait of Georgia.

I was accordingly concerned about finding a way over to French Creek, where I had to be this evening. The Lasqueti ferry crew was still on strike, and this summer we'd left the Grady at home. The only craft available to me was our small aluminum boat, and it would have been foolish to run over in that.

I motored to Lasqueti to beg passage with Aurel, but found the *Argent* snubbed tight to the dock. I wasn't sure if it was the weather that kept Aurel in port, or the case of beer at his side. Aurel just smiled when I asked him of his plans. Spying another case next to his drinking partner, I realized I'd have to find another way off-island.

Back on Olsen, I called several islanders who hired out their boats as water taxis, but couldn't find anyone willing to make the crossing in such high winds.

With my own distaste of unnecessary trips to the other side, I was reluctant to call on my friends to take me there. But I had to get off-island to attend to some pressing matters back at the office, so I finally called Ken and begged him for help. From our place on the edge of the Strait, I could see that the seas were settling down a bit. On my assurance that we wouldn't get hammered too badly, Ken said he'd be right over.

Though we encountered huge swells, the crossing went fine. Challenging, but thrilling as well. As with our decisions to settle in this wild place, the two of us were going where few others dared to go.

CHAPTER 65
OUR NEW PIRATE GUARD

In remote places, good conversation is very highly prized.
—Alexandra Morton and Billy Proctor, *Heart of the Raincoast*

September 28, 2001

Today I indulged in the simple rainy-day pleasure of tending a fire, alternately reading, staring into the flames, and going outside to retrieve more wood.

As the fire and I made our way through the day, the incense of woodsmoke and tree sap became my smell.

September 29, 2001

Though our ex-caretaker Larry now resided in an abandoned Lasqueti goat shed, enjoying only the merest approximation of human comfort, his eyes went wide with alarm when we inquired of his interest in returning to Olsen. His one pirate encounter had been one too many.

Accordingly we began fishing for a new caretaker. Our bait was the dream of living in Olsen's floathouse. Though the prospect of wintering on a remote island could tempt many, we knew that only someone very special would bite.

That someone was Kirsty Elliot.

Kirsty is a free-spirited woman in her mid-thirties, pretty, independent, and talented. She has biked her way around the world, lived in Canada's frozen Yukon, and always takes the road less traveled.

She plants trees and sews to support herself and writes poetry that deserves publishing. Her eyes also widened at the prospect of life in the floathouse, but in joy rather than fear.

Kirsty dove off the springboard of our island's magic into dreamlike dealings with the outside world. Her emails to us exuded her imagination and love of island life:

> *Hi there you two. Thank you so much for the use of the mellow gorgeous outboard motor!! I am glad it isn't an Evinrude. Baby drives a Mercury. I have borrowed Dick's boat, Rosanante, and covered her in plastic roses.*
>
> *I took my sewing machine to the craft fair last Saturday and now all the island girls are wearing kuku designs. My table was swarmed by girls wanting stretch denim skirts made on the spot and I had such a moment of clarity: let the bitches make their own clothes, I'm a poet, not a seamstress.*

***

> *Hi guys. I had my tea leaves read in Nanaimo and the woman said I lived surrounded in water and the place was very BLESSED.*
>
> *I am very excited to get back to my pirate watching post. I have a good message on the phone right now that starts: "if this is those pirates, don't even try coming here—"*

***

> *Did I tell you about my boat sinking incident? Everything is okay now, the motor is fine. I just finished patching the boat this evening at Ray's. I will tell you all about it. Give me a call when you know the exact day you're coming and I will dust and heat the place up and BAKE SCONES!! The windmeter was at 106 km/hr, and that is an official hurricane.*

I'm glad you got a bit of weather while you were here. It's so thrilling to be cozy while all hell breaks loose out in the forest.

***

I need you two to get the book that Alain gave me for Christmas. It is called Faerie-ality. It is all haute couture clothing for fairies, everything is made of leaves and petals and feathers. It makes me want to throw up because I can't wear rhubarb leaves and lily petals. And the shirt he gave me is out of this world. When I wear it I feel nervous that some woman is going to throw me down, scratch my eyes out and steal it. It is from Italy and is fluttery ragged silk and wool. I think it cost as much as the average lada.

I have been looking after Niabi's lovely little dog. She chased a deer off the island the first day she arrived and it swam way out to sea and Alain and I followed it in Rosey and the poor thing swam for nearly forty minutes. When it got out of the water it was tired and cold so Alain cuddled it for half an hour until the life came back in. When your man cuddles a wet deer it is hard to not fall more in love with him. Even more so when he tells you to meet the last ferry and pick up a present on the top shelf and it is a bouquet of stargazer lilies and orchids and you get to carry them home through the dark forest feeling like Miss Universe.

CHAPTER 66
THE STORM DRAGONS ATTACK

Tumbling together, the particles of air became a huge, unstoppable current. Some of them rake the earth ... pounding anything that stands in their way ... There is something much larger than me aloft out there. I am glimpsing, I believe, the garments of a passing god.

—Jan DeBlieu, *Wind*

October 25, 2001

The storm was one that all of us knew would eventually come.

Everyone who lived on these waters had tempted fate. And we were all aware that when we ventured forth in winds and waves that made our venturing pure foolishness, we cheated destiny.

Most times we laughed sheepishly afterward, eyes flickering downward as we admitted our stupidities: Dick owning up to clawing his way out to work on Olsen through fifty-knot winds with seven people in our four-meter aluminum boat, and me acknowledging that I'd crashed my way across the Strait in a gale that could have blown me over backwards.

But all of us knew of times when only a ghost lived to tell the tale, as in Verner's kayak trip through an April storm.

Deep down in our private thoughts, in those rare naked moments when as survivors we confronted our stupidities and fears, we expected retribution. We knew that the storm gods of the aborigines still ruled the wind and waters, and that a visit was due.

This morning a surreal calm stole over the world, the kind that exists in its purest form in the eye of a hurricane. In today's calm, nature held her breath. With her eyes closed and a smile on her face, she lulled us to take her for granted. At the same time, she was puffing her cheeks, drawing on storms deep in her lungs to deliver us a terrible blow.

Waiting for the storm, I felt the watchfulness of the world increase. Rocks, trees, and bay were listening. Though dawn had dispelled the darkness, a shadow of foreboding brooded over isle and sea.

The weather forecast had raised concerns in all of us who heard it. Storm-force winds were predicted for the Strait, and hurricane-force for the north end of Vancouver Island.

But far more nagging were the reports we received from our senses, senses sharpened by countless hours in the wind and waves discovering vestigial awarenesses that were typically ignored.

Living on our island had done this to us. Narrow misses had taught us to attend to the stream of subtle clues tendered by the sea and sky. Freed from distractions, we relied on what nature herself told us. Other blows had taught us lessons that barely broke the surface of consciousness, but which we remembered nonetheless.

As today's wind rose, we were beset by a stream of warnings that something ominous rushed toward us: changes in the way the wind buffeted us, unusual noises, differences in density of the air, and balance problems felt in the testicles.

On days like today, neighbor Eve wore her hard hat for necessary trips through the woods. All of us walked forest paths quickly, anxious to be clear of swaying trees that sloughed off limbs without warning. One such thigh-sized limb had narrowly missed Noel Taylor's head when she was walking through Olsen's woods in a blow.

Such storms were threshold events where nature would be reckoned with.

***

"We live at the junction of two oceans, one of liquid, one of air. The currents that gently ... [flow through the seas] are not unlike those that fill the atmosphere, responding to the tug of cold and warmth. It is easy to forget that air is a fluid and behaves as water does, curling into wrists and fingers, ripples and waves … Air and water, two great, encircling seas, similar in form, each shaping the other's flow" (DeBlieu 1999).

Immense rivers of air flow over us, placid and smooth when their movement is slow.

At other times, when the flow is violent, these currents have the power of mountain cataracts. Invisible dams collapse, unleashing torrents of destructive energy. Heaving mounds of turbulence burst skyward as the rivers crash over hills and mountains. Whirlpools and countercurrents spin off at their edges. Huge standing waves rise up as the wind's underbelly rebels at the friction of its passing. Waves that rear their heads and break. Exploding gusts to smite the unwary.

Today, the rivers tumbling above took control. Hovering gulls shot abruptly skyward, caught in runaway elevators of air. A duck was thrown against the cliffs by a sudden gust, and now floated dead on the waves. Even more notable were the birds cowering in the trees and on the ground. Birds that had abandoned their homes in the sky out of fear of its perils.

In the rising wind, ants retreated to their nests and deer went to ground in the woods. Small creatures shivered deep in their burrows, overwhelmed by the instinct to flee. Fish that usually fed near the water's surface dove deep and hid in protected crannies.

At the same time, small darting things that usually skulked at the fringes of my consciousness grew bold and swam forth through my thoughts, things that normally lived in nightmares.

Perhaps in response, all of the local boatmen and I found pressing things to do ashore, long neglected tasks that suddenly had to be done.

As afternoon bled into evening, we became increasing sure that tonight's storm would be different from other times of wind and waves. All of us—ants, deer, and fishermen—knew that in this blow our debts would come due.

***

When I clawed my way outside in the night to visit the outhouse, I found myself believing that the roaring wind was the breath of some mythical creature crouching just beyond the surrounding isles.

Whenever I blinked, in the fleeting instances that my eyes were closed, I caught glimpses of a demon of monstrous form. In its hunter's heart, it knew that small prey cowered on the islands before it.

Revealed as a spirit of malice that had been gnawing upon itself in the shadows, the wind launched itself upon the world. From somewhere beyond the trees I heard a roar, a venting of deep-chested anger backed by caverns of resonant lung space. I knew not what uttered that roar, but knew it befitted a creature of fantastic power and proportion.

***

Peering beyond the island's edge, I realized that for all the fear the dragon wrought ashore, she was immeasurably more terrifying at sea.

Every cell of every boatman bears the imprint of millions of years of terrestrial survival biology. In the most primitive levels of their brain stems, their senses orient them to the surface of the sea and the necessity of staying above it.

When the dragon attacks on water, the sea tilts at impossible angles. Boats drive into the waves, where experience shouts they shouldn't be. Green water crashes over the sides, invading our sanctuaries.

Our response is primitive and bone-deep. We are overwhelmed by a condition akin to shock, a slowing of mind and body. Judgment fails and seamanship deteriorates.

In *Heavy Weather Sailing* by Adlard Coles (1999), Bill Cooper recalls getting caught in Hurricane Alberta in 1982. "As I tried to gather myself to deal with matters, I felt all power to move leave me. I stood holding the leather covered wheel feeling strangely euphoric as if being drawn steadily upward off my feet. The feeling went on and on as if time had stopped, and I could not breathe, though my lungs were full. I could not move at all ... I had absolutely no sense of time ... Laurel describes me as standing motionless at the wheel, mouth wide open, with water streaming down me as if I were standing under a waterfall. I had to be roused to move. Presumably I was in a state of shock."

The toll taken by the incessant onslaught of a storm is further chronicled by John Wilson. Sailing from Scotland to Ireland in a 1979 storm, "I ended up so tired and cold that I was hallucinating while helming, steering for hours through brick railway arches as well as the breaking seas. I knew at the time this was a hallucination, but it didn't make it go away ... Much later, as the conditions improved, we sailed past a near-conical barren island, which then disappeared in a sudden mist. To this day I do not know if this island was real ... As we finally identified Heimay and made our way into the harbor, we made horrendous and quite elementary pilotage errors, and were lucky not to lose the boat among the rocks inshore" (Coles 1999).

For those caught out on the water tonight, there was no retreat. As the wind mauled the dark, frayed lines snapped and bad knots came loose. What had been minor problems quickly spawned a series of increasingly larger ones.

A blow that began normally enough had moved inexorably beyond normal. A storm surge raised the high tide higher, boosting the waves up to where they grasped at things stored beyond the water's customary reach. Wind and waves continued to build, revealing powers of disturbing strength and indifference.

***

Living on the water all of my life, I've known my share of calamities there.

Alone on a Hobie Cat turned turtle by gusting winds, I've drifted helplessly for kilometers. Windsurfing in the Columbia Gorge, I've broken a mast in thirty-knot winds and three-meter (ten-foot) swells and then been swept downriver in the barge lanes. Kilometers offshore on my sailboard in Hawaii, I've had the wind die and waited nervously in block-long swells, my legs treading shark-filled waters while I hoped for a gust to take me to shore.

I've been nauseated by seasickness, longing for solid ground under my feet. And I've watched the boom of Ken's jibing sailboat sweep the jaunty captain's hat off his head, and miss killing him by inches.

Another friend sailed into low-hanging power lines and was instantly electrocuted. Two other friends' boats were found drifting with no one on board, their bodies never found.

I've watched a Coast Guard team in front of our house chop its way through the bottom of an overturned catamaran in a rush to rescue people trapped inside the hull. And while hauling a ten-foot shark over the transom of a Lasqueti prawn boat, I've jumped back when it hit the deck to avoid its snapping jaws, and in that split second watched the captain's gaff whistle through the space where my head had just been.

Yet for all of this, and through a lifetime of friends telling similar tales, I have never had occasion to fear the sea. Not until living on the Strait of Georgia, where I've taken her true measure.

For though our island is solid rock, it lies like a toy upon the water. At times the wind and waves seem determined to wipe its diminutive smear off the surrounding blue.

In tonight's storm, I was grimly aware that standing on the shore of a tiny island was much different from standing on the edge of a massive continent. On our island, I could take no security in miles of backlands. The only escape was through the sea itself, a sea that bared fangs awash with spittle.

The storm in the dark bullied us with the fact that, for all our seemingly exalted accomplishments, in our bodily frame we bear the indelible stamp of our lowly origins. We are, after all, small animals living in the presence of much larger powers. The anger of tonight's sea exuded such power, a force that disdained man's petty concerns, demanding heathenistic worship and superstitious rites.

October 26, 2001

I slept late this morning, hungry for sleep after being kept awake much of the night by the wind. On arising, I padded to the window to check our boat. Double-anchored in the shelter of floathouse cove, she'd ridden out the blow without incident.

The wind and waves were still up, however, so I checked the weather radio to see what lay in store for us.

At the conclusion of the forecast, the Coast Guard reported that a fishing boat had gone down in the storm off Vancouver Island's north end. At first light, a crewman had been found alive in his survival suit.

Subsequent broadcasts told of the recovery of another member of the crew. Tragically, the second one was dead. Later a life raft was sighted, but the search plane couldn't tell if anyone was in it. Two crew members were still missing.

October 27, 2001

Switching on the weather radio, I was haunted by a sobering update to yesterday's tragedy. In waves the size of four-story buildings, the Coast Guard had plucked a survivor from the life raft. The last member of the crew, however, who'd been battered by the waves with just a float coat for protection, was predictably dead.

When friends kayaked over to pay us a visit, we were shocked to learn that one of the dead fishermen was Jan Vandendries, a friend from Lasqueti.

CHAPTER 67
MAYDAY!

"Steady, helmsman! Steady! This is the sort of weather when brave hearts snap ashore, and keeled hulls split at sea."
—Herman Melville, *Moby Dick*

Jan Vandendries loved to fish. When we ran into him on Lasqueti, he'd smile broadly as he talked of his life as a commercial fisherman. For years he'd been part of the crew of the fifteen-meter *Kella Lee*.

On October 24, as we were listening to the ominous forecast, the *Kella Lee* set out on a halibut trip. Their destination was a fishing ground northwest of Vancouver Island, an area for which storm-force winds were predicted. On board were friend Jan, Captain George Newson, Paul Sport, and Beachum ("Beach") Englemark.

As they fished and heard updates on the forecasted blow, the crew knew it was decision time. They could either pull their lines and run for cover, or stay and fish.

As the captain considered the perils of the approaching storm, the boat had managed only a moderate catch. Accordingly, he decided to keep fishing, telling the crew, "we're going to keep our lines down overnight, pull up on Thursday morning, and get our ass kicked on the way back in."

Everyone who lives on the water lives with unreliable weather forecasts. Predicted weather arrives early, late, or not at all. Fishermen thus make their own assessment of the weather and what to do about it. In doing so, they can be conservative or daring, respond to how much fish they are catching, and have varying degrees of bravado and faith in their boats.

Captain George made his own set of decisions that afternoon. The forecast called for sixty-knot winds the next evening. But all on board had been through such winds before, and George felt the *Kella Lee* would be closing on port when the worst winds broke.

What he didn't consider was a bomb storm. In a bomb storm, "explosive deepening" creates a sudden low-pressure hole in the ocean of atmosphere. As the surrounding air collapses in to fill the void, it explodes on the water unexpectedly and with incredible force.

Such a bomb storm ravaged British Columbia's halibut fleet in April 1985, blasting the north coast hours before it was predicted. Unleashing winds of surprising intensity, that storm left three fishermen dead.

As the *Kella Lee* crashed through rising seas toward Port Hardy, the weather service upgraded the day's forecast to hurricane-force winds of seventy knots. But the storm wasn't supposed to arrive in full force until about midnight, when Captain George expected to be safe in Port Hardy.

Tragically, events didn't unfold as expected. A bomb storm exploded, catching everyone off guard. The hurricane arrived three hours early, with shockingly vicious winds, and the men on the *Kella Lee* were caught out in the middle of it.

***

Wayne Bamford, of the Rescue Coordination Center, had only one word to describe the wind and waves that beset the *Kella Lee*. According to Bamford, as quoted in the *Mid Coast Beacon*, the conditions the men faced were "*horrendous.*"

At 9:45 PM, winds at Triangle Island gusted to eighty-eight knots. Steaming into the faces of thirteen-meter (forty-foot) waves, the *Kella Lee* labored up mountains of water. To keep her afloat, Captain George steered a zigzag track through the attacking seas. Though he doggedly returned to his course toward port, the winds only grudgingly ceded minor gains in that direction. They pushed relentlessly on the *Kella Lee*, striving to halt her in her wake.

At her normal cruising speed, the *Kella Lee* should have been closing steadily on Port Hardy. But in the conditions she was in, the fishing boat was lucky to claw out any progress over bottom. At times, simply holding her position was an accomplishment. She was at the mercy of the storm, with no ability to escape.

Picking his way through breaking waves, Captain George constantly worked the wheel in search of safe water. He had earlier deployed stabilizer fins over the sides to minimize side to side rolling. While George initially shot glances at the compass, trying to hold to a course toward port, eventually he steered only by feel.

When a boat surges over the tops of hurricane-driven waves, where it gets blasted by the full force of the wind, unnatural things happen. Speaking of the British Columbia hurricane of 1985, fisherman Fraser Dunn recounted, "You come up on these waves. They're a good forty feet, fifty feet, and they were only a hundred feet apart, or less, so it was straight up and down. You try to get the boat straight into the wind, and you get to the top of the wave and the wind would be so intense it would catch—and you'd be off a degree one way or the other way, it would blow you right on the side and you'd go gliding down the wave literally on your side … it was just an intense nightmare" (Keller 1997).

A rescue boat commands no magic in such waves, as the crew of the sixty-seven foot Coast Guard cutter *Point Henry* found out. Wayne Watson, awaiting rescue by the *Point Henry* in the same 1985 storm, watched the cutter get spun on the wave tops just like Fraser Dunn's fishing boat. "As the coast guard boat came up to the crest of a wave the wind would turn him and the white water would just engulf him. It was a terrifying thing to watch … he'd just turn and fall sideways and be engulfed in a mountain of white water thundering down" (Keller 1997).

The damage done to the 175-foot *George E. Darby*, a Coast Guard cutter that was running rescue missions in that storm, grimly illustrates the battering that a hurricane's waves can deliver. The *Darby's* captain, Monty Montgomery, was hospitalized afterward with a compression-fractured spine, and the *Darby's* half-inch steel bottom was so beaten in that she had to enter dry-dock for repairs.

Jan Vandendries and the rest of the *Kella Lee's* crew were grimly aware that the forces they battled were infinitely stronger than those that powered their boat. Increasingly at the mercy of the storm, they were witnessing a fundamental shift in their relationship with the sea. Wind and waves were no longer just matters of discomfort or inconvenience. Merely staying afloat required a furious spate of improvisation.

As the *Kella Lee* slammed into the seas, torrents of water washed over her deck. When the crew ventured outside, they fought to avoid being washed overboard. Scuttling from one handhold to another, they found that just standing was an overwhelming challenge.

Breathing was difficult when the men faced into the wind, which they did only reluctantly. Wind-driven spray drove into their skin like thousands of needles, threatening to damage unprotected eyes.

In this storm, the formidable seamanship of the crew was outmatched. Driving themselves and their boat beyond the breaking points of human and machine endurance, they squeezed into that narrow space between escape and disaster. They found themselves in survival conditions, where the sea commanded and they prayed for deliverance.

In such survival conditions, everyone believes in God. For among its many talents, the sea is an unfailing discoverer of weaknesses. And in its persistent assault on the *Kella Lee*, the sea found that an access hatch on the main fish hold had been swept away. Scrabbling excitedly at the point of vulnerability, the sea reached inward with its icy fingers. At first it did so secretly, giving silent notice that the crew had violated the first commandment of those afloat: above all, keep the sea outside of the boat.

At 11:00 PM on October 25, the *Kella Lee* was still approximately ninety kilometers from port. By then things had started to go seriously wrong, and the crew realized that their boat was taking on water. As Paul Sport watched, Jan calmly pulled on a survival suit. For a moment Jan struggled with its zipper, unable to close it around his neck. Failing in the attempt, Jan left it open and turned to more pressing matters.

***

Several light stations have been built in the area of the British Columbia coast where the *Kella Lee* fought its way forward. Their experiences give grim testimony to the extreme weather that haunts this area.

In Donald Graham's book, *Lights of the Inside Passage* (1986), George Smith, a keeper on Pine Island, said of one storm he went through: "On the eighth of this month we had a storm, it reached such an intensity that the A frame platform (for the winch) was floating up and down by the wind pressure underneath ... one serious blast pinned me against a building so tight I couldn't get off ... I arrived at the Fog Station by a combination of crawling and clawing."

In November 1948, a particularly nasty storm descended on the Egg Island light station. The keeper and his family cowered in the house as the wind and waves mounted. Then water gushed in through their bedroom window. Running from the house, the keeper turned when he heard his wife scream. "He looked behind as a big foaming sea roared wildly out of the mist and made for their abandoned home ... Everything was submerged in the raging acres of surf, and in retreat it carried off the entire station ... leaving only hollow concrete foundations full of curdled foam behind" (Graham 1986).

Cape Scott lies southwest of Pine and Egg Islands, jutting out into the Pacific at the northwest tip of Vancouver Island. Off Cape Scott lies Triangle Island, whose light station's records provide perhaps the best insight into the horrors that beset Jan and the crew. For it was off Cape Scott that the *Kella Lee* found herself that night.

Just building Triangle light station had been a challenge in itself. Gales pried off shingles and siding as quickly as the workmen nailed them down. Putty vibrated out of window frames before it could set, and carpenters wore safety harnesses to keep from being blown off their scaffolding.

Triangle's buildings were held in place by cables and turnbuckles, anchored by deadeyes cemented into the surrounding rock. Some were braced on all sides by huge beams that angled out from the eaves to the ground below.

"Even so," says Graham, "the dwellings teetered and swayed on their foundations so violently that their occupants became seasick. Windows bulged inward like lenses before they shattered. As a matter of routine, no one ever opened a door alone." (Graham, 1985)

All of the buildings were connected by cables that served as life lines, and in storms "men groveled on hands and knees" in their trips from one building to another. The first light keepers attempted to raise chickens and a cow, but these were blown off the island's cliffs by the wind.

In October 1912, Triangle Island was beset by 120 mile-per-hour winds. Chimneys were sheared off at their rooflines and a shed was blown off its foundation and over the cliff. Windows blew out of the radio house and doors tore off their hinges. Minutes later that house split in two, sending the radio operators crawling to the light keeper's home.

While other light stations were rebuilt after destructive storms, the Triangle Island Station was eventually abandoned. Defeating man's attempts to best them, the elements reclaimed the island and surrounding waters.

The first workmen on Triangle had, years earlier, found something that was perhaps an omen. "Crawling into a cave near the shore one evening, they held up their lanterns and recoiled in horror from a skeleton sprawled against the dripping rock wall, leering back at them, clad in a battered life belt and gum boots" (Graham 1985).

***

As midnight approached, things went from bad to worse aboard the *Kella Lee*. Forced onto her beam, the traitorous hull began gulping water. The rudder no longer responded and green seas broke over the vessel. Water rushed into the galley through its half-open Dutch door, and from there down-flooded the engine room.

Like a dying animal struggling to its feet, the *Kella Lee* lurched upright. Immediately she was blown down on her beam-ends again. With her flanks to waves, she pitched violently between vertical and her beam, thrashing the sea with her stabilizing gear

Realizing that the *Kella Lee* was going down, Captain George sent out a "Mayday." Looking at the men with the haunted eyes of one who has made some tragic miscalculations, he ordered them to abandon ship.

By this time, the crew had struggled into the *Kella Lee's* three survival suits. Captain George had given his personal suit to one of the crew and wore only a float coat.

Climbing to the top of the pilot house, Paul and Jan unlatched the pod holding the life raft and shoved it over the side. It immediately disappeared beneath the heaving boat. Moments later the raft inflated and rushed to the surface under the flailing boom, where its painter became tangled in the stabilizer gear.

Jan, Paul, and George piled into the bucking raft, but Beach could only jump into the frigid water and grab for its lifelines. Shoved underwater by the rocking hull, and repulsed by the flailing stabilizer gear, Beach let go and took his chances alone in the sea. In moments, he was joined by the others, who were thrown out of the raft as it jerked violently on the end of its tether. Paul and Jan managed to grab the bucking raft, only to watch Beach and George drift off into the dark.

Momentarily stunned by the disappearance of their two shipmates, Jan and Paul were yanked back to reality by their fear of being dragged under by the sinking fishing boat. In similar circumstances, men have been known to chew through rope to get themselves free.

As he struggled to liberate the tethered raft, Jan was thrown out and beaten away by the thrashing stabilizer gear. Paul stared at him in horror, for though Jan was only feet away from the raft, there was no way he could regain it.

Reaching out for his friend, Paul brushed Jan's arm with his fingertips. Jan just bobbed there in the water until he too was swept away into the dark.

For some moments, the *Kella Lee* thrashed on the surface like some pitifully wounded creature. But as her numerous interior spaces flooded, the weight of her metal hull finally pulled her beneath the waves.

Spewing trails of bubbles and debris toward the surface, the *Kella Lee* ran for the deep. Accelerating downward as bulkheads buckled and the hull coughed out air, the *Kella Lee* retreated from the storm that had assaulted her. Sinking in silence, she disappeared into the darkness of the abyss. Scattering fish, she crunched quietly into the bottom, leaned slowly onto her side, and was still.

***

Washed overboard, Jan confronted additional threats to those that had besieged Verner.

Jan had on a survival suit. Designed for quick entry during abandonment emergencies, it had seals at the neck and wrists and was fully insulated.

But Jan hadn't been able to completely close his suit or properly secure his face shield and hood. His head and neck, with their huge supply of blood coursing through vessels close to the surface, were exposed to the life-leaching cold of the wintery North Pacific.

Thieves sometimes work together, and hypothermia had an accomplice in its efforts to steal Jan's life. In thirteen-meter (forty-foot) seas and 100-knot winds, though buoyed by his immersion suit, Jan was just as likely to be taken by drowning.

As waves the size of small buildings toppled onto Jan, they drove him far below the surface. Knocking the wind from him with explosive force, they held him below in a swirling maelstrom. Tangling him in ropes of current, each tumbling breaker let him go only to deliver him to the hands of another.

Jan's survival suit was grossly outmatched. Though it floated him to the surface when the waters tired of holding him down, with each succeeding wave he got more out of breath, and less able to survive the next assault.

Spike Walker chronicles what it's like to be brutalized by breaking waves. In *Working on The Edge* (1991), Walker relates the experiences of John Magoteaux and Donny Channel. These two fishermen were among the crew of the *Master Carl* when she went down near Alaska's Prince William Sound.

Magoteaux remembers that when a breaking wave hit them as they drifted over an offshore reef, it "sent me shooting through the water, straight down, probably fifteen or twenty feet."

The same wave "smashed Channel under and knocked the wind from him. Submerged and blinded by the foamy froth, he felt himself being dragged into the depths and tossed wildly about by the brutal explosions of collapsing sea. The currents continued to pummel him, and he felt the icy rivulets of the Gulf of Alaska water pour in through the rim of his survival suit's hood."

"Driven down several fathoms below the surface, Channel covered his nose and mouth, and, holding on to what little air he had left, tried to keep from blacking out ... It seemed like whole minutes passed before he finally bobbed to the surface" (Walker 1991).

Jan experienced all of this as he was attacked by the storm. But it wasn't just the waves that threatened to drown him.

"In violent storms there is so much water in the air, and air in the water, that it becomes impossible to tell where the atmosphere stops and the sea begins" (Junger 1997).

Speaking of a helicopter rescue that was aborted for this reason, Sebastian Junger tells of why the pilot wouldn't allow his rescue swimmers into the sea. "They'd have died. In conditions like these, so much water gets loaded into the air that swimmers drown simply trying to breathe."

Smothered by the foam and blowing spray, Jan inhaled a froth of air and water with each gasping breath, water that pooled in his lungs and threatened to drown him.

***

Three hundred kilometers north of where I lay awake in the same storm, Coast Guard operators were monitoring Emergency Channel 16. After hearing Captain George's Mayday, their Search and Rescue coordinators came to some sobering conclusions.

There was no doubt that lives depended on getting the men out of the water promptly, and that the best thing for this task was a Labrador Helicopter. But the winds were too severe for a helicopter to safely deploy.

The nearby sixteen-meter (forty-eight-foot) *Cape Sutil* set out to find the *Kella Lee,* but the terror of the ride proved too much for the *Cape Sutil's* engineer. When another crew member found him sprawled in the galley experiencing chest pains, the *Cape Sutil* had to return to Port Hardy for emergency medical help. The thirty-nine-meter (128-foot) trawler *Frosti* was also in the area, but "We didn't go at first because it was blowing 80 to 100 and I had fears for our safety. The wind was so hard the radar wouldn't turn" (Skipper Brian Mose, *Mid Coast Beacon,* 2001). The most capable rescue craft was thus the Coast Guard's sixty-eight-meter (224-foot) *John P. Tully,* but the *Tully* was six and a half hours away.

A fixed-wing Buffalo aircraft was sent aloft and eventually spotted a light being waved frantically by someone in the water. Said copilot Jaques Robitaille in the *North Island Weekender,* "we attempted in vain to orbit the light," but "the horrendous winds blew us miles downwind in the time it took to make one orbit. I therefore had to rely exclusively on the GPS to guide me back to the light."

Despairing that "we were powerless to do anything for the people in the water," Robitaille and the Buffalo crew discussed a parachute jump into the sea. Careening through eighty-knot winds in the dark over thirteen-meter (forty-foot) seas, the men reluctantly concluded that such a jump "would be suicidal."

Before its dwindling fuel reserves forced the Buffalo to return to Port Hardy, the crew dropped a self-locating data marker buoy (SLDMB). Designed to drift near the man in the water, the SLDMB transmitted its changing position to a satellite overhead. This data beamed to a ground station, then fed into a Web site for search and rescue personnel. Steaming forward through the dark, the *Tully* utilized this data to plot a course toward what it hoped were survivors.

Peering through the dark at 6:03 in the morning, spotters on the *Tully* saw a light in the water ahead. In the illumination of paraflares dropped from the Buffalo they could tell they were approaching someone alive! After finally getting him aboard, they found out that they had saved Beachum Englemark. Beach had drifted for seven and a half hours over thirteen kilometers from where the *Kella Lee* went down.

Though another light and the life raft had been spotted earlier, they'd been lost in the frantic rescue attempt. As the search and rescue teams concentrated on saving Beachum, they were simply incapable of tracking multiple targets.

Four long hours after rescuing Beach, the *Tully* came upon a second person in the water. When he was finally laid on the *Tully's* deck, clearly having died some hours before, Beachum identified him as crewmate Jan Vandendries.

Hours later and more kilometers away, the *Tully* recovered the body of Captain George Newson. Still later and forty kilometers from the mayday point, a helicopter hoisted Paul Sport from his life raft. Sitting in the copter's cargo bay, Paul was grimly informed that he was only the second survivor of the ill-fated *Kella Lee*.

CHAPTER 68
A FOND FAREWELL TO ALLEN FARRELL

Death is only a launching into the region of ... the watery, the unshored.

—Herman Melville, *Moby Dick*

March 1, 2002

Today's late-winter sun sparkled lazily off the waters around us. Wildflowers graced Olsen's moss, and our eagles tended new eggs in their nest. False Bay's calm had forgotten all of winter's storms.

Walking around our island, I found myself drawn to the billowing rocks above its western shore. Here the island dropped off precipitously, sticking out defiantly into the Strait. Looking through the Finnerties to waters further north, I peered back through time to the hurricane that had taken our friend Jan.

To me that storm was a whirlpool. Though I stood far away from its center in place and time, I felt its vortex suck me into its maw. While self-awareness anchored me to our rocky island, I was unable to resist the pull of the hurricane. As my imagination took flight, it dropped me aboard the foundering *Kella Lee*.

Seeing me gazing northward through glazed eyes, Theresa climbed up and snaked her arm around my waist. Suddenly I was home, watching gulls wheel overhead in a blue sky. Ducks paddled lazily in the calm waters below, oblivious of my recent peril.

Walking down from the rocks and onto the trail through Olsen's woods, I pulled Theresa next to me in the joy of new-won life.

***

As Theresa and I hadn't seen our island neighbors for some months, we invited them over for dinner. Dick and Terry came in their canoe from Lasqueti and, after picking up Allen Farrell from his sailboat, Ray and Eve in their skiff from Higgins. Kirsty Elliot, our new pirate guard, joined us from the floathouse.

Though Allen was his usual spry and energetic self, he was shivering when he arrived. Nearing ninety, he still lived aboard the *China Cloud*, which could be frost-cold at floor level even with his woodstove going. To make matters worse, Allen was dressed in a threadbare coat which did little to warm him. Though he had much warmer things to wear, he preferred the ratty old coat he'd probably scavenged from the free store.

That coat *might* have kept Allen warm if he'd rowed himself over, but it did nothing to protect him from the chilly ride in Ray's motor boat. Allen had lived on the water far too long not to have anticipated this, but he liked his plaid rag. To him it was his dinner-party best. So that was that, and he walked in chilled to the bone.

Though Allen was a bit embarrassed from the fuss we made over him, he happily slipped on a sweater of mine and sidled up to our woodstove. Soon he was smiling and delightedly eating smoked salmon, warmed by the attention as much as the fire. A while later, he moved from the woodstove to our blazing fireplace, where he stayed for the rest of the evening.

March 2, 2002

Today dawned sunny but cold. Invigorated by the winter sun, island trees have flooded the Strait with oxygen. Days of calm have pooled new air on the water, where it is cleansed by fog and scrubbed by ripples and clouds. This morning I drew it deep inside me, savoring its purity.

Much to my surprise, in early morning I spied Allen rowing himself out to Olsen. The *China Cloud* was anchored in Mud Bay, a five-kilometer (three-mile) round-trip away. As the tide was out, Allen had to land on the tide flats at the end of the back pass and walk the rest of the way through mud and oysters and broken clam shells. As he approached our floathouse, I was shocked to see that Allen was barefoot!

Allen stayed only five minutes, having rowed all the way out just to make sure that Kirsty knew that she was invited to that afternoon's pie eating contest.

When Allen started to take his leave, both Kirsty and I tried to coax him into socks and gum boots. But Allen waved us off good-naturedly, reminding us that he often went months without shoes.

Mid-March 2002

A number of tales are circulating about Allen, or perhaps just different versions of the same tale. There is a common thread in all of them—that Allen had decided to die and was taking steps to hasten his own demise. He'd told several Lasqueti friends that he was tired of living and wanted to join his departed wife Cheri in the afterlife.

One Lasquetian reported finding Allen lying beside a dirt road, shoeless and inadequately clothed. When he tried to help, Allen ran barefoot into the woods.

In another account, Allen was sitting on the road without any clothes on, and similarly ran away into the forest when help was pressed upon him. In both instances, he made it clear that he wanted no assistance or interference.

Several days ago, some friends went out to visit Allen on the *China Cloud*, where they found him cold and sick. Although they were able to persuade him to accompany them home, and succeeded in warming him up, Allen remained stubbornly infirm. In short-order, he was ferried off to a Vancouver Island hospital. While his body clung to life, it was obvious that his spirit had fled. Lonely and cold, his body soon followed.

Allen had always been a man of strong passions and beliefs. Though his motorless boat drifted with the tides and was pushed by the winds, he pursued whatever he wanted with calm determination.

When Allen chose his time to die, he went at it with the same pluck that people so admired him for. He announced that he was leaving life's port, said his good-byes, got himself sick, and sailed off into the beyond.

May 10, 2002

Lasquetian friends had planned a ninetieth birthday bash for Allen on May 10, and since everyone had already made arrangements to attend, the date was kept and the party changed to a wake. Word went out for all to bring some type of small boat to set adrift in memory of Allen.

On what would have been his ninetieth birthday, a crowd of Allen's friends gathered on the shores of Mud Bay, his favorite Lasqueti anchorage.

A microphone was set up on the grass overlooking the bay, and as a potluck dinner got under way, many of Allen's friends stepped up and shared their remembrances of his incredible life afloat.

When bellies were full and stories told, friend Dazy brought out Allen's ashes in a large bowl. Each of us took a small handful and placed it on our homemade boat, then proceeded to the water's edge. After lighting candles and placing them on our boats, we launched our hulls onto Lasqueti's waters.

As the afternoon waned, a dreamy flotilla assembled on the bay. Some boats were fanciful pieces of hull-shaped driftwood topped with juniper branch masts and whimsical sails. Others were classic children's creations—pointed pieces of lumber with square chunks of wood nailed on top. Some had been rough-hewn with machetes, others painstakingly hand carved and perfectly detailed. There were tugs and fishing boats and schooners and junks, yawls and canoes and catamarans and outriggers.

Karl Darwin had fitted his craft with a slow fuse, fireworks, and a cabin full of black powder, intending to blow it to smithereens in a hail of rockets and explosions.

Some people lovingly tended their crafts, guiding them toward deeper water from their rowboats. Oblivious to the chilly water, several children waded into the bay to shepherd the fleet toward the bay's small mouth.

We launched ninety boats, one for each of Allen's years. As the tide ebbed, a ghost breeze carried Allen into False Bay for the last time.

Making our own departure as afternoon faded into dusk, Theresa and I motored slowly among the spirit-craft sailing toward open water. With us were friends Maria Coffey and Dag Goering, who had sailed with Allen and chronicled his life in *Sailing Back in Time*. Cutting our engine, we bobbed silently in the fleet of flickering candles.

CHAPTER 69
COMING FULL CIRCLE

According to Celtic tradition, the earth has "thin places," where spirit and matter meet, where humans can touch the divine ...
—Maria Coffey, *Explorers of the Infinite*

I have been shaped by those island times, and find it difficult now to achieve any kind of distance from them. The place has entered me. It has coloured my life like a stain. Almost everything else feels less dense and less intense than those moments of exposure ... I have never known a place where life is so thick, experience so immediate or the barriers between self and the world so tissue-thin.
—Adam Nicholson, *Sea Room*

May 12, 2002

Summer is approaching, and Theresa and I are readying our island home and boats for an extended stay. After a morning of launching kayaks and sweeping forest paths clean of arbutus leaves, I indulged my desire to explore a midden on an uninhabited Lasqueti cove. Climbing into our aluminum boat, I set out full of anticipation.

My passage took me across False Bay and into the open waters of the Strait. I'd fished here countless times and knew where the island ended in underwater cliffs. In the deeps beyond were silver salmon and creatures of the dark, gibbering salinae and the silent bones of the drowned.

From where I motored offshore, the mouth of the cove was perfectly camouflaged, disappearing into the surrounding rock. Only when I snuggled up to Lasqueti did the entrance to this intimate refuge materialize before me.

The cove proved a microcosm of our island world, and my afternoon there a condensed version of our experiences here. As I boated slowly into its clear, shallow waters, my hands rested on gunwales polished by the countless feet of prawn line that had passed over them. I calmly scraped my bow up on the rocky beach, a bow dented and scratched from hundreds of landings, some easy like this one, many more violent.

A rusty fishhook caught my eye from its resting place between my floorboards, just as it had caught denizens of the deep. Forgotten in our boat, it waited patiently for someone to bend and retrieve it, as did the arrowheads I was seeking on this seldom-visited shore.

Looking out from the cove to the Strait beyond, I thought back on the endless hours I'd spent gazing at those waters. Though in ways I thought I knew each drop of water personally, the sea was too elusive for that. While today it had a Buddha's calm, my boat's broken welds showed that the sea was fickle and indifferent and careless and brutal. The barren rock of the cove's entrance attested to the Strait's fits of temper, showing that the sea did whatever it wanted with complete impunity.

Remembering the shrieking winds and brutal waves of the storms I'd been through, I realized that they were the roaring forge in which I'd been heated and pounded into an islander. I'd emerged from this furnace permanently altered. Its hammer strokes of terror and awe had worked me, as they had all who live here.

Walking up the shore, a flash in the rocks caught my eye. Stooping down, I picked up a frosted piece of beach glass. It could have been a broken porthole from some storm driven wreck, a piece of a glass ball launched from exotic shores, or simply part of a bottle that had drifted here on the tides. Soon it would be sanded to nothingness by the patient waters of time—its footprints gone forever.

Beyond the beach logs rose the midden, an aboriginal shell pile built through thousands of years. The abandoned summer camp above had gone feral and then wild. Old trees grew where ancient shelters had stood. Though the echoes of fire-lit dances were gone forever, a jade adz I found teased spectral totems from the surrounding woods.

Rubbing my find between my fingers, I smelled ancient cooking fires above the beach. In the woods nearby, an angry spirit father chastened his young son for losing his prized chisel.

Though the months of cold and dark were melting, as I walked into the forest I encountered reminders of their fury. At the edge of the trees was an old-growth beach log, impossibly long and thicker than I was tall. Tossed up by the Herculean forces of some winter storm, it shrank my scrotum as I imagined the seas that pitched it there.

Far beyond and into the trees, large chunks of Styrofoam littered the forest floor. Thrown up by the waves and snatched by incredible winds, they'd been blown deep into the home of deer and raccoons, surprise visitors to the private world of wild creatures.

Back on the beach again, I clambered over logs and ducked under low-hanging limbs as I explored the shore. Luxuriating in the sun, I wondered what native lovers had lain here, perfectly twining with the beauty of the coast, reveling in this wilderness home of the gods.

Selected Bibliography

Ambrose, Stephen, *Undaunted Courage*, Simon & Schuster, New York, 1996.

Ames, Kenneth and Maschner, Herbert, *Peoples of the Northwest Coast*, Thames and Hudson, New York, 1999.

Bailey, Maurice, and Maralyn, *117 Days Adrift*, Sheridan House, New York, 1992.

Blanchet, M. Wylie, *The Curve of Time*, Seals Press, Vancouver, Canada, 1968.

Bown, Stephen, *Madness, Betrayal and the Lash: The Epic Voyage of Captain George Vancouver*, Douglas & McIntyre, Vancouver B.C., 2008.

Burney, James, *Journal of James Burney*, 1778, http://www.hallman.org/indian/cook.html.

Burroughs, William J., *Climate Change in Prehistory*, Cambridge University Press, New York, 2005.

Cannings, Richard and Sydney, *Geology of British Columbia*, Greystone Books, Vancouver, Canada, 1999.

Cook, James, *Journal of James Cook*, 1778, http://www.hallman.org/indian/cook.html.

Coles, Adlard, *Heavy Weather Sailing,* International Marine, Camden, Maine, 1999.

Conover, David, *Once Upon an Island,* John Hawkins & Associates, New York, 1967.

Corsin, Trevor, *The Secret Life of Lobsters,* Harper-Perennial, New York, 2004.

Crawford, William, *Mariner's Weather,* W.W. Norton, New York, 1992.

DeBlieu, Jan, *Wind,* Mariner Books, New York, 1999.

Doig, Ivan, *The Sea Runners,* Mariner Books, 2006.

Ellis, Richard, *The Search for the Giant Squid,* The Lyons Press, New York, 1998.

Fortey, Richard, *Life,* Alfred A. Knoph, New York, 1998.

Gill, Paul, *The Waterlover's Guide to Marine Medicine,* Fireside, New York, 1993.

Glavin, Terry, *The Last Great Sea,* Greystone Books, Vancouver, Canada, 2000.

Graham, Donald, *Keepers of the Light,* Harbour Publishing Ltd., Madeira Park, B.C., 1985.

Graham, Donald, *Lights of the Inside Passage,* Harbour Publishing Ltd., Madeira Park, B.C., 1986.

Haddaway, Husain (Translator), *The Arabian Nights II,* Everyman's Library, New York, 1995.

Heaney, Seamus (Translator), *Beowulf,* Norton, New York, 2001.

Holmes, Hannah, *The Secret Life of Dust*, John Wiley & Sons, New York, 2001.

http://earthquakescanada.nrcan.gc.ca.

Jewitt, John, *White Slaves of the Nootka*, Heritage House, Surrey, Canada, 1994.

Junger, Sebastian, *The Perfect Storm*, W.W. Norton, New York, 1997.

Keller, Keith, *Dangerous Waters*, Harbour Publishing, Maderia Park, B.C., 1997.

King, James, *Journal of James King*, 1778, http://www.hallman.org/indian/cook.html.

Konner, Melvin, *The Tangled Wing*, Henry Holt & Company, New York, 2002.

Kunzig, Robert, *Mapping the Deep*, W.W. Norton, New York, 2000.

Lansing, Alfred, *Endurance*, Carroll & Graff Publishers, New York, 1959.

Manby, Thomas, *Journal of the HMS* Discovery *and* Chatham, *1790-1793*, Ye Galleon Press, Fairfield, WA, 1992.

Mason, Elda, *Lasqueti Island – History and Memory*, Morriss Printing Co., Victoria, Canada, 1976.

McPhee, John, *Annals of the Former World*, Farrar, Straus and Giroux, New York, 1998.

Melville, Herman, *Moby Dick*, Modern Library, New York, 1998.

Menzies, Gavin, *1421: The Year China Discovered America*, Harper Collins, New York, 2003.

Mid Coast Beacon, Port Hardy, B.C., October 31, 2001.

Mithen, Steven, *After the Ice*, Harvard University Press, Cambridge, 2003.

Morton, Alexandra, *Listening to Whales*, Ballantine Books, New York, 2002.

Morton, Alexandra, and Proctor, Billy, *Heart of the Raincoast*, Horsdal and Schuburt, Victoria, 2001.

Natural Resources Canada, 2008, http://gsc.nrcan.gc.ca/marine/sponge/paleo_e.php.

Nicholson, Adam, *Sea Room*, Farrar, Straus and Giroux, New York, 2001.

North Island Gazette, Port Hardy, B.C., October 31, 2001.

Olsen, Scharleen, an unpublished account of "Captain Frank Barker's 38 years with General Construction Company of Seattle, from information obtained from Captain Barker on March 9 & 10, 1998."

Orr, Elizabeth and William, *Geology of the Pacific Northwest*, McGraw Hill, New York, 1996.

Patterson, Kevin, *The Water In Between*, Doubleday, New York, 2000.

Philbrick, Nathaniel, *In the Heart of the Sea: The Tragedy of the Whale-ship Essex*, Viking, New York, 2000.

Quammen, David, *The Song of the Dodo*, Simon and Schuster, New York, 1976.

Quimby, George, *"Japanese Wrecks, Iron Tools and Prehistoric Indians of the Northwest Coast,"* Arctic Anthropology, Vol. 22, No. 2, 1985.

Raban, Jonathan, *Passage to Juneau*, Pantheon Books, New York, 1999.

Renner, Jeff, *Northwest Marine Weather*, The Mountaineers, Seattle, 1993.

Roberts, Callum, *The Unnatural History of the Sea*, Island Press, Washington D.C., 2007.

Robitaille, Jacques, *Rescuer Recalls Fateful Night*, North Island Weekender, Campbell River, B.C., Nov. 17, 2001.

Roche, Judith and McHutchinson, Meg, *First Fish, First People*, University of British Columbia Press, Vancouver, 1998.

Sagan, Carl, *The Dragons of Eden*, Ballantine Books, New York, 1977.

Spielman, Andrew and D'Antonio, Michael, *Mosquito*, Hyperion, New York, 2001.

Stevens, William, *The Change in the Weather*, Random House, New York, 1999.

Stewart, Hilary, *Indian Fishing*, University of Washington Press, Seattle, 1977.

Sturgis, William, *Journal of William Sturgis*, 1799, http://www.hallman.org/indian/sturgis.html

Thompson, Richard, *Oceanography of the British Columbia Coasts*, Canadian Special Publication of fisheries and Aquatic Sciences 56, Ottawa, 1981.

Valliant, John, *The Golden Spruce*, Norton, New York, 2005.

Van Dorn, William, *Oceanography and Seamanship*, Cornell Maritime Press, Centreville, Md., 1993.

Walker, Chip, *Thumbs, Toes and Tears*, Walker and Company, New York, 2006.

Walker, Spike, *Working on the Edge*, St. Martin's Press, New York, 1991.

Weisman, Alan, *The World Without Us*, St. Martin's Press, New York, 2007.

CPSIA information can be obtained
at www.ICGtesting.com
Printed in the USA
LVHW111400120221
679178LV00033B/182